"Fidelity to Freud's method in this book featuring contributions by many eminent psychoanalysts, becomes the creative spur towards bold new theories and ideas on the centrality of the body in psychoanalysis. The multiplicity of approaches guarantees a multidimensional and insightful journey that dares to tread new paths while remaining grounded in inalienability of the Freudian perspective.

The academic rigor of *On the Body* makes it stand out and I have no doubt that it will great interest to those working in the field of mental health."

—**Antonino Ferro**, President of the Italian Psychoanalytic Society, and Training and Supervising Analyst in the American Psychoanalytic Association

"The authors demonstrate that if today's psychoanalysis wants to remain relevant, the body of the drives should be restored to a central position. Yet our world is dramatically changing. *A Psychoanalytic Exploration of the Body* raises fundamental questions that stem from philosophical and clinical thoughts on the body in post Freudian psychoanalysis. The complexity of infantile and adult sexuality is explored here, and this exploration gives rise to fascinating elaborations on the role of technology, gender, transgenderism. Every analyst should read it."

—**Marilia Aisenstein**, a training analyst and the former president of the Paris Psychoanalytic Society

"This volume explores the dynamics between the experience of the biological body as the primary source of ego development, and the dissociation between the sexual body and the psychological determination of individuals' core gender identity. This dissociation is explored from multiple viewpoints: controversies regarding drive theory, identity diffusion related to severe psychopathology, sociological and political assertion of multiple core gender potentials, and new psychoanalytic findings regarding early development. It is a complex, challenging, thought provoking volume that presents important controversies in contemporary psychoanalytic thinking."

—**Otto Kernberg**, M.D., Professor of Psychiatry, Weill Cornell Medical College, Director, Personality Disorders Institute, New York Presbyterian Hospital

"This book reclaims a fundamental connection/integration of the contemporary psychoanalytic mind with the reality of the body of drives. Like a tree's branches, post-freudian achievements and visions have made psychoanalysis an advanced science and practice, but now we need a harmonious re-integration of the trunk of that analytic tree: as Freud asserted, body and its drives are the basis for a deep psychoanalytic view. This is the role of this wonderful book in our contemporary psychoanalytic literature."

—**Stefano Bolognini**, psychiatrist, training and supervising analyst of the Italian Psychoanalytical Society and the President of the International Psychoanalytical Association

"This fascinating collection of essays proposes to restore and elaborate original conceptions of drive and body sidelined in contemporary psychoanalysis, and thereby reopen their exciting intellectual and clinical potential. The complex theoretical contributions by brilliant and erudite scholars offer a fresh take on the existing body of thought on sexuality and drive in psychoanalysis. Based in primarily French traditions, On the Body offers rich and radical reflections on the body and its psychic repres   ⋯ ⋯ ⋯ ⋯ ⋯ ⋯ ⋯ and enlighten readers of all backgrounds."

—**Jessica Benjamin**, auth
Recognition Theo

A Psychoanalytic Exploration of the Body in Today's World

A Psychoanalytic Exploration of the Body in Today's World: On the Body examines the importance of the body in everyday psychoanalytic practice and beyond. Written by world leading clinicians and international scholars, this important book aims to relocate the psychoanalytic body in the modern, more challenging world. Bringing together perspectives from across the range of psychoanalytic schools of thought, it covers essential analytic topics such as family and parenting, sex and gender, illness and psychosomatics, and concepts of the body in infancy.

Though in Freud's writing the intertwining of body and psyche is fundamental, psychoanalytic thought has sometimes downplayed or ignored this idea. This book returns the body to its rightful place in psychoanalysis, and brings the body into the contemporary world of technology and change, offering fresh insight into the sick body, the sexual body, the speaking body, the body of the changing family in which the traditional gendered labels no longer fit seamlessly, gender dynamics and much more.

A Psychoanalytic Exploration of the Body in Today's World gives renewed and increased emphasis to an essential tenet of psychoanalysis. With contributions from some of the most important modern psychoanalysts, this book will prove an essential work for both psychotherapists and academics.

Vaia Tsolas is a psychologist and psychoanalyst on the faculty at Columbia University Psychoanalytic Center and Albert Einstein Medical School, teaching Freud and Lacan. She is the director of Rose Hill Psychological Services. She is the winner of the IPA Sacerdoti Prize, Columbia Ovesey and Klar best teacher awards.

Christine Anzieu-Premmereur is an M.D., Ph.D. and Psychoanalyst, Member at the Columbia University Psychoanalytic Center, Member at the Société Psychanalytique de Paris and the New York Psychoanalytic Institute. She is currently the director of the Parent-Infant Program at the Columbia Psychoanalytic Center and Assistant Clinical Professor in Psychiatry at Columbia University.

A Psychoanalytic Exploration of the Body in Today's World

On the Body

Edited by
Vaia Tsolas and
Christine Anzieu-Premmereur

LONDON AND NEW YORK

First published 2018
by Routledge
2 Park Square, Milton Park, Abingdon, Oxon OX14 4RN

and by Routledge
711 Third Avenue, New York, NY 10017

Routledge is an imprint of the Taylor & Francis Group, an informa business

© 2018 selection and editorial matter, Vaia Tsolas and Christine Anzieu-Premmereur; individual chapters, the contributors

The right of the editors to be identified as the author of the editorial material, and of the authors for their individual chapters, has been asserted in accordance with sections 77 and 78 of the Copyright, Designs and Patents Act 1988.

All rights reserved. No part of this book may be reprinted or reproduced or utilised in any form or by any electronic, mechanical, or other means, now known or hereafter invented, including photocopying and recording, or in any information storage or retrieval system, without permission in writing from the publishers.

Trademark notice: Product or corporate names may be trademarks or registered trademarks, and are used only for identification and explanation without intent to infringe.

British Library Cataloguing-in-Publication Data
A catalogue record for this book is available from the British Library

Library of Congress Cataloging-in-Publication Data
Names: Tsolas, Vaia, editor. | Anzieu-Premmereur, Christine, editor.
Title: A psychoanalytic exploration of the body in today's world : on the body / [edited by] Vaia Tsolas & Christine Anzieu-Premmereur.
Description: Abingdon, Oxon ; New York, NY : Routledge, 2018.
Identifiers: LCCN 2017025248 | ISBN 9781138065468 (hardback) | ISBN 9781138065475 (pbk.) | ISBN 9781315159683 (e-book)
Subjects: LCSH: Mind and body. | Human body. | Psychoanalysis.
Classification: LCC BF161 .P786 2018 | DDC 150.19/5—dc23
LC record available at https://lccn.loc.gov/2017025248

ISBN: 978-1-138-06546-8 (hbk)
ISBN: 978-1-138-06547-5 (pbk)
ISBN: 978-1-315-15968-3 (ebk)

Typeset in Times New Roman
by Apex CoVantage, LLC

For Ariadne and Michael for the continuous inspiration, creativity and love.

Contents

Notes on contributors xii
Notes on editors xiv
Acknowledgements xv

General introduction 1
VAIA TSOLAS

PART I
The body in our changing world 13

1 Introduction 15
   VAIA TSOLAS

2 Empathy machines: forgetting the body 17
   SHERRY TURKLE

3 Changing attitudes about sex: a dual inheritance perspective 28
   ROBERT A. PAUL

4 Modern gender flexibility: pronoun changes and
   the body's activities 42
   ROSEMARY H. BALSAM

PART II
The body in the changing family 61

5 Introduction 63
   VAIA TSOLAS

6	Introduction to "Transformations of *parentality*" JULIA KRISTEVA, TRANSLATED BY EDWARD KENNY ROSEMARY H. BALSAM	66
7	Transformations of *parentality* JULIA KRISTEVA, TRANSLATED BY EDWARD KENNY	68
8	The sibling body-ego JULIET MITCHELL	75
9	Perspectives on the body Ego and mother-infant interaction: I've got you under my skin CHRISTINE ANZIEU-PREMMEREUR	89

PART III
The sexual body, the speaking body and the sick body 101

10	Introduction MARIA CRISTINA AGUIRRE	103
11	Body and soul, a never-ending story PAUL VERHAEGHE	105
12	Somatic ailment and death drive: dangerous liaisons PANOS ALOUPIS	120
13	What is alive in the ill body? Affect and representation in psychosomatics MARINA PAPAGEORGIOU	130

PART IV
Sex, gender and infantile sexuality 141

14	Introduction CHRISTINE ANZIEU-PREMMEREUR	143
15	Foreign bodies: the body-psyche and its phantoms DOMINIQUE SCARFONE	146

16	**Botched bodies: inventing gender and constructing sex**	159
	PATRICIA GHEROVICI	
17	**Repudiation of femininity and the aftermath on the female sexual body**	174
	VAIA TSOLAS	
18	**Concluding remarks**	187
	CHRISTINE ANZIEU-PREMMEREUR	
	Index	189

Notes on contributors

Maria Cristina Aguirre, Ph.D., is a Lacanian psychoanalyst, trained in Paris, France. Member of APM, APA, MLS (New Lacanian School), the World Association of Psychoanalysis (WAP), NEL (Nuevo Escuela Lacaniana), Coordinator of the New York Freud Lacan Analytic Group (NYFLAG). Practices in New York City.

Panos Aloupis is an M.D. (Psychiatrist), Ph.D. (Psychologist) and Psychoanalyst (SPP-Paris Psychoanalytic Society) member of the IPA, consultant at IPSO – Pierre Marty (Paris), member of the editorial board of Revue Française de Psychosomatique.

Rosemary H. Balsam F.R.C.Psych. (London); M.R.C.P. (Edinburgh); is an Associate Clinical Professor of Psychiatry at Yale Medical School; Staff Psychiatrist at the Dept. of Student Mental Health and Counseling; Training and Supervising Analyst at Western New England Institute for Psychoanalysis. Her special interests are in gender and body issues, especially female development. Recent book: *Womens' Bodies in Psychoanalysis*, Routledge 2012. Recent article: "Freud, The Birthing Body and Modern Life" (2017), *Journal of the American Psychoanalytic Association* 65(1):61–90.

Patricia Gherovici, Ph.D., is a psychoanalyst and analytic supervisor. Co-founder and director of the Philadelphia Lacan Group, Associate Faculty, Psychoanalytic Studies Minor, University of Pennsylvania (PSYS), Honorary Member at IPTAR (the Institute for Psychoanalytic Training and Research) in New York City, and Member at Apres-Coup Psychoanalytic Association New York.

Julia Kristeva is Director of the Institute for the Study of Texts and Documents at University of Paris VII and Visiting Professor at Columbia University. She is the recipient of France's distinguished "Chevalière de la légion d'honneur" and in 2004 won the Holberg International Prize for her "innovative explorations of questions on the intersection of language, culture and literature [that] have inspired research across the humanities and the social sciences throughout the world". A practicing psychoanalyst, she is a careful reader of Freud, and finds his voice in such contemporary concerns as desire, love, revolution, the poetic, the soul, and faith.

Juliet Mitchell is a Professorial Research Associate and Founder/Director of the M.Phil./Ph.D. Programme in Psychoanalytic Studies at UCL Psychoanalysis Unit. She is also the Founder/Director of the Centre for Gender Studies at the University of Cambridge, a Research Fellow at the Department of Human Geography, University of Cambridge and Fellow Emeritus of Jesus College, University of Cambridge. She is a Fellow of the British and International Psychoanalytical Societies and a Fellow of the British Academy.

Marina Papageorgiou is a psychologist, psychoanalyst, psychosomatician, clinical psychologist in the Center of Treatment of Pain, University Hospital Avicenne, University Paris XIII, Member of SPP (Psychoanalytic Society of Paris), Member of IPA (International Psychoanalytic Association), Member of IPSO Paris (Institut Psychosomatique de Paris) and Director of the editorial board of Revue Francaise de Psychosomatique.

Robert A. Paul, Ph.D., is Charles Howard Candler Professor of Anthropology and Interdisciplinary Studies at Emory University. A training and supervising analyst, he is also Director of the Emory University Psychoanalytic Institute.

Dominique Scarfone, M.D., is an honorary professor at the Departments of Psychology and Psychiatry of the Université de Montréal and a training and supervising analyst in the Canadian Psychoanalytic Society and Institute (French Montreal Branch).

Sherry Turkle, Ph.D., is the Abby Rockefeller Mauzé Professor of the Social Studies of Science and Technology in the Program in Science, Technology, and Society at MIT, and the founder (2001) and current director of the MIT Initiative on Technology and Self. Professor Turkle received a joint doctorate in sociology and personality psychology from Harvard University and is a licensed clinical psychologist.

Paul Verhaeghe, Ph.D., is on the faculty of psychological and educational sciences, department for psychoanalysis and counseling psychology at Ghent University (Professor Ordinarius).

Notes on editors

Vaia Tsolas, Ph.D., is a psychologist and psychoanalyst on the faculty at Columbia University Psychoanalytic Center and Albert Einstein Medical School. She is the director of Rose Hill Psychological Services. She is the winner of the IPA Sacerdoti Prize, Columbia Ovesey and Klar best teacher awards. Dr Tsolas teaches Freud/Lacan at Columbia Psychoanalytic. She chairs the scientific meetings for APM. She is the author of *Sweet little deaths of everyday life: A psychoanalytic study on the feminine* (2008) and numerous articles on issues of otherness, body and gender.

Christine Anzieu-Premmereur is a Psychiatrist, Ph.D. Psychologist, Adult and Child Psychoanalyst and member of Société Psychanalytique de Paris. She is on the faculty at the Columbia Psychoanalytic Center, Director of the Parent-Infant Psychotherapy Program. Author: *Play in Child Psychotherapy. Psychoanalytic Interventions with Parents and Babies. Process of Representation in Early Childhood. Capacity to Dream in Children*, and *Attacks on Linking in Parents of Young Disturbed Children*.

Acknowledgements

This book that has come out of the APM symposium *On the Body* would not have been possible without the help of Edith Cooper, Lila Kalinich, George Sagi, Stuart Taylor, Jonathan House, Bob Michels, Bonnie Kaufman, Edward Kenny, Aerin Hyun, Anand Desai, Judy Mars and the APM council members; David Gutman, Marvin Wasserman, Jules Kerman, Juliette Meyer, Talia Hatzor, Hillery Bosworth, Dina Abel, Harvey Chertoff and Jonah Schein.

For invaluably encouraging my writing and thinking, I want to thank my associate editor, Christine Anzieu-Premmereur. I have greatly enjoyed and benefited from my editorial work with Christine, who is an ongoing joy to work with and provides an abundance of psychoanalytic ideas.

Diane Robinson, my freelance copy-editor for this book, deserves many thanks. Kate Hawks, Kerry Boettcher and Charlotte Taylor have been most helpful on behalf of Routledge.

My most special thanks goes to my husband Michael, who has been the co-creator of the symposium and of this book from day one and has been my editor, and my inspirational partner at every step in the gestation of this book and a continuous wellspring of resourcefulness, psychoanalytic inspiration and true creativity. My special gratitude also goes to my eight year old daughter Ariadne, who aspires to be a writer herself, and has put up with my preoccupation and long hours of working on this project for the last three years, observing with unlimited curiosity the process of writing.

General introduction

Vaia Tsolas

Throughout Freud's writings, the intertwining of body and psyche was elemental. Hysteria revealed to Freud that infantile sexuality has a general traumatic nature that has to be repressed. This revelation in turn gave birth to the concept of the repressed unconscious and to the birth of psychoanalysis as a distinct discipline.

As psychoanalysis has evolved since Freud's time, in a world that has changed so dramatically, the relationships among repression, infantile sexuality and the unconscious continue to demand rigorous exploration. One line of thought suggests that the changes in our contemporary world have decentered repression from infantile sexuality. Thus, Anzieu (1990) points out that

> in Freud's time the repressed was that part of psychic life that related to sex: that is why he understood what sort of desires hysterics were expressing through their bodily symptoms. Now that the sexual is no longer taboo and with the loosening of morality, the development of contraception, and access by women and the young to sexual freedom, the repressed of today is the body.
>
> (p. 898)

In the view of many contemporary psychoanalytic theorists and practitioners, the role of infantile sexuality and its relationship to repression and the body has suffered a virtual, or total, eclipse, obscured by the emergence of the object relationship, or simply the relationship (See Greenberg & Mitchell, 1983). Many other theorists, spearheaded by but not limited to the followers of Jacques Lacan, continue to emphasize and to build theory and practice around Freud's foundational views of infantile sexuality and repression, and their connection to the unconscious and the body. The work of a number of such theorists, Lacanian and non-Lacanian alike, is represented in the current volume.

Before we proceed with this introduction however, let's elaborate on the question of what the body is that we psychoanalysts have as the object of our inquiry and how is it different from the biological body or the organism. This distinction, moreover, runs parallel to another distinction; that between the instinct and the drive.

Unfortunately, instinct and drive have been used as synonyms in English as a result of Strachey's erroneous translation of Freud's texts.

> Whereas the category of instinct covers a whole series of received animals' behaviors, mainly concerned with the preservation of the species (reproduction) and of the individual for the purposes of the species (survival), behaviors that vary little from one individual to another, the concept of drive introduced by Freud is radically different from that of instinct.
>
> (Mieli, 2017, p. 24)

Eating disorders, as one of many examples, highlight the difference between instinct and drive, as the drive to recapture the lost satisfaction overrides and opposes the instinct for preservation.

Condensing Freudian theory, I might run the risk of oversimplifying by saying, for heuristic purposes, that what accounts for the separation of instinct from drive is the lost original experience of satisfaction. The infant cries as need arises and the breast appears without a prior anticipation. This first satisfaction, being imprinted in the psyche as the primary memory trace of satisfaction, will launch the mental apparatus into a *push* to refind this original lost satisfaction without ever being able to reproduce it as it once was. When the need reappears, satisfaction will be sought via hallucinatory reactivation of the memory traces of prior satisfaction.

Freud (1900) states that:

> As a result of the link that has thus been established, next time this need arises as psychical impulse will at once emerge which will seek to re-cathect the mnemic image of the perception and to re-evoke the perception itself, that is to say, to re-establish the situation of the original satisfaction. An impulse of this kind is what we call a wish; the reappearance of the perception is the fulfillment of the wish.
>
> (p. 565)

Wish (desire) to regain the prior lost satisfaction rather than need (instinct) puts the psychic apparatus to work and mental life is born in the hallucinatory reproduction of the traces of perception. It is at this point and onwards that we can't speak of instinct alone, but rather of drive. In Freud's words, the drive is "the measure of the demand made upon the mind for work in consequence of its connection with the body." (1915, p. 122). This demand for satisfaction originating in the soma (the erogenous openings/zones of the body that involve the other) reaches its aim via the interchangeable part objects.

Hanna Segal (1997) points out, "I have always disagreed with the translation of Trieb as 'instinct.' I agree with Bettelheim that the best translation is the French 'pulsion'. The nearest in English would be 'drive'." (p. 21).

Furthermore, it is the body of the drives that we believe to be the object of psychoanalytic inquiry, rather than the body of the instincts; and it is this body that this book is intending to decipher.

Anzieu (1990), in revising the Lacanian motto "the unconscious is structured like a language," states pointedly that "the unconscious is structured like the body" and by so doing he differentiates this body from the body as studied and represented by anatomo-physiologists. It is rather the "body of the phantastic anatomy of hysteria and infantile sexual theories (as Freud clearly showed); and, more fundamentally still, in a more primary and archaic manner, the body as source of the first sensory-motor experiences, the first communications, and the oppositions that relate to the very basis of perception and thought." (p. 626). In other words, it is the libidinalized body trying to recapture the primordial loss of original satisfaction and not the organism that pushes the mind to tie excitations into mental representations and unconscious phantasy.

It is undeniable today that in the evolution of psychoanalytic theorizing and the vast majority of current psychoanalytic thought, the body of the drives has suffered a virtual aphanisis. This book *On the Body* brings together the thoughts, theories and clinical praxis of many of the world's most eminent psychoanalysts with the goal of returning to its proper place the body that Freud so brilliantly investigated.

On the Body is not simply an archeological excavation and restoration of the Freudian edifice; it also strives to illuminate and recenter the psychoanalytic body in a contemporary world that often appears to use technology to obscure loss, the fragility of our bodies and the ultimate limit, that of death. To this end, *On the Body* strives not only to return the body to the consulting room and its technical consequences, but also to examine the threats and challenges that this body of our being faces in the trend toward the post-human.

The clinical and intellectual significance of returning the body to the forefront of psychoanalytic discourse is urgent; and yet, as Sherry Turkle's contribution signals, the virtual obliteration of the Body from psychoanalytic theory is symptomatic of larger and hugely momentous cultural changes. In a world in which artificially "intelligent" computers (that have, of course, never experienced emotions and are devoid of anything resembling an unconscious) are being touted and promoted as the therapists of the future, a book heralding a return to the body is beyond vital and urgent. It is imperative!

The editors of *On the Body: A Psychoanalytic Exploration of the Body in Today's World*, as well as the eminent psychoanalysts collaborating in it, share the belief that psychoanalysis as it is widely practiced currently is drifting ever farther away from many of the primary concepts that anchor Freud's theorizing and that remain today as quintessentially imperative for a coherent and salutary psychoanalytic theory as they did over 120 years ago. We believe that for psychoanalysis to remain relevant, the body (in general) and the body of the drives (more specifically) must be restored to the central position that Freud understood it to occupy. Without this restoration, psychoanalysis is on a clear course to become yet another victim of the mergers and acquisitions of the non-corporeal corporate medical world. *On the Body* strives not only to return the body of the drives to the consulting room, but also to examine the threats and challenges that this body of our being faces in the trend toward the post human. The book also looks at the impact on behaviors, sexuality and psychosomatics of a body that has been affected by new technologies and transformed through medical and sociological changes.

If psychoanalysis is, indeed, to survive as a clinical and intellectual discipline that remains meaningfully distinguishable from theories and practices that gravitate increasingly toward the observable, quantifiable demands of the corporate and "post-human" (the driverless car of being), then it must rally its forces as best it is able to give full voice to a meaningful, well-thought-out and articulated alternative. As a group, the collaborators in this endeavor believe that this alternative must be anchored *On the Body*.

To a certain degree, recent psychoanalytic publications reveal a de facto collaboration in reclaiming in the psychoanalytic endeavor one or another view of the body. Historically speaking, as noted above, in the evolution of psychoanalytic theorizing, the body was extinguished from contemporary psychoanalysis as a consequence of leaving behind the Freudian drives in favor of a privileging of the object. This book, very specifically, and other recent books, more collaterally, further the mission of reminding psychoanalysts and psychoanalytically informed academics that the body and the mind of Freudian psychoanalysis cannot be considered apart from each other.

Other works, including those written from a relational and/or object relational perspective have sought to rescue the body from being thrown out with the bathwater of the drives, but the challenge remains. For example, in the Relational Perspectives Book Series in *Relational Perspectives on the Body*, Lewis Aron (2000) reminds us that before his death, Steve Mitchell informed relational theorists that, in rejecting drive theory, they ran the risk of a simultaneous rejection of the body. Aron goes on to point out how central a role sexuality plays in the rolling out of the complex relationship between patient and analyst. Jessica Benjamin's work, while staying clear of the intrapsychic drives, returns the body to the consulting room by rooting it instead in the relationship between two subjects (Benjamin, 2017).

From an object relational framework, Alessandra Lemma's work on the body, such as in her book *Minding the Body: The Body in Psychoanalysis and Beyond* (The New Library of Psychoanalysis, 2014) focuses on a range of subjects, such as the function of breast augmentation surgery, the psychic origins of hair, the use made of the analyst's toilet, transsexuality and the connection between dermatological conditions and necrophilic fantasies in order to demonstrate patients for whom the body is the primary presenting problem or who have made unconscious use of the body to communicate their psychic pain.

The Embodied Subject: Minding the Body in Psychoanalysis (2007) edited by John P. Muller (Editor) and Jane G. Tillman (Editor) takes a broad perspective, bringing together a wide range of both philosophical and clinical thoughts on the role of the body in post-Freudian psychoanalytically informed work. Furthermore, Rosemary Balsam's book *Women's Bodies in Psychoanalysis* (2012) argues that the female biological body, including the "vanished pregnant body," has been largely overlooked in psychoanalytic literature. She highlights the importance of thinking about the body's contribution to gender, rather than continuing the familiar postmodern trend of repudiating biology and perpetuating the divide between the physical and the mental. Balsam's chapter in our proposed book, and in fact the entire book, expands upon these ideas which view the body (biological) and mind (psychological) as an entity rather than as a duality.

On the Body comprises four sections, each with several major contributions.

Part I: The body in our changing world

The body is where the mind of the subject is rooted and, perhaps, the body is where the repressed/unconscious of our postmodern digital era resides as well. The papers in this section explore various ways in which the disembodiment of the body in the world of technology as well as the use of the body in the changing norms of gender fluidity, sexuality and reproduction are shaping our psyche.

Dr. Turkle appeals to the power of presence that she advanced in her recent books *Alone Together* (2011) and *Reclaiming Conversation* (2015) to explore the disembodiment that comes from using our digital devices in a flight from conversation. Here she explores the implications of the world in which more people would rather text than speak to each other face to face. In addition, Dr. Turkle explores what it means for our bodies that we have become open to interacting with machines as if they were invested with the same richness of human experience that we have when we were dealing with actual people. She also extends this exploration to the arena of psychotherapy itself as it becomes threatened by automated therapists and automated programs.

From his dual inheritance theory (genes strategy and cultural strategy), Dr. Paul's paper takes an anthropological point of view to examine the ways in which contemporary social changes in the structure of marriage and reproduction have evolved and impacted the world at large and the practice of psychoanalysis as a cultural phenomenon in specific. By examining an aspect of the real body, namely its sexual functions, Dr. Paul elucidates how from the time of the Greeks onward our civilization has been obsessed with the idea of creating humans, or good enough substitutes, by non-sexual mechanical means. In vitro fertilization (IVF) serves as an example of the contemporary disconnect between sex and reproduction with new consequences for the society and the individual. Paul goes back to Freud's unanswered question: is the malaise of civilization due to restrictions of our own sexual urges facing cultural constraints, or inherent in sexuality itself? He argues that it is both, but also that in our times it has a specific configuration brought about by the evolution of our sexual norms and cultural values where there is a disconnect between sex and reproduction; this disconnect recasts gender roles and many other organizations of sex in mutual, egalitarian terms. Similarly, psychoanalysis, given that it is a cultural phenomenon, has evolved accordingly. It has moved from the asymmetrical practice between the analyst and the analysand, where the focus was on interpretation and resolution of conflict with the goal of enhancing the ability to enjoy heterosexual genital intercourse and reproduction, into an egalitarian relationship, where the emphasis is on the dyadic relationship and on the exploration of a wide range of sexual practices disconnected from the goal of reproduction. Bountiful examples, both contemporary and historical, enrich this exposition.

In her 2012 book, *Women's Bodies in Psychoanalysis*, Balsam argued that psychoanalysis in the USA abandoned the psychological potentials of the material body, because the prevalent ego psychology was still in the dark ages in relation to women. "American psychoanalysis," she said, "had abandoned prematurely the continuing exploration Freud had begun of the body as a central psychic focus." Building on this, the author focuses on the intriguingly flexible genders that are enacted in life now, so much more freely than even just a few years ago. Especially given the myriad technological and social changes that impact the body, she writes about their relation to the psychic representation of individuals' bodies. Balsam observes that the ascent of relational theories has brought about a descent in the importance of the material body. In light of this, she explores essential questions: Where does the natal material body currently stand in dilemmas about flexible genders and also transgender roles and enactments? What does it mean to include active sex behaviors in gendered expressions that operate in progressive intimate partnerships? Where does the vitality of the body's natally endowed reproductivity become channeled, if unexpressed or inexpressible within a gender portrait that is born "she," but subsequently self-labeled "he"/"they"/ "ze"? (The same question goes for the natal "he"). And where does the material body or the altered material body place itself in debates about parenting and modeling internalization for the sex and gender patterns of nurtured children?

Part II: The body in the changing family

The Body in the Changing Family begins with Kristeva's chapter on the effects on the body of transformations of parentality. Kristeva defines the body as the psychosomatic construction that is formed as the speaking subject emerges in the relationship with the parental, where the parental is sexual difference, the third between the mother and the father. As analysts, Kristeva argues, we cannot speak of the body clinically without a theory of parentality in the evolving structure of the contemporary family. In our secular world, and with the help of technology and lawmakers, differences between sexes seem obliterated, heterosexuality extremely fragile, and the imperative to develop a new discourse of parentality becomes an emergency. Who is a mother and who is a father in our postmodern world where the Third is a disseminated One of incommensurable singularities? We need to develop a discourse of parentality on a case-to-case basis today without losing the necessity of sexual difference, which Freud conceptualized as the cornerstone of our psyches.

In this chapter Juliet Mitchell uses the "law of the mother" to address the psychological body via the sibling trauma. Her thesis applies both an inner and an outer framework. The inner framework is the "lateral body" of the bisexual social subject while the outer framework argues that psychoanalysis traditionally privileges the vertical axis of human parent and child to the neglect of the horizontal axis of lateral relations. Mitchell suggests here that although Freud always described the traumatic effects and theoretical importance of the next sibling's birth, this left him even more emphatic about the dominance of the Oedipus/castration complex and the Law of the Father on the vertical axis. Looking laterally along a horizontal axis, the mother intervenes between siblings to prohibit murder and incest. This "The Law of the Mother" precedes "The Law of the Father" (Lacan/Freud) since it comes in response to the trauma of the arrival of a younger sibling. The mother's prohibition operates only on the horizontal axis between her children. She clarifies that if we see that with the vertical and the horizontal axes, their similar desires and prohibitions are distinct ways of handling the fact that we are all "born under one law but to another bound," then we can realize that there is room for both.

Christine Anzieu-Premmereur adds a rich clinical component to this section. Her chapter focuses on the difficulty of treating children with severe defects of representation, children who are "deprived of life," who were never able to develop symbolic representation. From the Freudian notion of the embodied self to the development of a sexual body and a body Ego, Anzieu-Premmereur's chapter expands on the role of the body in Ego integration during early childhood, with clinical vignettes of babies and toddlers in session with their parents. The author also integrates infant researching, showing the importance of body sensations and their psychical assimilation. Anzieu-Premmereur asserts, with references to Spitz, Winnicott, Grotstein and Lombardi, that imitation, mirroring dyadic relations, holding and handling are at the forefront of maintaining a centered body ego. Infant observation and psychoanalytic interventions with disturbed young children show the role of the intersubjective relationship between parents and babies, and inform the therapeutic technique.

Part III: The sexual body, the speaking body and the sick body

"The ego is first and foremost a bodily ego: it is not merely a surface entity, but is itself the projection of a surface" (Freud, 1923, p. 26). In this section, the chapters explore the intertwining of sex and representation and its imprinting on the body that enjoys, speaks and gets ill.

Verhaeghe opens this section with a playful comment that psychoanalysis renders the binary "body and soul" less offensive by relabeling it sex and representation. He argues that Lacan's final theory understands the gap between the body and soul as a circular, but not reciprocal, relationship. In early Lacan, we find the mirror stage. The infant acquires an organized bodily awareness by identifying with the image presented by the mother. The resulting self-consciousness – "I have a body" – is deceptive because it originates outside the "self."

In Lacan's next period the accent was on the primacy of the drive, which Freud considered "a measure for the amount of work asked from the psyche because of its connection to the body." According to Lacan, this work is endless because the real part of the drive – object a – can never be represented. Compared to the first theory, the roles are reversed, as it is the organism that contains an original cause. It is the body that has an "I." Causality is at the core of the final theory, where we find Lacan's version of the immortal soul versus the temporary body. The organism functions as a cause, in the sense that it contains a primal loss and a tendency to remediate it; this is the loss of eternal life, which paradoxically enough is lost at the moment of birth, the moment that we are born as an individual with a particular sex. This primordial loss sets into motion a circular but not reciprocal process with the aim of undoing the loss and a return to the previous state of being. This "circular but not reciprocal process" runs as follows: by becoming a body, we lose eternal life. In trying to undo this loss, we become a subject but lose our body. In trying to regain the body, we become a man or a woman. The accompanying phallic interpretation of the loss is applied retroactively to all the preceding instantiations, such that each loss gets interpreted in a phallic way. The original circular but not reciprocal relationship between life and death, between organism and body, between jouissance and subject, is reproduced and worked over in the relationship between man and woman.

Aloupis presents the clinical case of a man suffering from heart disease in order to illustrate the dangerous liaisons between the somatic ailment and the death drive. Freud's 1930 letter to Pfister says: "The death instinct is not a requirement of my heart, it seems to me to be only an inevitable assumption on both biological and psychological grounds."

Viewed in this light, Aloupis argues, psychosomatics studies the path from instinct to drive, from the soma to the body. Using and expanding Freud's economic point of view in reference to the death drive and psychic trauma, he illustrates that the somatic disorder constitutes a trauma, insofar as the person is subjected psychically to an aggression that actively invades his/her psychic space, requiring adjustments and readjustments for which the subject may not be ready or adequately equipped to face. Using the Winnicottian concept of impingement, Aloupis illustrates how the trauma of the somatic ailment can be experienced as an impingement of a surplus of traumatic excitation that cannot be worked through (metabolized), psychically provoking, in return, aggressiveness and destructiveness that can go as far as putting the body in danger. As for Winnicott, where the space between mother and child is essential for the good enough mothering function to take place, the distance from the object is important for the treatment of psychosomatic patients. The therapist in the role of the good enough mother should take into account the effects of the death drive, facilitated by projective identification, in order to evaluate the danger it represents, but also its stratagems, adjustments and its role in the psychic conflict.

Papageorgiou, coming from the Paris school of psychosomatic, but with a focus different from Aloupis, elaborates on the original and rigorous conception of the processes of somatization through the lenses of affect. In this evocative clinical chapter, a patient who suffers from severe diabetes enters therapy to deal with the distress and anxiety associated with his illness, only to discover that he is a man who suffers from alexithymia (no words for feelings). The analyst utilizes her own preconscious mental functioning to help this somatic patient mentalize his own affect. Papageorgiou builds on Andre Green's situating affect at the core of mental functioning and Claude Smadja's original concept of the silence in psychosomatic praxis that describes the operational state in which the subject has become devoid of affect as a particular thought. Such children always behave well, having received the message from the mother that they cannot cause her any trouble by having their own affective and instinctual reality. Thus, the analyst must use her preconscious to decipher the patient's unarticulated affect and to facilitate the patient's capacity for mental functioning, lifting the burden from the body.

Part IV: Sex, gender and infantile sexuality

It was Freud's assertion, not only that children were sexual, but also that human sexuality was polymorphously perverse in nature, that made him unpopular in his times. In our theorizing, the notion of infantile sexuality has been repressed. Ironically, sexuality today is polymorphous beyond Freud's imagination, thanks in part to the technologies that transcend the natal body. This section explores the complexities of these phenomena.

Scarfone, the scholar of Laplanche, expands on Freud's theory of trauma in this chapter, elaborating on "beyond the pleasure principle" with regard to the repetition compulsion. More specifically, he focuses on how the psyche is embodied in trauma and examines what is in common between a phantom pain, a curse-utterance in aphasia and a fetish in order to delineate more ordinary processes in infancy where the body-psyche stumbles on the repressed infantile sexuality of the caretaker.

"If we needed an additional argument in favor of the view that the psyche is embodied, phantom pain offers a most convincing one," Scarfone states. This embodiment, Scarfone specifies, is an embodiment-with-unconsciousness, which offers a caveat against the illusion of a direct access to the body. In other words, the body from the psyche's perspective is a foreign body. Thus, psychoanalysts are concerned with a different body from the body studied by biologists. Similar to phantom pain, in Freud's book on aphasia, aphasic patients are still able with great excitement to say afterwords a vigorous curse, which were the last words produced before the injury. In both cases, the subject, unprepared in the face of tragic loss, is left hanging to the last intense speech or motor residues that remain frozen due to the trauma.

An interesting comparison with a fetish, where the problem is once again one of disappearance, however imaginary, illustrates the same phenomenon. In this case the phantom limb becomes the foot or shoe, a material substrate for the missing body-part (the penis). Scarfone highlights that the common denominator in these three cases is that the psyche, in the face of being unprepared, is trying to transform passivity into activity and in this way re-establishing the integrity of the narcissistic image. Scarfone's elaboration of Freud with Laplanche states that infants, no matter how active they are, remain unprepared and helpless to deal with the repressed Infantile sexuality (the Sexual for Laplanche) embedded in the adult messages.

In this chapter, Gherovici, the well-known author of *Please Select Your Gender* (2010), remarks on the lack of psychoanalytic discourse on transgenderism in order to assert that developing a discourse on transgenderism will reorient our practice and improve it. She beautifully illustrates that the historical backdrop of this lack resides in the ever persistent predominance of dichotomies of mind/body and sex/gender. From a Freudian/Lacanian perspective, Gherovici highlights instead the disjunction we see in transgender subjects between their experience of their bodies and the given natal body, in other words between having a body and being a body, to point out that this disjunction is not unique to the transgender subjects but to any human subject. This disjunction springs from our own sense of castration.

According to Freudian and Lacanian theory, there is constitutionally always something out of sync in human sexuality. Gherovici proposes that doing something with this disjunction between our experience of our sexual bodies and our sexual bodies themselves is a complex lifelong process of embodiment and that it is a particular challenge today given the plethora of gender categorizations and options that technology makes possible. The contemporary American belief in technology and self/reinvention converts gender transition into a commodity, a personal choice available to those who can afford it, Gherovici states. This ideal, presented to us as another form of a more perfect union between our sexual bodies and our social identities, denies the ever-persisting discord between the two and, at the core, is the discord between language and sex. In this gap between the two is the arena where every subject tries to embark on its own individual journey, the place where sex needs to be symbolized and gender needs to be embodied.

Tsolas' final chapter presents two clinical cases of female patients to explore the link between repudiation of femininity and masochism in the face of a harsh early maternal superego. The author suggests that anal defenses in these cases restrict the penetration of libido into the ego and block the binding of energy into representation, leaving the body abandoned to carry the unsymbolized mark of defect even at the cost of extinguishing life itself, as in the second case. The hypercathexis of these patients' intellectual capacities serves to push away incestuous wishes and oedipal guilt associated with parricide in an attempt to repair the father by thinking, overvaluing thought and signification. Both patients suffer from the unseen beatings of a phallic, harsh, and hypervigilant superego, the humiliations of having a defective feminine body that does not work and the overflow of jouissance that breaks through as unbearable realistic anxiety.

The first patient, Anna, is a successful writer who presented initially to treatment suffering from vaginismus and a masochistic relationship with a long term boyfriend. Her recent immigration from the east to the west, from a culture that prioritized the needs of the family over the individual's to a culture that valued the opposite, highlighted Anna's conflict over sacrificing, for the father, the weak castrated mother and with that, her adult female sexuality. The second patient, Matilda, is diagnosed with terminal cancer around the same time her father was diagnosed with cancer. Matilda, in the intergenerational chain of female subjectification and reactive rage to male domination, assumed the role of the one who is supposed to set the record right; her role, to be like a man and to prove how it is possible for a woman to do it all. A successful business woman who managed to get married and to be a mother later in life, she came too close to proving to all generations before her that she was the woman who had it all; then, at the moment of her triumph, a very aggressive tumor appeared to return her to the mark of her birth. Was she being punished because she finally had gotten it all or was this her final challenge to prove herself? Was she dying instead of the father, for the father? The unfolding of these cases will be discussed in reference to Schaffer's notion of repudiation of the *feminine dimension,* Kristeva's reading of Freud's "child is being beaten" and Chasseguet-Smirgel's work on feminine guilt and the Oedipus complex to suggest the challenges to transcend the anal/phallic maternal superego and to acknowledge sexual difference.

References

Anzieu, D. (1990). *A Skin for Thought: Interviews with Gilbert Tarrab on Psychology and Psychoanalysis.* London: Karnac Books.

Aron, L., & Anderson, F.S. (2000). *Relational Perspectives on the Body.* London: Routledge.

Balsam, R. (2012). *Women's Bodies in Psychoanalysis.* New York, NY: Routledge.

Benjamin, J. (2017) *Beyond Doer and Done To: Recognition.* Theory, Intersubjectivity and the Third. New York and London: Routledge.

Freud, S. (1900). The Interpretation of Dreams. *Standard Edition,* 4. London: The Hogarth Press.

Freud, S. (1915). Instincts and Their Vicissitudes. *Standard Edition,* 14. London: The Hogarth Press.

Freud, S. (1923). The Ego and the Id. *Standard Edition,* 19. London: The Hogarth Press, pp. 12–66.

Freud, S. (1930). Civilization and Its Discontents. *Standard Edition,* 21. London: The Hogarth Press, pp. 64–145.

Gherovici, P. (2010). *Please Select Your Gender: From the Invention of Hysteria to the Democratizing of Transgenderism.* New York and London: Routledge.

Greenberg, J., & Mitchell, S. (1983). *Object Relations in Psychoanalytic Theory.* Cambridge, MA: Harvard University Press.

Lemma, A. (2014). *Minding the Body: The Body in Psychoanalysis and Beyond* (The New Library of Psychoanalysis). London: Routledge.

Mieli, P. (2017). *Figures of Space: Subject, Body, Place*. Translated by Jacques Houis. New York: Agincourt Press.

Muller, J.P. (2007). Introduction. In Muller, J.P., and Tillman, J. (eds.), *The Embodied Subject: Minding the Body in Psychoanalysis*. Plymouth, UK: Jason Aronson Inc., pp. vii–xiii.

Segal, H. (1997). On the Clinical Usefulness of the Concept of the Death Instinct. In Spillius (ed.), *Psychoanalysis, Literature and War*. London: Routledge, pp. 14–21.

Turkle, S. (2015). *Reclaiming Conversation: The Power of Talk in a Digital Age*. New York: Penguin Press.

Part I

The body in our changing world

Chapter 1

Introduction

Vaia Tsolas

Just as it is often proffered that Freud's hysterics, so critical to the very development of psychoanalytic thought, represent an emotional embodiment of the repressed sexuality of Victorian times that coincides with the industrial revolution, it may be argued that the contemporary psyche and its pathologies are shaped fundamentally by the disembodiment of the body in the world of technology that recasts the use of the body in the changing norms of gender fluidity, unrepressed sexuality and reproduction. The following section explores this argument from the sufficiently triangulated perspective of three psychoanalytic voices to facilitate charting the reader's course through the challenging currents and turbulence of the contemporary body politic.

Building on her impactful book, *Reclaiming Conversation* (2015), Sherry Turkle explores the impact of our digital age on human interactions. She contends that ever so often now, we interact with machines 'as if' they were embodied with the richness of human experience, thus enhancing the risk of treating other humans as if they too were disembodied, rendering conversation irrelevant as a result. Her research unearths college students who can be looking directly at their professors and typing on their phones at the same time, revealing an undetected split attention that signifies their virtuosic capacity to leave their bodies behind in surrogacy.

Turkle's writing illustrates, with various examples, that technology's appeal rests on the promise that it will solve our problems and will help us lead a life that is "friction free." "*Perhaps we have always wanted to run from our bodies, from the anxieties of embodied empathy, of being together in this messy way, and now we are given a chance?*" Turkle questions what the implications for the body are in the digital culture (what she calls "the culture of forgetting") in which increasingly more people would rather text than converse face-to-face, rely on empathy machines to imitate affect and reach out to sociable robots to erase loneliness and replace human relatedness. And Turkle also questions psychoanalysts themselves who have given in to the use of disembodied technologies such as Skype.

Robert Paul builds on his dual inheritance theory (genes strategy and cultural strategy), using psychoanalytically informed anthropology to examine contemporary social changes in the structure of marriage as they have evolved and impacted the world at large and the practice of psychoanalysis as a cultural phenomenon in specific. Beginning with the real body of sexual functions, Dr. Paul contends that civilization has been obsessed with the idea of creating humans, or good enough substitutes, by non-sexual mechanical means. The contemporary disconnect between sex and reproduction, and the consequences of this disconnect, jump off the page with IVF. Paul returns to Freud's unanswered question: is the malaise of civilization due to restrictions of our own sexual urges facing cultural constraints, or inherent in sexuality itself? He argues that not only is it both, but also that in our times it has a specific configuration brought about by the evolution of our sexual norms and cultural values where there is a disconnect between sex and reproduction; this disconnect recasts gender roles and many other organizations of sex in mutual, egalitarian terms. Similarly, psychoanalysis, as a cultural phenomenon, has evolved accordingly. It has moved from the asymmetrical practice between the analyst and the analysand, where the focus was on interpretation and resolution of conflict and inhibition of libido with the goal of enhancing the ability to enjoy heterosexual genital intercourse and reproduction, into an egalitarian relationship, where the emphasis is on the dyadic relationship and on the exploration of a wide range of sexual practices disconnected from the goal of reproductive copulation.

The author of *Women's Bodies in Psychoanalysis* (2012), Rosemary Balsam argues that ego psychology tipped psychoanalysis in the United States away from the psychological potentials of the material body, because it remained in the dark ages in relation to women. While Freud had begun an exploration of the body as a central psychic focus, American psychoanalysis prematurely abandoned continuing this fertile exploration. In the current section Balsam focuses on modern gender fluidity and its relation to the psychic representation of individuals' bodies in the context of burgeoning technological expansion of possibility. In her paper, Balsam suggests that modern gender plurality is demanding a transformation of personal pronouns in our common language and this seems to signal a profound change in era. She carefully explores essential questions about the natal material body in the context of gender fluidity, transgender roles and enactments. This chapter explores many compelling questions via clinical vignettes about the vicissitudes of the natal body's vitality in the context of our current technologically engendered multiplicities.

References

Balsam, R. (2012). *Women's Bodies in Psychoanalysis*. Hove: Routledge.
Turkle, S. (2015). *Reclaiming Conversation: The Power of Talk in a Digital Age*. New York: Penguin Press.

Chapter 2

Empathy machines
Forgetting the body

Sherry Turkle

Digital culture is a culture of forgetting (Turkle, 2015). Most specifically, it tempts us to forget what it can only simulate: the body. In every relationship, digital culture challenges us to reaffirm our commitment to presence and the significance of "being there."

One might think that psychoanalysis – so profoundly rooted in things of the body – would be immune from such temptations. But it is not. Today, many analysts do psychotherapy, psychoanalysis, and even training analyses (analytic sessions in which analysands are trained to become analysts themselves) using Skype and FaceTime. This may begin as a convenience – for example, a large market for classical analysis opened in China just as the market for it was closing down in the United States. Skype sessions were first presented as better than nothing–the patient was at a distance and other options were not available – but they ended up being justified as simply better, a method that frees and disinhibits analytic interaction.

Indeed, analysts have joined the culture of forgetting, to the point where it makes sense to ask if they will defend physical presence as the gold standard for the development and expression of intimacy and empathy. This question takes on greater importance because, in the larger culture, empathy has become a contested terrain. Some psychologists contrast it unfavorably with concern and rational compassion, presented as more global and less discriminatory (see Bloom, 2016). In the day-to-day, we subvert empathy by using technology to distract ourselves from the conversations that nurture it. And taking a longer view, technologists propose machines as relational substitutes for people, machines that could only ever offer *as-if* empathic connection (see Turkle, 2015).

Who are we becoming as we become drawn to a life without contingency, one that seeks connection without physicality, one that my engineering colleagues like to talk about with the phrase "friction free?"

As I ask this question, I note this paradox: Our society seems eager to put aside our bodies when we communicate with intimates, yet we are ever more concerned with our bodies' upkeep. Across generations and gender lines, we care more about fashion, fitness, make up, and cosmetic surgery than ever before, while caring less about the body's presence in relationships. We have a stake in our bodies becoming ever more perfect so that we can "wear" them, and healthily, but we are alienated from what they do for us relationally, where we become content with stand-ins for physical presence.

The robotic moment

I talk about our reaching *the robotic moment* (Turkle, 2011), not because we have built machines worthy of talking to us about personal matters (because we have not) but because we are willing to talk to unworthy machines. We become accustomed to digital interlocutors, from robot dolls to online agents. We take machines that have not lived the arc of a human life, that have not lived in a human body, and treat them as if they could fully share our human experience.

We invest in what people readily call "empathy machines," a phrase that undermines the meaning of empathy because it has no room for embodied experience. So, for example, we are tempted by companionship and even therapeutic dialogue with computer programs that are designed to pass a new kind of Turing test. This time we are not fussing about whether a computer is intelligent (that was so 20th century!); the new test is whether a machine can simulate affect. In Turing's behavioral test, seeming to be intelligent was intelligence enough. Now, seeming to have empathy is proposed as what it will take to qualify you as empathic enough to serve as a companion and even as a psychotherapist. The psychotherapist programs are still primitive but in the robotic moment, we declare ourselves ready for them before they are ready for us.

The assault on empathy

The "silent spring" is a phrase that Rachel Carson coined to denote a shared recognition that technology, despite its many marvels, was contributing to an assault on the environment (Carson, 1962). Now, we recognize its assault on empathy. The research is compelling. One study that reviewed thirty years of studies that measured empathy among college students found a 40-percent decline (Konrath, O'Brien, & Hsing, 2011). Since most of the change was in the final decade of the study, the researchers linked the empathy gap to the presence of mobile communication. Indeed, research shows that the presence of a phone on a table during a conversation, even a phone turned off, does two things: the conversation turns to more trivial matters and the people in the conversation feel less connected to each other (see for example Przybyliski & Weinstein, 2012).

Even a silenced phone creates distance between us. Our phones also undermine our connection to ourselves, our capacity for solitude, and this from the earliest ages. There are baby bouncers and potty trainers with a slot for a phone or a tablet. By the time people are in college, solitude has become painful, almost impossible to sustain.

In one experiment, college students were asked to sit alone without a book or a phone for fifteen minutes (see Wilson, Reinhard, Westgate, Gilbert, Ellerbeck, Hahn, Brown, & Shaked, 2014). Although the students began the experiment saying they would never consider it, after six minutes a significant number delivered electroshocks to themselves rather than spend those minutes in quiet reflection. These results are not surprising. When people are alone, for even a few moments, in a line at the supermarket or at a stop sign, we see that they reach for a device.

We struggle to pay attention to ourselves just as we struggle to pay attention to each other. The two go together. We need the capacity to be alone to be able to fully attend to each other. If you can't gather yourself to yourself, you can't come to another person and really hear them, you can't see them as an individual rather than projecting onto them what you need them to be. Without the ability to be content in solitude, we risk using other people almost as spare parts to buttress our fragile sense of self (see Ornstein, 1978).

Human relationships are rich; they're messy and demanding. These days, when we flee conversation to communicate behind the safety of a screen or divide our attention between the people we are with and the people "in the phone," we try to clean up our relationships with technology. We forget the difference between conversation and mere connection. *This isn't just a side effect. We have to consider that it has become the desired effect.*

What our phones allow us to avoid

People talk about being addicted to their devices; it is important to remember that their attachments express both what they want their phones to provide and what they want their phones to help them avoid. What I hear most is that a phone allows you to avoid moments of boredom and anxiety. One young woman I interview talked to me about her "seven-minute rule." She explained that it takes seven or eight minutes to know if a conversation is going to be interesting. As she spoke she seemed so wise. But she quickly explained that she doesn't have the patience to put in that time. She doesn't like "the boring bits" in conversation. She goes to her phone as soon as there is a lull in a conversation. The "lull" makes her anxious.

But research is making it ever more clear that what people are now experiencing as a moment of "feared boredom" (that "lull") can be a driver to reach within yourself or to look deeper into others. Anxiety may signal that you are stretching yourself in a new direction (for an overview see Schooler, 2009); it may signal that you're learning something new, something disruptive, something alive. And, of course, it is often when we stumble, or are silent, that we reveal ourselves most to each other. We lose each other if we can't tolerate silence or the "boring bits."

But these days, we become accustomed – on social media – to seeing life as a kind of steady feed. *It is always changing, always new.* We turn a lull or a moment alone into problems that need to be solved. And people try to solve them with technology. We slip into thinking that always being connected is going to make us less lonely. But we are at risk, because it is actually the reverse. Here, the psychoanalytic tradition offers a formulation that captures our risk: If we don't teach our children to be alone, they will only know how to be lonely (for elaboration see Winnicott, 1958).

The researcher who led the study that found that empathy was down 40-percent among college students was depressed by her findings. She told me that she wanted to do something constructive, so when the empathy study was over she went on to make "empathy apps" for the iPhone. The notion here is that technology has created a problem that technology can solve. So, if children can't relate, there might be an app for that. Or they might do well with machine confidants, or programs that will serve as psychotherapists, or robots that will read to them, or dolls that can befriend them. All of these are "empathy machines."

Empathy machines: machine confidants

In 2011, when Siri was introduced, I was on a radio show discussing it with a panel of engineers and social scientists. The conversation began with how this computer agent was able to answer factual questions but was also programmed to give shockingly lifelike answers to questions about one's emotional life – many of these were responses pre-programmed into the system by Apple to make Siri seem smarter than it was. The topic turned to how much people like to talk to Siri, part of the general phenomena that allows people to feel uninhibited when they talk to a machine; they like the feeling of no judgment. One of the social scientists on the program suggested that soon a somewhat smoothed out Siri could serve as a psychiatrist. It didn't seem to bother him that Siri, in the role of psychiatrist, would be counseling people about their lives without having actually lived one. If a program can *behave* like a psychiatrist, he said, it could *be* a psychiatrist. If no one minded the difference between the "as if" and the real thing, let the machine take the place of the person. This is the new pragmatism of "the robotic moment."

These days, we are close to living in the world that social scientist envisaged. Conversational programs have matured. They are better at behaving as if they were psychiatrists, but one thing has stayed constant – for all that they are able to pretend, machines that talk to us as though they care about us do not know the arc of a human life. They can only deliver performances of empathy and connection, and yet people persist with the idea that we can get empathy and connection from the world of apps – things that have no bodies and lives. *The assault on empathy and its connection to human embodiment does not come from what computers can do but from how the very prospect of artificial intelligence has changed who we are as people and what we consider essential to our humanity.*

Consider a mother who tells me that she is pleased that her daughter, a ten-year-old, "vents" to Siri. The girl feels free to let her feelings out to the computer agent. The mother continues: With people, her daughter is more likely to play the role of the "good girl." Isn't her self-expression with technology a good thing? There is no simple story to tell here: One of the most important lessons of childhood is that saying something angry to a parent doesn't destroy a parent; that the fantasy that one can destroy a parent with words is only that, a fantasy. This lesson, that words don't destroy, frees up the capacity for feeling and expressing emotion. You risk sidestepping this crucial lesson if you suggest that you can only say hard things if you express yourself to a machine. That's exactly what this mother does not want to teach her daughter. And yet to many it seems a clean solution.

Now consider "Hello Barbie," a sociable toy robot that comes out of the box, announces that it is your friend and has been pre-programmed to know that you have a sister and to say that it has a sister too. The doll may go on to share that "she" is often angry at "her" sister. What about you? And how are things at school? In all of this, the child is asked to enter a pretend world of feelings. An as-if world of a doll pretending to have a life in a body, a life born of a mother. Perhaps, even, a life in conflict with that mother or with a father. Hello Barbie pretends empathy but has none to give. And it does not allow the space for imaginative, projective play that the old fashioned, silent Barbie did. With a traditional doll, a young girl who had just broken her mother's crystal might put her dolls in detention. Play space was a way to work through the turmoil of one's inner life. Hello Barbie has its own agenda.

Like all sociable robots, Hello Barbie connects with people not so much through its smarts, but by the way it gives us clues that it understands and cares about us. These days, sociable robots are targeted for the very young (this year the big toy craze is the Hatchimal, a robot that seems to develop under your care) and the very old. For years I brought sociable robots (most in the shape of robotic pets) to nursing homes. The robots were able to fool older people into thinking they were recognized and understood (Turkle, 2011). In that setting, I had a moment of reckoning. To an older woman who had lost a child, I gave a "Paro," a robot in the shape of a baby seal. The Paro made sounds and movements that convinced this grieving mother that the robot understood her problem. She began to confide in it, and to comfort it when it showed sadness, because she thought it was grieving for her. As all of this unfolded, those of us who had brought the robot into her life stood around amazed. Spectators. But we were so pleased that this woman was talking to the robot that we had stopped asking: Who was listening to this woman? Isn't that the question that defines the compact among generations? *That we will listen to each other*. To understand her problem, a death, you had to live in a body. You had to understand mortality. And loss. I think you had to have had a mother.

We forget this compact between generations, a compact that implicates our bodies, when we imagine robotic companions for the elderly. In my research, I've found that in considering robotic companions, people begin with the idea that there is "nobody there to do those jobs." The robot is better than nothing. And then we begin to argue that the robot is better than something: It is always available. So handy. No older person ever need feel alone. And then, people take a critical step. They change their criteria about what is valuable. Efficiency and cost become the new metrics and the inanimate creature becomes better than anything, more reliable than what life could ever provide. But life, embodied human life, can provide what robots cannot: a person who has lived a life, a person who can be empathic.

The same "better than nothing to better than something" argument is used to consider how artificial intelligence might come into other aspects of our affective lives. For example, it is used to argue the merits of robots reading to children: the robot readers will always be there. Many children have no one to read to them, so the robots are better than nothing. But once developed, we are drawn to substitutions. We change our metric for assigning value and place a higher and higher value on what is always available. And that will always be a machine. We forget that reading to a child is an occasion to talk about the human stories in books, conversations that can only take place with a reader who has lived a human life. Reading to a child is a chance to talk about your feelings about the stories. It is a chance to talk about your family, your history. It is a chance to teach about the embodied life. On some level we know this. And yet we are drawn to fantasies of a world of automatic readers. Technology can make us forget what we know about life.

Avoiding presence: fighting by text

People turn texting, email, and chat into empathy machines when they use them for "conversations" that only a few years ago would have been considered the kind of conversations that a dining room table was made for: the conversations of family discord. I study families who take presence out of difficult family conversations and prefer to "fight by text." By this they mean that they air family grievances online. When they do this, as my colleagues at MIT would say, life proceeds in a manner that is more "friction free."

So, for example, parents and children who "fight by text" tell me that if they don't meet face-to-face they stand a better chance of being "heard out," and so they are more open in expressing their feelings. It's easier to express yourself, they say, if the other person isn't in the room. It's worth pausing on this: It is, after all, the presence of the other person and learning how our words affect them that teaches us how to put ourselves in the place of the other. And for children, watching how this unfolds (and that their elders *care* about how this unfolds), teaches that empathy is a value.

Telling a family member that you will get back to them when you have composed yourself is a time-honored way of handling a difficult turn in a relationship. What is different in the many families who talk to me about "fighting by text" is that what was once a moment now becomes a method. My concern is that it may send the message to family members that in general, you are so reactive you won't try to process your feelings in real time, and perhaps you don't think they can. And even if you don't think you are saying these things, this may be what your child or spouse or partner may hear.

Fighting by text, where you put the emphasis on getting the "right" message out, also sets the expectation that you, too, will require crafted responses. It suggests that you are trying for some perfect response. Indeed, it implies that you think there is a way for people to talk to each other in which each party will say the *right* thing.

Analysts fall for an empathy machine

Families take presence out of family meetings and argue that this is a good thing because it opens up the conversation. These days, therapists, too, from cognitive behavioral therapists to analysts, have also taken their bodies out of the room. They've been tempted (because it is *so* tempting) to move from occasionally doing a session by phone or Skype with a traveling patient to doing more and more of it and envisaging whole treatments using it.

On one level, the enthusiasm of analysts makes no sense at all. Analysts have been the most eloquent champions of presence. Their tradition explores how when people deeply listen to each other, they have bodily experiences of each other's words. So, in sessions, analysts and analysands get sleepy, get headaches, want to get up and stretch. That bodily experience is in part a reaction that demonstrates the deep connections and complexity of the work. As a treatment unfolds, it is explicitly part of understanding the transference and countertransference. But beyond the therapeutic context, that understanding of how bodily experience is part of intimate conversation is part of how the psychoanalytic tradition contributes to the culture: We are with each other body and mind, words and bodies, all tied together. Yet even analysts, who have brought us the most moving writing about the importance of presence and the body in treatment, have been quick to forget its importance (On this point, see Isaacs Russell, 2015; Miller, 2014).

Within the analytic community, the idea of analysis by Skype has become increasingly banal. A recent webinar on virtual practice sponsored by the International Psychoanalytic Association was almost celebratory in tone. To listen to the presenters, there was not much reason to treat the doors opened by new technology as anything but a gift (www.ipa.world). As one strained to connect with the image of the presenters on the screen, it was hard to believe that they were arguing for the virtues of electronic presence. And yet they were: the preoccupations of the webinar were mostly logistical. We have normalized machine-mediated psychoanalysis. But we must step back to understand what is being lost. It is not too late to make the corrections.

Here we have a profession that has given us some of the most sophisticated writing on the relationship between words and the body. And yet, faced with technology, it can become naïve. One analyst told me that on Skype she feels a quickening, things feel more intense than when the patient is with her in the room. I felt sad when I pointed out to her the significant literature on online life and hypervigilance. Online, we are put into a state of hypervigilance. It is natural to feel that quickening. It's exhilarating, but it is very precisely not the relaxed, free floating attention that psychoanalysis suggests as the necessary path to access her patient's unconscious process and her own.

Why are the princes of the relationship between mind and body so quick to abandon the body and what it brings to our understanding? We know that there is a financial incentive to analyze people and even do training analysis at a distance. One can reach people in far-flung locations. But is there something more? *Perhaps we have always wanted to run from our bodies, from the anxieties of embodied empathy, of being together in this messy way, and now we are given a chance?* Psychoanalysis, in all of its "impossibility," is stressful on the mind and the body of the analyst. Distancing oneself makes it easier. And so now we allow ourselves a high-tech way out, a way to think that we are doing more or less the same thing as before. Indeed, perhaps *better* than we have done before, by certain metrics. Better, because with distance we can focus on the words. We can easily and unobtrusively record sessions and have an exact transcription of what occurred. We can work even when illness or travel or vacations might have impeded treatment. If these become our metrics, analysis on Skype or FaceTime isn't just better than nothing, it can be better than anything.

Technology encourages us to change our metrics for evaluation, and to forget the original nature of our enterprise. This was the logic by which robot pets became better than "real" pets. The robot pets will always be there, they will always be loving in their behavior, they will never die. And this is the logic by which machine psychotherapists will be better than people. They will be available to everyone. They will be democratic, scientific, and, of course, they build on the behaviorism and pragmatism of the robotic moment: If the programs can fake conversation, they can do the job. A human body and its experiences are not required. An as-if relationship is relationship enough (Morris & Picard, 2012).

The larger culture: fantasies of the friction-free

Over decades, and across generations, I have been talking to people about their lives with technology. I ask them, always, to tell me if they have any ideas about how they would like technology to change their lives. The conversation comes back, again and again, to images of a life with less emotional wear and tear. Among engineers, I have said that the phrase that comes up to describe this life of less stress is "friction free."

So, for example, in my MIT world, there has for decades been talk about how wiring up every object on the Internet ("the Internet of things") would make life easier. Now that this program is fast becoming everyday reality, I am reminded of an early demo that showed how one could order coffee on the network and the barista at your favorite coffee shop would have it prepared to your exact taste when you arrived. Meanwhile, you would get to the shop on a route mapped out by your phone that would avoid your ex-lovers, ex-spouses, and anyone you had tagged as a difficult person. Only a few years ago, that was a demo. Now, there is *Cloak*, an app for your phone. *Cloak's* tagline is "Incognito mode for real life," and it offers its users the ability to "avoid exes, co-workers, that guy who likes to stop and chat – anyone you'd rather not run into." It is the beginning of the friction-free life because the real world is mapped onto a virtual grid and your body only travels in non-confrontational space. But who said that a life without conflict, without dealing with the past, or without rubbing up against the troublesome people in it was good? Who said that not having to be reminded of past mistakes, with past pain, made up the good life? Was it the same person who said that life shouldn't have boring bits? When did these images of life without boring bits become our aesthetic? When did we decide that these were problems that we wanted technology to help us solve?

That's a trend: the idea that just because technology can help us solve a problem means that it was a problem in the first place. What technology critic Evgeny Morozov calls "solutionism," suggests a methodology for understanding our moment: What are the problems we imagine that we want technology to help us solve? (Morozov, 2012). These days we seem vexed by the body's role in generating empathy and intimacy. We'd rather relate on our screens. If only empathy could bypass bodies! If only machines could generate it! Perhaps possess it. Or at least facilitate it. For me, virtual reality, by definition, takes the body as a problem it can solve. It accelerates the move to take empathy (an offer of understanding in the particular case, an offer that demands conversation) and replace it with concern or compassion, something you can feel when you project yourself into the world in the machine.

Being there

These days we are most likely to meet virtual reality (VR) in the form of films to watch with goggles that make us feel that we are "there." For example, the filmmaker Chris Milk has made a VR film, *Clouds Over Sidra*, in which you feel you are sitting on the floor next to a twelve year old girl in a Syrian refugee camp in Jordan. Milk says: "Virtual reality makes anyone, anywhere, feel local. It works like an empathy system." (Milk, TED Talk).

Virtual reality begins with a certain humility. It presents itself as something that is better than nothing. Right now, all of us can't be in a refugee camp, so VR lets us experience the camp. But VR moves quickly away from humility. *An empathy system*. Milk says that *Clouds Over Sidra* provides "an empathic experience" that will make us understand, connect, and feel at one with Syrian refugees.

Milk showed *Clouds Over Sidra* at the 2016 World Economic Forum in Davos. And following that, he gave a TED talk that included a film of him showing the VR film at Davos. In the TED talk, we see rows of men in suits in a climate controlled room wearing goggles. The men are not cold or tired or hungry. They have not travelled to a refugee camp. They are not meeting any refugees, talking to them, or sharing their food. But through their goggles, they have the VR experience of being among them.

Over the past decades, social media enabled the development of social norms that discouraged friends from visiting each other and excused colleagues from showing up to what used to be shared work spaces. Then, we began to use smartphones as a way not to look at each other when we gathered together. Phones relieved the anxiety of conversation and physical presence. Now, we are enthralled because VR use makes us feel "as if" we are in a refugee camp. Substitution isn't the intent. But we have learned that substitution is always a subtext.

As Milk puts it, "VR makes anyone, anywhere, feel local." Here is what needs vigilance: The feeling of local becomes local enough. Just as when you talk to a computer program that passes the Turing test for a psychotherapist, the feeling of being in a conversation becomes conversation enough.

Milk's film is a technical wonder. But Milk says that films such as these "will make us more human." That is not clear at all. VR makes it easier for us to *see* classes of people up close, people who would have been distant from us. But we are quickly learning the limits of disembodied seeing. On March 16, 2016, the ravaged city of Aleppo was presented to the world in a virtual reality film. Naturally, news stories about this wrenching film cited Chris Milk. This film, said the critics, would be the "ultimate empathy machine." (Nudd, 2016). But clearly, our technological fantasies are just that. It will take more to realize our humanity.

The fantasies around VR as an empathy machine remind me of my studies of the first generation of people who wore Google glass. They talked about their hope that if their spouses, boyfriends, and partners had Google glass, they could watch a recording of the world from their point of view and how sharing a perspective would improve their relationship. They told me that talking was so hard, so emotionally fraught, and that they loved the idea that they could just hand over how they saw the world – their actual perspective – on tape so they wouldn't have to explain.

And they talked about political hopes for glass as an empathy machine. Some said that if a white person could see the world from the point of view of a person of color, even if they didn't know a person of color, the white person could understand their experience. It would be like being there, certainly better than trying to get into someone else's head by talking with them. "Talking," said one young man, "is so complicated, unscientific and subjective." Glass could make empathy objective. These are similar fantasies to those I hear when people talk about virtual reality. And they are not so far from new musings about what "rational compassion" has over empathy. Rational compassion has a surgical precision. Empathy is sloppy. It leads us to odd preferences; the odd human preferences of embodied selves, subject to fatigue, infatuation, arousal. Empathy is a local, particular, uncomfortable emotion. Perhaps VR fails as an empathy system because, disembodied, we are left with compassion, a more global and feel-good feeling – or a feel-bad feeling. Either way, we get to it without being there or by connecting to a person we care about.

I think of the researcher who was depressed when she found an empathy gap and wanted to build apps for the iPhone. It is always easier to build an app than it is to have a conversation, and no matter how impressive the art, it is always easier to make a movie than it is to visit those refugees. *But tempted by empathy machines, it is important to remember that we, embodied, are the empathy app.*

Every technology challenges our human values, which is a good thing, because it causes us to reflect on what these values are. Empathy machines raise the concern that we will model who we are on their limitations and human absence will come to seem sufficient unto the day.

References

Bloom, P. (2016). *Against Empathy: The Case for Rational Compassion*. New York: Harper Collins.
Carson, R. (1962). *Silent Spring*. Boston: Houghton Mifflin.
Isaacs Russell, G. (2015). *Screen Relations: The Limits of Computer-Mediated Psychoanalysis and Psychotherapy*. London: Karnac Books.
Konrath, S.H., O'Brien, E.H., & Hsing, C. (2011). Changes in Dispositional Empathy in American College Students over Time: A Meta-Analysis. *Personality and Social Psychology Review*, 15:180. doi: 10.1177/1088868310377395.
Milk, C. (2015). How Virtual Reality Can Create the Ultimate Empathy Machine. *TED Talk*. www.ted.com/talks/chris_milk_how_virtual_reality_can_create_the_ultimate_empathy_machine.
Miller, P. (2014). *Driving Soma: A Transformational Process in the Analytic Encounter*. London: Karnac Books.
Morozov, E. (2012). *To Save Everything, Click Here: The Folly of Technological Solutionism*. New York: Perseus.
Morris, R., & Picard, R. (2012). Crowdsourcing Collective Emotional Intelligence. *Proceedings of CI*. www.robertrmorris.org/pdfs/Morris_Picard_CI2012.pdf.
Nudd, T. (2016). Amnesty International Unveils Incredible VR Experience Showing Devastation in Syria. *AD Week*, March 14, 2016. www.adweek.com/adfreak/amnesty-international-unveils-incredible-vr-experience-showing-devastation-syria-170202
Ornstein, P., ed. (1978). *The Search for Self: Selected Writings of Heinz Kohut (1950–1978)*, Vol. 2. New York: International Universities Press.
Przybyliski, A., & Weinstein, N. (2012). Can You Connect with Me Now? How the Presence of Mobile Communication Technology Influences Face-to-Face Conversation Quality. *Journal of Social and Personal Relationships*, 30 (13):1–10. doi: 10.1177/0265407512453827.
Schooler, J., cited in Glausiusz, J. (2009). Devoted to Distraction. *Psychology Today*, March 1, 2009. www.psychologytoday.com/articles/200903/devoted-distraction.
Turkle, S. (2011). *Alone Together: Why We Expect More from Technology and Less from Each Other*. New York: Basic Books.
Turkle, S. (2015). *Reclaiming Conversation: The Power of Talk in a Digital Age*. New York: Penguin.
Wilson, T.D., Reinhard, D.A., Westgate, E.C., Gilbert, D.T., Ellerbeck, N., Hahn, C., Brown, C.L., & Shaked, A. (2014). Just Think: The Challenges of the Disengaged Mind. *Science*, 345(6192):75–77. doi: 10.1126/science.1250830.
Winnicott, D.W. (1958). The Capacity to Be Alone. *International Journal of Psychoanalysis* 39(5):416–420.
http://www.ipa.world/IPA/en/What_is_Psychoanalysis/Webinars/en/IPA1/Webinars/New_technologies_webinar.aspx?hkey=d70d4590-49b6-4e03-8b35-f298c25767a2

Chapter 3

Changing attitudes about sex
A dual inheritance perspective

Robert A. Paul

Introduction

The socio-cultural world that produced psychoanalysis at the turn of the twentieth century is no longer our world. Not the least of the changes that have occurred since Freud developed his original ideas are those having to do with sexuality – precisely the area in which Freud made so many of his most far-reaching and still controversial contributions. My aim is to examine these changes by putting them in historical and socio-cultural context; then to offer a theoretical way to understand the nature of these changes based on the theory of dual inheritance (which I will explain in due time); and to give some ethnographic data that illustrates my thesis. I write here primarily as an anthropologist rather than a psychoanalyst; my topic is an examination of an aspect of the real body, specifically its sexual functions, as a basis for understanding how our cultural attitudes about sex have changed, and, hence how psychoanalysis has changed with them.

Let me begin by reminding you of what Freud saw as the place of sex in civilization in 1930:

> Present-day civilization makes it plain that it will only permit sexual relationships on the basis of a solitary, indissoluble bond between one man and one woman, and that it does not like sexuality as a source of pleasure in its own right and is solely prepared to tolerate it because there is so far no substitute for it as a means of propagating the human race.
>
> (1930, pp. 103–104)

Of course he goes on to add this qualification: "Everybody knows that [this prescription] has proved impossible to put it into execution, even for quite short periods" (Op. cit., 104).

Freud acknowledged that this was the ideal, but only for certain classes of society, and that the rules were more malleable in the case of men than of women. While marriage of the kind Freud described was normative for bourgeois society in Vienna (as elsewhere), there were also flourishing demimondes for those with other sexual preferences, prostitution was rife, and women of the lower classes often served as mistresses for men, single and married, of the bourgeoisie.

Nonetheless, Freud said that we can't assume that just because civilization does not always achieve its aim, "such an attitude on the part of society is entirely innocuous." (*Loc. cit.*). After asserting that the sexual life of civilized people was severely impaired by the restrictions placed on it, he then suggested that "sometimes one seems to perceive that it is not only the pressure of civilization but something in the nature of the function itself which denies us full satisfaction and urges us along other paths." And he concluded: "This may be wrong; it is hard to decide" (*Loc. cit.*). This is the question upon which I hope to shed a little light.

Changes in attitudes about sex from Freud's time to ours

The picture Freud drew of the attitude of society to sex in 1930 is, of course, still with us in many quarters; but alongside that attitude, whether it persists as a traditional cultural system or is a more self-consciously codified orthodoxy developed as a reaction against the changes that have occurred, there have emerged, mostly in liberal urban centers, a new set of sexual practices and discourses about them that are radically different from the hetero-normative monogamy to which Freud alluded.

Among the most notable of these changes are the dramatic reconceptualization of women's gender roles; the unlimited discussion and depiction of sexual practices of all kinds in the realm of allowable public discourse; the de-stigmatization of same-sex partnerships culminating in the legalization of same-sex marriage; the de-stigmatization of single-parenthood and especially single-motherhood; the decline in the social and cultural importance of marriage and the growing prevalence of divorce; and in general greatly expanded opportunities for and tolerance of pre-, extra- and non-marital sexual practices of (almost) all kinds.

What was the social context for these changes?

The nineteenth century witnessed the beginning of a fertility decline in the Western world that has continued, with fluctuations over time, to this day. In bourgeois society, and to a certain extent in other classes as well, the ideal of large families gave way to a preference for fewer children. This was both a norm and a reality. It seems that children went from being an economic asset, as agricultural or factory laborers, to a liability, as success in bourgeois life demanded a large investment of effort, time, and money in children's education. Changes in women's lives also played a role: at one and the same time, Victorian women were confined to the household with little to do other than try to give quality time to their children, while improvements in the education of women made them frustrated with their lot (as Breuer and Freud noted of the hysterical women they treated [1895]) and led women to question the demand that they be mere reproducing machines.

In order for this reduction in family size to happen, ways had to be employed to control fertility. Traditional methods for birth control had long included delayed weaning, abstinence, late marriage, coitus interruptus, various folk remedies, and abortion. But the late 19th century, responding to the implications of the newly arising preferences for reduced fertility, saw the invention of progressively better contraceptive methods. These included the sponge or pessary, the diaphragm, the condom, first made of animal tissue and later of rubber, and the rhythm method based on the calculation of when ovulation was unlikely. These methods, however, were less than foolproof; and some required mechanical precautions prior to every act of intercourse and thus tended to interfere with the spontaneous enjoyment of the act (see McLaren, 1990).

In 1960, the birth control pill was approved in the United States by the FDA and became widely available. It put reliable and affordable responsibility for long-lasting fertility control into the hands of women, and did not interrupt the prelude to intercourse. It had the obvious consequence of allowing not only marital but also non-marital heterosexual intercourse to proceed with only a low risk of pregnancy for the woman (Eid, 2015). And in 1973, the Supreme Court decision in Roe v. Wade made abortion legal in the U.S., further reducing the concern about intercourse leading to unplanned or unwanted births. (Needless to say abortion rights are under vigorous attack in many quarters as we speak.)

Perhaps an even more decisive development that occurred, also in the 1970's, was the introduction of reproductive technologies that eliminated the need for intercourse altogether as the prerequisite for conception. This was overtly intended to help infertile married couples, but it obviously also enabled un-coupled women or Lesbian couples to procreate. In vitro fertilization, surrogacy, and a host of other techniques completed the process whereby what was true in Freud's day – that as he put it "there is so far no substitute for it [sexuality] as a means to propagate the human race" – was rendered "no longer operative". Copulation no longer always carried the possibility of conceiving a child, whether wanted or unwanted; while having a child no longer required copulation.

Another cultural and technological development that accelerated concurrently with the trends I have mentioned deserves our attention. From the time of the Greeks onward, our civilization has been fascinated, if not obsessed, with the idea of creating humans, or good-enough substitutes for or approximations of them, by non-sexual means. One has but to think of the stories of Cadmus sowing the dragon's teeth that turn into men, or Pygmalion carving a female statue that comes to life; to continue through the alchemists' fantasy of producing a homunculus unclouded by carnal taint; to the vogue for automata in the 17th century that inspired Descartes to opine that animals, and even humans, were only machines; and on to the iconic stories of Frankenstein, Pinocchio, and Rossum's Universal Robots, the artificial workers in *R.U.R.*, Karel Capek's great prophetic play (1920). These were all precursors, in fantasy, of what has now become a vast technological reality: the thriving fields of artificial intelligence and robotics, about which Sherry Turkle (2011) has written. These endeavors bid fair to make actual humans less and less necessary to sustain the economy or to do many of the jobs that currently must be done by live humans. The fantasy that our machines will shortly overmaster us is a favorite theme in works of futuristic fiction, such as the films *2001: A Space Odyssey* and *Blade Runner* along with many others.

What do all these parallel developments add up to? They speak to both a wish for and, in the last few decades, the reality of a situation that separates the act of heterosexual intercourse from procreation, both by preventing conception, and by circumventing the need for it, either by achieving biological conception by other means, or by creating humans, or passable simulacra of them, by non-biological, non-sexual means.

According to the quotation from Freud with which I began, one might suppose that this would mean that, with the need for it gone as the only way to procreate new generations, civilization would redouble its efforts and eliminate sexuality from the social realm entirely; but of course that is the opposite of what happened. In the last decades discourses of sexuality have poured into the public sphere in a torrent, and the things I listed above came to pass. Having gotten rid of the necessary link between copulation and procreation, civilization reversed itself: now, to reframe Freud's formulation, we might say that society does not particularly like procreation for its own sake, but focuses instead on sex as a source of pleasure, including not only purely sensual pleasure but also the pleasure of romantic love. What are we to make of all this from the point of view of a contemporary anthropological theoretical understanding of human society and culture?

Dual inheritance

The contemporary neo-Darwinian theory of evolution holds that sexually reproducing animals such as mammals are governed by the imperative to maximize inclusive reproduction, that is, to evolve behaviors as well as physical traits that will best ensure that their genes, or their close genetic relatives' genes – or more accurately alleles – will survive and flourish in future generations, in comparison with those of others of the same species. This means in principle that each phenotypic organism, in seeking to optimize its own fertility, is in competition with all other organisms of the same sex. This is especially true of males, as is borne out by the empirical observation of most mammal species. This is so because of the different proportional investments of time and energy each sex makes to procreation in many mammalian species including humans (see for example Konner, 2015).

This being the case, any species that evolves to take advantage of the many benefits of social life – and there are quite a number of these – has to find ways to manage the potential for competition among members of the same group so as to minimize it. The study of mammalian social behaviors reveals many strategies for accomplishing this, which I cannot delve into at any length here, but they range from brutal male-male combat, such as that between male elephant seals, at one extreme, to the secretion of oxytocin that turns otherwise promiscuous voles into devoted monogamists at the other. The important point for present purposes is to identify the specifically human approach to enabling a social life that is, if not completely harmonious, then harmonious enough to get by, in the face of a genetic propensity to rivalry related to the quest for sexual reproductive advantage.

The human solution has been to evolve a second source of information alongside the genetic one, one that is external to the organism and constitutes a collective phenomenon that can be shared by many people. This is what we term "culture"; its prototypical exemplar is language which, like the genetic code transmitted in DNA, is a generative code composed of elementary binary oppositions. While the genetic code operates from inside the nucleus of each cell in an organism's body, the cultural code exists in what may be termed the public arena, that distinctively human social realm within which everyone who has learned the code can and does participate, albeit in different roles and statuses. Any human being in the course of its self-development from embryo to mature adult uses instructions from both the genetic code and the cultural code to complete what Maturana and Varela (1980) have usefully called its "autopoeisis", or self-creation. The existence of the two parallel channels of information transmission, one genetic, the other cultural, is the situation referred to by the term "dual inheritance".

Dual inheritance theory, as an outgrowth of the theory of biological evolution redesigned to accommodate human society, was first developed by two biologists, Robert Boyd and Peter Richerson in the 1970's and is now a robust research field in its own right (Richerson & Boyd, 1985; Boyd & Richerson, 2005).

In 2015, I published a book, *Mixed Messages*, in which I further developed the theory from the standpoint of comparative sociocultural anthropology. Boyd and Richerson had argued that humans have two different adaptations leading to the formation of two different kinds of social groups; one of these is the circle of close genetic kin, as predicted by the principle of inclusive reproductive fitness. The other is what they call "tribal" society, an overarching social grouping that binds numerous small family units into larger and larger collectivities as populations grow with technological advances and societies become more complex.

In my book, I pointed out that these two kinds of social formations result from and entail two very different strategies. One is the strategy of the genes, which favors behavior leading to inclusive fitness and is by that token competitive and limits prosocial behavior to the immediate kin and, to a lesser degree, to the affines with whom the law of exogamy and the prohibition of incest require close kin to mate and reproduce. But it is the cultural strategy made possible by shared codes of signs and symbols expressed and transmitted in the public arena that is able to overcome the competitive forces inherent in the genetic program and to make possible relations of amity among genetically un- or distantly-related individuals who identify with one another by virtue of sharing the same cultural codes, just as biological kin share some of the same genetic code. Among these cultural codes are rules governing sexual behavior, which every society requires so that competition for mating opportunities does not become a free-for-all. These vary widely across the ethnographic record, but all human societies have some system or other for determining whom you may or may not take as a partner for what is socially recognized as legitimate sexual reproduction.

A further and very important implication of this duality is that the genetic code and the cultural code are transmitted across generations via two different methods. The former, up until the 1970's and the introduction of new reproductive technologies, could only be accomplished by heterosexual copulation; it therefore could only involve the sharing of genetic information between two people. The cultural code, however, is a system of meaningfully shaped forms inscribed in external media such as sound waves or light waves, transmitted in the public arena where the information encoded in the signs and symbols of culture enters the sense organs of as many people as are within reach of the transmission, whether that be oral, gestural, or magnified by technological means such as via radio waves. (I am exemplifying this right now by writing to all of you at once.)

This means that there is an inherent conflict in the human organism and in traditional human societies between behaviors advancing the genetic program, of which the one essential requirement is heterosexual copulation; and those advancing the cultural program, which must modify, contain, and regulate copulation so as to enable the wider tribal society to emerge and sustain itself. In my book I have detailed some of the myriad ways different societies accomplish this. Even in societies more sex-positive and/or pro-natalist than ours, as a consequence of this conflict the wider culturally constituted social system not only regulates but disallows to some degree the intrusion of reproductive copulation into the public arena created by cultural symbolic communication. At the very least, to cite a clear example of what I mean, in almost no human society is marital reproductive copulation regularly performed in public, nor, in most though hardly all cases, is explicit reference to it allowed in the discourses of the public realm. This was certainly true of the 19th century sociocultural milieu that produced Freud and psychoanalysis – though as Foucault (1990) argued the discourse of that era was permeated by indirect and veiled incitements to sexuality. This made for the ubiquity of the *double entendre* in which sexuality, ever-present as it actually is, was frequently the subtext of many overtly permissible communications. Officially at least, in Freud's day, as Mark Twain, one of Freud's favorite authors, is probably apocryphally credited with remarking, "everyone talks about the weather but no one does anything about it; nobody talks about reproduction but everybody does something about it".

It is well to note that the basic human social form as posited by Boyd and Richerson, requiring two different kinds of social groups, one constituted by procreating couples and their offspring, and another formed by cultural symbol systems uniting these basic units into larger wholes, was already evident to Freud. As he wrote in *Civilization and Its Discontents:*

> In no other case [that of a couple in love] does Eros so clearly betray the core of his being, his purpose of making one out of more than one; but when he has achieved this in the proverbial way through the love of two human beings, he refuses to go further.
>
> So far, we can quite well imagine a cultural community consisting of double individuals like this, who, libidinally satisfied in themselves, are

connected with one another through the bonds of common work and common interests . . . But this desirable state of affairs does not, and never did exist . . . [Civilization] favours every path by which strong identifications can be established between the members of a community.

(1930, p. 103)

Freud suggests that "civilization" accomplishes this feat by drawing libidinal energy away from real sex and, as "friendship", overcoming the divisive effects of human aggression. A key dimension of that human aggression, I would propose, has as its evolved basis the inherent competition among individuals, and in particular males, for reproductive success dictated by the genetic program; while cultural symbolism, by mimicking and redirecting energies drawn from the realm of reproduction and the erotic, in the process Freud termed "sublimation", creates ties of attraction that offset the fragmenting effects of competitive destruction.

Dual inheritance in action in ethnography

Even limiting myself to Western societies, I can cite a wide arc of possible resolutions of the conflict between sexual and cultural reproduction and their manifestations in social forms. For example, at one extreme is the southern Italian village studied by Edward Banfield (1958), in which an ethos he calls "amoral familism" dictates that each nuclear family operates alone, and no significant social groups emerge. The result is that much-needed community tasks that would require broader cooperation among families do not happen. At the other extreme would be the example of the early Israeli socialist *kibbutzim*, which militantly opposed the nuclear family in favor of the community. This system separated parents from their children, who were raised and educated by the group as a whole through professional caretakers and teachers, as described by Spiro (1970). Both of these are, of course, extreme, even aberrant cases: Banfield's village was not typical even of southern Italy, and the radical *kibbutzim* devolved, in fairly short order, to the more usual Western situation featuring nuclear families as the basic reproductive and developmental groups within a wider communal structure.

As this last point – the rapid disintegration of the practice of communal child-rearing – demonstrates, one of the greatest adaptive advantages that having a cultural symbolic system has for a society over a social system dominated only by the genetic program is that it can adapt and change on a much more rapid time scale than the slow process of natural selection, which requires statistical shifts in births and deaths in populations and therefore takes many generations. This, indeed, is presumably why natural selection tolerated and even encouraged the evolution of a cultural system in humans in the first place.

A particularly clear example of such rapid change (relatively speaking) is that of Ireland, which has been much studied because of its dramatic demographic characteristics (on the demographics and marital practices of Ireland, see Daly, 2006; Guinnane, 1997; Salazar, 2006). In the century or two before the 1840's,

Ireland's economy rested on two staples, grain raised for export, and potatoes raised for subsistence. In that era, marriage rates were high, fertility was high, and it was all sustainable because the potato requires very little space to grow in proportion to the amount of nutrition it supplies, thus avoiding the dangers of the fragmentation of land parcels over generations. The disastrous potato blight of the 1840's changed all that. After that terrible decade, livestock production requiring larger acreages replaced grain agriculture for export, and the small to middle-sized farm system emerged in the countryside. These farms were worked by a single nuclear family as tenant farmers, following the so-called stem family system of inheritance. In this system, only one son – this was a strictly patriarchal and patrilineal system – could inherit the property, so as to keep it intact and prevent it from subdividing over generations into useless tiny parcels.

The result was a rather unique pattern of late marriage (because the father held on to power until he died, and only then could the chosen son come into his own); and very high rates of celibacy for the other children, male or female, who would not inherit land and so could not marry. At the same time, fertility within the population that did marry was unusually high, large families being the desired norm; while the illegitimacy rate among the unmarried remained remarkably low. This pattern was sustainable only because of the large-scale emigration that Ireland experienced following the famine, in which non-inheriting individuals started new lives in cities or in America and elsewhere. Those unmarried persons remaining at home served as labor on the farm, and lived alone or in non-sexual households, or, often enough, entered the church as priests or nuns. This last pattern in turn strengthened the Catholicism that barred contraception, encouraged marital fertility and condemned extra-marital sex of any kind, thus providing ideological support for the whole system.

Despite the downsides of this system, the cultural norm for large families in the Irish countryside lasted well into the twentieth century. In their classic ethnography of the farming communities of the Irish countryside, Arensberg and Kimball (1940) wrote:

> [F]or the small farmers marriages are for the purpose of producing children and assuring continuity of descent and ownership. They are "forever". They are indissoluble . . . They lead to children if one is fortunate and strong and potent. . . . Thus marital and sexual success has but one criterion. One proves one's worth sexually in the marriage bed, which in turn is the childbirth bed.
> (pp. 207–208)

It was a man's duty to keep his wife, as they said, "in the milk" as much as possible. Marital sex might also be pleasurable, but that was a side benefit. And any other sex was a scandal; non-marital sex, especially among women, meant social ruin, usually leading to emigration to escape the inevitable public shame.

With the introduction of more effective contraception as the 20th century progressed, and with the rapid urbanization that resulted from the stem family system, with non-inheriting people seeking other forms of work as the modern industrial age emerged, this system underwent dramatic change. The in-turned familism of the small farmers had been offset not only by the all-encompassing institution of the church, but then also by the collective militant movement that led to the liberation of Ireland from British colonial rule in 1920. National identity thus gained pride of place over family loyalty. Or, in dual inheritance theory terms, a cultural norm favoring the tribal system prevailed over one favoring the genetic program.

By the late twentieth century, Ireland presented a picture much more in keeping with the prevailing demographic trends of the western world in general. Instead of a small percentage of marriages but with very high fertility in those unions, the pattern flipped around to one of widespread marriage but with very low fertility within each family. Like the rest of Europe, Ireland lost overall population. To counter this decline, Ireland resorted to one frequent method of non-biological social reproduction: immigration from other parts of Europe. By the beginning of the 21st century, even that pattern had evolved further: single motherhood, which had previously been enough to lead to disgrace and exile, now grew rapidly, and many heterosexual couples, as elsewhere in Europe, refrained from the formality of marriage. In 1996 Ireland amended its constitution to lift the prohibition of divorce; and, as if to put an exclamation point on the dramatic shift in sexual attitudes, in 2015 Ireland became the first country in the world to legalize same-sex marriage by a national plebiscite, in which support for such unions won a lopsided victory. This in a country in which, only two decades earlier, homosexuality had been illegal.

What this very abbreviated history reveals is a situation in which a social system governed by cultural norms that favor the social formations shaped by the priorities of the genetic program gave way to one in which the cultural system suppresses the centrality of sexual reproduction as a normative value and substitutes national identity and individual equality. In this system, marriage as the institution that sacralizes and legitimizes both sex and reproduction loses its force, and these procreative functions can be carried out on the initiative of consenting free agents of any self-determined sexual identity, including by adoption or new reproductive technologies, without the state or the church regulating anything.

Under a cultural system adhering to the imperatives of the genetic program, a system like the one described for pre-modern Irish farmers would be expected: marriage was for sex and sex was for marriage, because both had only one essential purpose, namely abundant procreation. Since marriages were largely arranged, romantic love was an add-on that was by no means expected or normative. And when Arensberg and Kimball say that there is only one criterion for success, namely procreation, they are echoing what contemporary evolutionary theory says of all life forms: that their only requisite task is to reproduce themselves, and their genes along with it; even survival itself is, ultimately, only a means to that end.

The new sexual ethos

With the uncoupling of the reproductive function of sex from either procreation, which can be managed without it; or from sexual pleasure, which can be had without the consequence of pregnancy and the heavy and fraught responsibilities it imposes on those who will take care of the resulting child, all the changes I mentioned at the beginning of this paper, and many others besides, follow as night the day. Heterosexual genital intercourse goes from being the only allowable and culturally valorized form of sex to being just one among a vast array of sexual practices; gender, which was defined, for example in the Irish case, both by social and economic roles and also by the implications of sexual reproduction and childcare, ceases to be paramount or even necessary. In the post-industrial world, both sexes can perform most of the necessary tasks of society equally well, since they involve intelligence or manual and other skills not linked to the body parts pertaining to sexual reproduction. Marriage for heterosexual couples becomes less necessary and even desirable, since multiple sequential (or simultaneous) pairings are possible without harm or consequence, and adoption makes it easy to "blend" families or to reproduce without sex. And in this new world, sexual reproduction, though not sex itself, changes from being a sacred blessing, to its default human position as something with the whiff of scandal and "animality" or, to use Stephen Mitchell's (1988) evocative word, the "bestial", associated with it.

Let me give just one concrete example of this latter phenomenon from the recent and ongoing political struggle over same-sex marriage in the United States. Somewhat ironically, while for heterosexual couples, as we just saw, the value of marriage and a resulting family as the goal of one's sexual striving and the guarantor of social acceptance has been greatly reduced, for queer people, marriage has become valued precisely because it has come to symbolize the social acceptance and valorization of same-sex preferences and practices that had previously been strongly stigmatized.

One of the leading intellectuals providing the grounds for opposition to same-sex marriage is Robert George, a professor of jurisprudence at Princeton University. He has written widely arguing from an essentially Catholic "natural law" standpoint that marriage is a conjugal relation that is "begun in commitment and sealed in sexual intercourse". But how does that exclude same-sex marriage? Because, George argues, heterosexual union produces offspring within the natural unit of the family with parents of different sexes providing different strengths for the children. He writes that heterosexual union is "completed in the act by which new life is made" and therefore is "especially apt for and deepened by procreation" (cited in Stern, 2013, p. 2).

In short, George has presented a picture of the desirable, or "natural" marriage at the heart of which is potentially fertile sexual union, and thus a perfect representation of the aims of the genetic program. For George, the trouble with the "revisionist" view of marriage is that it is not "conjugal", in his sense, but instead is based on an emotional tie, accompanied by consensual sexual union. For him, this is inherently unstable, because emotions are fleeting and volatile; while the commitment to marriage and procreation (even if the marriage should in fact prove infertile) leads to families that are inherently permanent, not only because of the vow but because of the reality of the link, real or intended, to future generations. This, in short, is a clear statement of a set of norms guided by the genetic principles I have described.

On the other side of the argument, Mark Joseph Stern (2013) attempts to rebut and refute George's arguments by making several points, such as that same-sex couples can of course create stable families with children by adoption or, in the case of lesbians, via intercourse or non-coital means of insemination. But what I want to point to in Stern's argument is how well it illustrates the predictions of what would follow from a perspective that favors the cultural symbolic program and does not valorize, but rather devalues, the centrality to life and society of biological procreation. Stern's arguments favor "love" – the mutual affective bond between two free individuals regardless of gender – over fertile sex as the key essential ingredient in marriage.

Granting that the stability of family life is a virtue, Stern writes that what is in dispute "is how you get there. According to opponents, to achieve this sharing, commitment, and stability, a penis must ejaculate in a vagina. What a base view of commitment this is. In George's primitive understanding, marriage isn't about love or raising children. It's about copulation" (2). Stern continues, "supporters of gay marriage aren't questioning the biology of procreation. They're questioning its relevance. Reducing marriage to intercourse isn't scientific. It's coarse" (2).

My reason for raising this hot-button issue is not to take sides or argue for or against same-sex marriage (though I will say for the record that I strongly support it). It is to hold up these contrasting views as perfect exemplars of how two different political and social ideologies can be distinguished entirely on the basis of whether they see fertile copulation as the highest value and sine qua non of human social life or whether they see it as "base, primitive, and coarse", to quote words Stern uses in his essay. What this brief snippet exemplifies is that a single objective fact about the human body and its sexuality, namely that until recently it had to copulate to reproduce, but that it no longer does, determines entire strongly, even violently, held and contested views about the meaning and purpose of life and the nature of society.

I would contend, further, that, through this lens one can understand a great many of the "social issues" that have polarized American society in our times, including women's roles and rights, abortion, disputes about transsexuals in bathrooms, "religious liberty" bills that condone discrimination against gay people, and even race: consider the case of Rachel Dolezal, the NAACP president, born to "white" parents, whose claim to be black opened a controversy about whether it is biological descent or the voluntary adoption of a culturally constituted identity that determines one's racial identity. In all these cases, the issue revolves around the relative value or relevance of sexual reproduction and the family structure and family values that accompany it in the total picture of the ideal society.

From the perspective of dual inheritance theory this polarization is hardly an arbitrary one; the basic givens of human nature prescribe that conflicts like this will be played out in any and every society, and will be resolved, insofar as resolution is possible, by more or less ingenious and successful compromises and workarounds, often employing myths and collective fantasies that only make sense in the context of dual inheritance. And this same conflict, I would argue, is repeated in the human breast, where, as Freud showed us, prosocial actions vie with selfish ones evolved to advance our reproductive fitness – that is, sex and aggression, not to put too fine a point on it – in an ongoing and not always successful struggle to achieve internal harmony. Indeed, Freud anticipated much of my whole argument when he wrote these lines:

> The individual does actually carry on a double existence: one designed to serve his own purposes and another as a link in a chain, in which he serves against, or at any rate without, any volition of his own. The individual himself regards sexuality as one of his own ends; while from another point of view he is only an appendage of his own germ-plasm [read "DNA"], to which he lends his energies, taking in turn his toll of pleasure. . . . The differentiation of the sexual instincts from the ego-instincts would simply reflect this double function of the individual.
>
> (1914, p. 78)

Conclusion: two observations about the relationship of all this to psychoanalysis

First, to return in closing to Freud's unanswered question about whether the "malaise in civilization" we experience is due to the restrictions imposed on us by culture or is somehow inherent in our sexuality itself, the answer is that it is both; it is in the nature of human sexuality that it must coexist with a cultural system that delivers to us as a species all sorts of benefits and advantages, but also necessitates that our sexuality be constrained in ways that are frequently less gratifying than it seems by rights ought to be the case. Dual inheritance theory thus coincides with and lends support to fundamental psychoanalytic notions about the inherent status of conflict in human life, in large part about the organization of sexual life, in people and in societies.

And second, I have depicted the trajectory of the evolution of our sexual norms and values from a cultural system in which the then-necessary connection between sex and reproduction established the primacy of heterosexual monogamous marriage; to one in which the disconnect between sex and reproduction has refocused our erotic values to ones emphasizing the dyadic relationship itself, and recasting gender roles, same-sex love, and many other aspects of the organization of sex in mutual, egalitarian terms.

At the same time, psychoanalytic technique itself has moved away from an asymmetrical and patriarchal practice in which a primary focus is on resolving, through interpretation, internal obstacles to an ability to perform and enjoy heterosexual genital intercourse; to one in which a more mutual and egalitarian relationship is explored between the analyst and analysand, and a wide range of sexual practices are accepted and understood in the context of relationships, rather than as determined by the progress or inhibition of the development of the libido towards the goal of reproductive copulation. In this respect, psychoanalysis as a cultural system has itself paralleled the evolution of the attitudes to and practices of sexuality and marriage prevalent in the culture in which it is situated. This should not surprise us; psychoanalysis is a cultural phenomenon, and it too changes along with the rest of culture.

References

Arensberg, C.M., & Kimball, S.T. (1940). *Family and Community in Ireland*. Cambridge, MA: Harvard University Press.

Banfield, E.C. (1958). *The Moral Basis of a Backward Society*. New York: The Free Press.

Boyd, R., & Richerson, P.J. (2005). *Not by Genes Alone: How Culture Transformed Human Evolution*. Chicago: University of Chicago Press.

Breuer, J., & Freud, S. (1895). Studies on Hysteria. *Standard Edition*. London: The Hogarth Press, 2.

Capek, K. (2004/1920). *R.U.R.* London and New York: Penguin Classics.

Daly, M.E. (2006). *The Slow Failure: Population Decline and Independent Ireland, 1920–1973*. Madison: University of Wisconsin Press.

Eid, J. (2015). *The Birth of the Pill: How Four Crusaders Reinvented Sex and Launched a Revolution*. New York: W.W. Norton.

Foucault, M. (1990). *The History of Sexuality, Vol. 1: An Introduction*. New York: Vintage.

Freud, S. (1914). On Narcissism: An Introduction. *Standard Edition*. London: The Hogarth Press, 14:73–102.

Freud, S. (1930). Civilization and Its Discontents. *Standard Edition*. London: The Hogarth Press, 21:64–145.

Guinnane, T.W. (1997). *The Vanishing Irish: Households, Migration and the Rural Economy in Ireland, 1850–1914*. Princeton, NJ: Princeton University Press.

Konner, M.J. (2015). *Women After All: Sex, Evolution and the End of Male Supremacy*. New York and London: W. W. Norton.

Maturana, H.R., & Varela, F.J. (1980). Autopoeisis and Cognition: The Realization pf the Living. *Boston Studies in the Philosophy of Science*, 42. New York: Springer Netherlands

McLaren, A. (1990). *A History of Contraception: From Antiquity to the Present Day*. Oxford and Cambridge, MA: Basil Blackwell.

Mitchell, S.A. (1988). The Metaphor of the Beast. In Mitchell, S.A. (ed.), *Relational Concepts in Psychoanalysis: An Integration*. Cambridge, MA: Harvard University Press, pp. 67–93.

Paul, R.A. (2015). *Mixed Messages: Cultural and Genetic Inheritance in the Constitution of Human Society*. Chicago: University of Chicago Press.

Richerson, P.J., & Boyd, R. (1985). *Culture and the Evolutionary Process*. Chicago: University of Chicago Press.

Salazar, C. (2006). An*thropology and Sexual Morality: A Theoretical Investigation*. New York and Oxford: Berghahn Books.
Spiro, M.E. (1970). *Kibbutz: Venture in Utopia*. Cambridge, MA: Harvard University Press.
Stern, M.J. (2013). *The Sexual Fetish of Gay Marriage Opponents: Defenders of DOMA and Proposition: 8 Say Marriage Isn't About Love or Parenting: It's About Coitus*. www.slate.com/articles/news_and_politics/jurisprudence/2013/03
Turkle, S. (2012). *Alone Together: Why We Expect More from Technology and Less from Each Other*. New York: Basic Books.

Chapter 4

Modern gender flexibility
Pronoun changes and the body's activities

Rosemary H. Balsam

Modern gender plurality is demanding a transformation of personal pronouns in our common language. This seems to signal a profound change in era. Some experiential implications will be examined through clinical vignettes. More questions will be raised than answers offered about the use of the body in the service of modern gender fluidity, in terms of its articulation with the sexed natal body, erotics and ability to produce a child. One wonders if our psychoanalytic theories, established in an older day, may have their limits in this arena. For example, may aspects of our digital age catalyze novel forms of mentation that may take part in the enactments and living out of non-traditional forms of gender identities?

Introduction

Steven Reisner, a New York psychoanalyst, tells in the *New York Times* about his 16-year post analytic check up with the late Dr. Martin Bergmann, then 100 years old. He writes,

> [he] looked me squarely in the eye, and . . . said, "You will not be fully yourself until you are wholly aligned with your sexuality." I tried to soften what he was saying. "You mean my life drive?" He shrugged "No, not your life drive, that's not your problem. Your *sexuality*."

Reisner goes on,

> Martin's generation of psychoanalysts had worked to tame sexuality, focusing instead on a more general need for relationships. This gentler version has become prominent in today's psychoanalytic circles. This was half the problem. But for Martin . . . [t]he other half . . . was the problem of how to connect intimately with other people without compromising the productive disturbance that comes from true, physical sexual drive – what Freud called the "mischief maker."

(2016)

These days I freshly puzzle about these majestic psychic integrations of instinctual drive and object relations that used to be more fashionable. As Reisner points out, the scene of greatest interest is currently object relational, or relationships in general with their intersubjective unconscious components. Few current schools of thought pay attention to the material body, let alone *privilege* it, ever since ego psychology and conflict/drive theory first became actually derided, especially as an aspect of the American Psychoanalytic Association's 1985 political wars when the psychologists fought the hegemony of the power of the medical profession in psychoanalysis in the United States, and also the ascension of and popularity of the Relational School in the 1980s that often defined itself against the rigidities of mainstream ego psychology. For a variety of both rational and political reasons drive theory became a whipping boy. The topic of this book speaks to the plethora of issues that involve the body in the contemporary world and how timely it is now that some of these wars are less acute, together to expand and restore the balance of our thinking about the body.

Consider a modern parade of the body's stunning capabilities. Consider the miraculous coming back to life that happens with heart, lung, liver and kidney transplants; and even face transplants, first successful in 2011, that alter the subjectivity of identity; the heroic salvage of human limbs; since the millennium, tiny robotic hands that operate on fetuses still inside the womb; or the long strenuous but successful maintenance of life in the face of many deadly cancers. The modern body is frequently stressed by "eating disorders" in the young, in males now as well as females; or punished and celebrated by extreme exercise in the service of staying upbeat with endorphins; or in the spectacularly decorated body displays in elaborate tattoos, and apparent excesses of painful and extreme grooming in the removal of genital and other body hair (reported by participants as mainly in the interests of "cleanliness" – whatever that means! But for the enhancement of eroticism in oral or anal sex): the ubiquity of cosmetic surgery, or extreme makeovers that are stared at by millions of viewers on reality TV; or the phenomenon of the French artist "ORLAN", who uses her body as a surgical canvas for public display. It is trite to say that *all* of these dramatically shifting corporeal states demand an enormous flexibility of their bearers' psyches.

Flexible genders

I would like to focus on the intriguing flexible genders that are enacted in life now, so much more freely than even just a few years ago, and try to think about their relation to the psychic representation to the individuals' bodies.

Since the 1970s, (Stoller 1968/1994; Money 1988) the natal body clearly has been unmoored and removed from any insistent or necessary tether to gender expression. This is both embedded now in our social culture and in psychoanalytic theory. Medically assisted means by which babies are conceived and come into the world loosen and challenge the psyches of people to the intimacy of their bodies so that a dialectic is necessarily introduced between the forces of objectification of these bodies and their owners' subjectivity. At an extreme, a sperm that is desired but not loved is joined with an ovum that is (for better or worse) *not* imbued with self-love – being not of the same make as the mother.[1] This female will carry and give birth to this child, and as a newly birthed mother may hand it to another woman or man, who will in turn become the psychological parent who loves and raises this child into a modern family that can be single mothered, same-sexed male or female partnered, or with differently sexed partners, married or unmarried and regularly blended with other children as siblings, half-siblings or same-nesters. What emotionally very complex demands exist within all those steps in all those systems! We have no way of comparing this to times past either. Emphatically, this chapter is not nostalgia for "the good old days". We just know for sure that the environmental conditions are changed. Times past – who is to know, really, what vast or even greater psychic demands there were, say, on a woman who lost six children out of ten 10 born to her, or on the psyches of those assailed with famine, war or pioneering in this vast land? We see the social effects of these more in other parts of the globe and still within some sectors of our own society, but there are now new demands too, related to peacetime and prosperity.

The body in our times in the West, is undoubtedly much more malleable by human will than in any previous era. I want to make much of this modern shift of circumstance. Increased knowledge of the body's function has obviously vastly aided our sophisticated surgical, hormonal and immunological technologies. The body in this era actually can be engineered with a certain amount of success. Offspring too can be engineered – with attention to ethics, hopefully – and chosen to avoid certain genes bearing congenital illness. Without the great medical advances in biological medicine it would not be possible to try to achieve aims of both gender flexibility and procreative desire. And without individual social push to change gender rigidities, we may not have spurred medical research to such an extent. The body's fate is bound intimately into the fate of the psyche, and thus "the ego is first and foremost a bodily ego" (Freud, 1923, p. 27) in some measure still holds for me.

Side by side with the mobility of sexual and gendered behaviors, the subject's own natal biology retains a powerful brute ungovernable aspect. It moves with its own genomic patterning, its secret strategies for health and sickness and its capability or futility to multiply – all, in large part, entirely *unbidden by* the subject's will. Cells can go haywire; the blood can flow from wounds in an unstoppable fashion; the delicate brain can be assaulted by external and internal physical traumata. The bones and joints can fuse or yank awry. There are airborne, blood-borne and insect borne infections everywhere in the global atmosphere. We can combat with the scientific powers at our disposal many personal psychic disaffections and ills, but the body ultimately is still the master over us: no matter *how* elaborate, intelligent and exquisitely sensitive our thinking; or – importantly – how powerful and pleasurable are our wishful omnipotent fantasies.

Postmoderns and the body

Freud himself wavered between sociocultural and biological notions of sex and gender. He laid down early, especially in the 1905 "Three Essays", developmental grounds for the familiar complex view of infantile "polymorphous perversity" and how "sexuality" (as was then called this sex/"gender" blend), expressed itself in physically sensual polyvalent modes that became patterned gradually and woven into adult behaviors. The body's interactions with the person's subjectivity and vice versa were once central in these descriptions. However a welcome (and pragmatically useful) breaking up of the old catch-all concept "sexuality" was introduced by feminist critics in the 1960s and 70s, and by John Money, and in our field by Robert Stoller in 1968. A sharper conceptual division between the categories of "sex" and "gender" was introduced. This was a sea change. Sex was now "biological" whereas gender was psychical. This freed the gendered personality and actions from natal genital anatomy, and opened enquiry about any fixity to notions of so-called "femininity" and "masculinity".

This initially helpful division of labor was later reversed, seen as retrogressive, and was re-structured by academic non-scientists such as the philosopher Judith Butler and many academic and psychoanalytic postmodern thinkers. Once again sex and gender were united – just as in Freud's pre-gender concept of the blended shopping-bag "sexuality", but very unlike Freud, as the postmodern philosophers' intention was to question any link at all between gender and sex to the biological body. Just as a reminder, I quote Judith Butler: According to her, "the ostensibly natural facts of sex [are] discursively produced in the service of other political and social interests." (1990, p. 7). Butler concludes, "If the immutable character of sex is contested, perhaps this construct called 'sex' is as culturally constructed as gender; indeed, perhaps it was always already gender, with the consequence that the distinction between sex and gender turns out to be no distinction at all." (Butler, 1990, p. 7). The new/old blend, then, is due to "social constructivism" and is the absolute opposite of a binary "biological essentialism" (attributed to Freud and other thinkers, especially those in the medical profession. A reminder on "biological essentialism" is that if one were born with male or female reproductive organs, a prescription for behavior followed for exactly matching "masculinity" or "femininity"). Biological essentialism was a seriously erroneous concept, and flew in the face of clinical experience. The concept of "the ego is first and foremost a bodily ego" was not subjected to revision, but rather tended to sunset with biological essentialism. Rightly, the socially constructed categories of so-called "femininity" and "masculinity" were interrogated, and now open to revision.

The downside of this liberation is, alas, that in many psychoanalytic camps, biology and the material body have almost became bad words – as if they have nothing at all to do with a "true in-depth" psychological formulation that any self-respecting psychoanalyst may create. Writers, especially those of the Relational school, have moved to transcend division between sex and gender by using the concept of "embodiment". This certainly keeps alive clinically a sense of the individual's struggle with her or his body, but it does not attempt to create individual histories of living within that body – in fact, they offer that looking for such a history may be a defensive maneuver to bind anxiety, and propose that chaos theory is more apt to psychoanalysis than looking for living history (Harris, 2004).

In my 2012 *Women's Bodies in Psychoanalysis*, I have taken the tack that psychoanalysis in the United States abandoned the psychological potentials of the material body much too soon in the 1970s, leaving the prevalent ego psychology still in the dark ages in relation to women in particular. This lag has not been recovered. We abandoned prematurely the continuing exploration of the body as a central psychic focus that Freud had begun. Sheer clinical embarrassment in the office rendered untenable, trying loyally to uphold concepts like universal penis envy, and universal notions of a female as a castrate, in the face of the many women patients who defied its truth. By the 1970s women patients were much more confidently vocal in their complaints. I have come to believe that using the Oedipal myth is highly problematic in efforts to uphold the universality of the Oedipus complex (as seems axiomatic in the service of analysts' identities). The mythic basis requires that females continue to be seen as derivatives of male dominance. I am fully on board with triangular patterning in object and drive derivatives as signaling increased emotional maturity (the main developmental import of the Oedipal complex), but this feature of psychic life can be encompassed and is discussable without Oedipal insistence.

"Oedipal" dynamics, as they now stand, promote theoretical foreclosure and abiding misunderstanding of the strong and prolonged relationships of girls to their mothers into adulthood that are doomed, pre-judged and unexplored as pathological by "pre-Oedipal" labeling as necessarily "immature". Female to female maturational progression is left under-theorized and we pretend that we know more than we do. The quality of this interaction may, for example, be a noticeable gender difference from males evolving with their mothers. Life-long mother-daughter bonds may be an unexplored feature of having *like* bodies that only reach their maximal corporeal maturity later in life during the twenties in pregnancies and birthing. These are times when a woman's mother manifestly and unconsciously internally plays a vital role. This suggests a different corporeal developmental timetable and a differing object relational patterning than those males expressing their body maturity (for a fuller discussion of the limits of Oedipus, see Balsam, 2015). The female procreative body all along has been virtually ignored in all developmental schemes that involve unconscious life.[2] In the contemporary fast breaking news of dislocating of the body from socially gendered activities, internally developmental female body representations can be further "disappeared". Yet, with the new opportunities for pregnancy that as yet have no psychoanalytic theoretical "place" as it were, we can be in an exciting pioneering position to try to understand anew how indeed the sexed natal body may or may not be linked to gender and psychically integrated – or not – in life progression.

Contemporary questions

Here are a few of my questions: Where does the natal material body currently stand in dilemmas about flexible genders and also transgender roles and enactments? What does it mean to include active sex behaviors, the work of "the mischief-maker", in gendered expressions that operate in progressive intimate partnerships? Where does the vitality of the body's natally endowed reproductivity become channeled, if unexpressed or is inexpressible within a gender portrait that is born "she", but subsequently self-labeled "he"/"they"/ "ze"? (The same question goes for the natal "he"). And where does the material body or the altered material body place itself in debates about parenting and modeling internalization for the sex and gender patterns of the nurtured children?

I have many more questions and few "answers" – but I believe that admitting our genuine ignorance is a better approach to our patients than pretending that we "know", either through global declarations that thinly disguise despairing value judgments, or relying on our old understandings with just a few tacked on disconnected minor modifications to acknowledge consciously only the presence of our formidable biological and procreative as well as sexual bodies. If the body still played a central role in a general theory of mind, the changed view of women as equals would need to be formulated into that general theory. This, of course, would shift the view of male development also, even though aspects of male development as presented by Freud may still hold. Among those who see the body as key and each sex's body as differently represented in the mind's functioning, Julia Kristeva, (e.g., 2014) the French, contemporary analyst whose work in the maternal sphere is highly aware of its deep presence in issues of sex and gendered living: so is the work of the Middle group London analyst Joan Raphael-Leff (e.g., 2015), and in the past, the Nicaraguan Marie Langer (1952): so was Helene Deutsch (1945) in her clinical work – (though her theory was erroneous as she was a flagrant biological essentialist with the narrow view that as a woman one is not fulfilled unless one has a child). Many contemporary, especially North American, analysts have contributed valuable papers, including those who write about shifting views of the male body e.g., Fogel (1998). Bibring (1959) and Benedek (1952) are among those who developed pregnancy and parenthood as "special" life events – but as a sidebar to a theory of mind – and therefore limited themselves more to adult experience of "crisis" (if normative), without including childhood developmental emphasis as an underpinning.

Gender through the lens of changing pronouns: what does this mean for the body?

In September 2015, following a pioneering 2014 action at Vermont University, Harvard allowed its students for the first time to choose their preferred gender pronouns. Thus, as well as he and she, "zie" "e" and "they" can now be used on registration forms. Yale expanded gender-neutral housing to sophomores beginning in the fall of 2015. The Office of LGBTQ Resources is including a project to install at least one "All Genders" restroom in 85-percent of Yale's buildings by the end of this school year (Wang, 2015). Many therapists in their offices have been privy to genderqueer patients' agonies and humiliations provoked by their non-conforming gender apparel and appearance, in being seen and encountering reactions against them inside a toilet of the other sex. There is a societal tectonic shift going on, and the recent demand in language change is a momentous reflection of this. Changes in personal pronouns go to the heart of the sense of self and personal identity. The effort of the changed personal pronoun is to present the person as "gender-neutral" instead of narrowing the specifics to "his" or "hers". See Table 4.1[3] for some personal pronouns that are in usage now.[4]

English teachers have had questions. Ardis Butterfield, a Yale Medievalist, says, "A new pronoun . . .[is] so difficult in English", she said. ". . . we do have a gender neutral pronoun 'it', but it is not used [for] people without seeming rude". Other English teachers fear the risk of sounding illiterate: "If you use 'they' for an individual, do you say 'they is' or 'they are'"? (*Yale Daily News*, Feb 10, 2015). However, another teacher in the *New York Times* (Jan 30, 2016) points out that "As a gender neutral pronoun 'they' has been useful for a long time . . .[It is] found in the works of Chaucer and Jane Austen." The advantage of "they" over some of the other variants is that it already is familiar in the evolving English language. English has met these personal language shifts before. How uncomfortable we once were with the revival of "Ms". in the 1970s, until it came to be widely perceived as socially helpful. Ms. was only one of several abbreviations for "Mistress" in the 17th and 18th centuries, and represents a return to the state that prevailed for 300 years, together then with the use of Mrs. for any especially respected adult woman regardless of marriage. Nowadays Ms. applies to all females and not just the social elite. There was the Early Modern English style of using "thee" "thou" and "thine" too, by now faded (Bennett, 2016).

Table 4.1 Personal pronouns

1	2	3	4	5
e/ey	em	eir	eirs	eirself
he	him	his	his	himself
[name]	[name]	[name]'s	[name]'s	[name]'s self
per	per	pers	pers	perself
she	her	her	hers	herself
sie	sir	hir	hirs	hirself
they	them	their	theirs	themself
ve	ver	vis	vers	verself
zie	zim	zir	zirs	zirself

Source: University of Wisconsin, Milwaukee's LGBT Resource Center. ©2011 The University of Wisconsin-Milwaukee LGBT Resource Center

And take the Royal "We." It was first used in 1169 in England, when Henry II declared the doctrine of the "divine right of kings" – "we", meaning that "God and I . . . " rule together (Campbell, 2014). That version of being a monarch is subject to no earthly authority, and is not subject to his people, nor to the aristocracy (nor, from the Protestant point of view, to the Catholic Church). "By the Grace of God," attached to the titles of a reigning monarch carries this meaning. We have modern secular examples of the Royal "we" – indicating self-inflation (without the monarchy) these days. The redoubtable Miss Piggy for example, of the Muppet Puppets, used the Royal "we" on occasion, and also the English Prime Minister, Margaret Thatcher indulged the plural pronoun in her day – (to the outrage of many English citizens!) – when she grandly announced that "we" had become a grandmother. The personal pronoun in English has had experience in flexibility before. Some survived – some didn't last.

The contemporary malleable pronoun is not just what is "politically correct" for a transgendered or genderqueer person. The change affects how we relate to "he" and "she" too, and the cis-gendered population. We are stirred to uproot categories of what we thought of as established knowledge or certainty in analytic listening to individuals' pursuit of genderqueer destinies. In turn, this stance can help us shift foreclosed received knowledge about heterosexuality also. Befuddlement about our inner registrations and signals from the human body is just further exposed by the new manifestations of great interest in living out the fluidity of gender. We need to admit that what we think we know may not hold, and in re-thinking and re-hearing we may even be able to re-visit the long suppressed female body procreative abilities – but maybe with less moral certainty about which "she/zie or they" should employ these biological resources. The body, malleable in its own right, unmoored from definite gender categories thus becomes more in need of fresh exploration.

Clinical situation

My supervisee, a white heterosexual female straight psychologist, recently married, gifted in her profession, and just starting to build her private practice in a liberal New England college town, is very eager to come across as agreeable to her new graduate student patient. Bobbi is a tall, cropped-hair graduate student sitting before her, legs tightly crossed, rounded hips, faint breast shapes and wearing a preppy shirt and college-stripe conservative tie. The student strongly and flatly states: "People need to call me 'they'. That pronoun appropriately addresses my gender status. 'He' or 'she' is ill-matched to me, and much too limiting." The therapist thinks with relief that in the room they need no other pronoun than "you." But of course the therapist and supervisor betray their confusion, shown in the extra effort to try to sort out the right usage of this "neutral" pronoun while the threat of being offensive to the patient is ripe within the tension of these uses of familiar vs. unfamiliar everyday language and can wreck a budding therapeutic alliance. "They," (Bobbi) were struggling in an everyday uphill battle to correct the terminology of the populace. In fact, it is in supervision that the therapist refers to Bobbi as "they," which is hard to get used to. What takes the place of the usual singular pronoun for me, I notice, as the supervisor, is a kind of "we" sense surrounding Bobbi, that is gradually responsively forming in my mind – as if there are two of them to listen to rolled into one – and I wonder what this plural sense means. I day-dream in listening to the troubles with her dismissive, angry self-blaming mother, that it must be easier for Bobbi to relate to the original family world as two – as twins maybe, who could make themselves heard better or protest more effectively than one alone – a boy and a girl together against that world?

Danielle Quinodoz, in 1998, wrote about one of the very few actual reported psychoanalytic treatments of a transgender woman, Simone, aged 38, and the manner in which she adapted to her patient within the transference-countertransference ambiance with a fantasy as if she were pregnant with a child about whom she did not yet know its gender. Her patient, born male, had always felt a stranger among boys, and at age 18 had had a vaginoplasty and accompanying hormone treatments. From one sector of her mind the patient would say, "I know that I have not become a woman even if the surgeons have given me a vaginoplasty. I shall never be able to be a woman, but only have the appearance of one; for me, that is already not so bad" (p. 96). And in another sector, "But I still have my penis! It is not missing! It has been used to make a vagina; it has only had its function changed!" (p. 96). Bobbi, our patient, also contains and projects a "they" sense which is much more graphic than a person who contains a conflicted he/she model that assumes woven strands of male and female identificatory elements in a way that I am more used to. Bobbi prefers sex with identified heterosexual men or women. They are not interested in a partner who is identified as a homosexual. In Bobbi's case, each gender representation is *almost* fully accommodated, but still not fully inhabited. One seems to cancel the other out, but they seem to appear separately. Is *that* what Bobbi means by the "neutrality" that is intended in Bobbi's use of "they"? The *unconscious* effort then would be to try to keep in neutral position in order to be unidentifiable as either a "she" like mother, whom Bobbi happens to fear and despise at the moment, or "he" like father with whom Bobbi is angry for abandoning the family. *Is* that, in fact, I ask myself, a *lack* of integration of both gendered trends internally? Are the parental images too much at war inside Bobbi? Or am I off on a bourgeois path of assumption that singular means just that, and I am unconsciously trying to mold her to singularity, unable to accept that inside Bobbi there are two shades of genders but none that dominates? I need to retranslate Bobbi's duality of gender back into its own terms – where bourgeois straight people allow grossly insufficient space, as far as Bobbi and many others are concerned, to hear this condition as *gender neutrality* . . . it seems more *multigendered*, to me than "neutral". Bobbi's young therapist, meanwhile, simply becomes easier with the "they" of Bobbi. They are opening up to the therapist's focus on Bobbi's own experiences and their current manifest struggle against any strong feelings that are betrayed in the office by Bobbi's flatness of affect, while endowing their words with vivid language. Unfortunately for our purposes of learning more, the therapy is college-based and cannot be of analytic intensity – though it must be said that Bobbi prefers the shorter form of Tx. "They" don't want to become too intimately known.

Other experiences

Anecdotes from clinical practice with college students show the current familial confusions with the pressure of this social change. A middle-aged mother told me with embarrassment that her daughter's love partner referred to "zirself" as "ze". The tone was outrage: "Can you believe it?" she said, while privately I thought, "Well yes, indeed I can". The mother told worriedly how her daughter shared, "What *really* turns me on is the sight of zie's figure with long straight dark hair at the back, flowing in zir walk, and when zie turns around it takes my breath away to catch sight of zir strong manly jaw and grunge beard." The mother stumbled over the words, ill-concealing her distaste and discomfort. Of course the subtext directed to me was many a mother's age-old complaints about things she disapproves of in her grown children: "What have I done wrong in my daughter's growing up?" The mother wept, "If only she were just *gay*, I wouldn't worry so much." That statement would not have been possible not so long ago. In contrast to being "odd" in the old biological essentialist system of "straight means childbearing" with an assumption that "gay is childless", the appeal of a grown child being gay for some families nowadays, I believe, is that "gay" is a *cis*-gendered position (meaning a person who wants to express sexuality that is concomitant with their natal material body). That is an example of contemporary freedom in setting free childbearing from mandatory gender identity. A gay woman, after all, may just as well as a straight one in today's less restrictive atmosphere present her parents with a grandchild. And a gay man is as expected to yearn to be a "Dad" as a straight one might.

Why now?

Why is this the time for such profound social change to prove so ripe? The idea of a "gender spectrum" has been around for many years. We thought we knew a lot about this internal gender spectrum (e.g., Chodorow, 1994), which is still the case. But why *now* do the millennial Generation and the iGeneration effectively act to reify these wishes? Wishes about becoming "the other" in gender expression arouse from the deep (as well as pleasures and envy), uglier primal passions in humans about who is sanctioned to procreate. Rebelliousness and the urge to differentiate generations is nothing new in propelling "difference". Combine these combustibles with heady reified possibilities opened by modern medical technology, modern surgery and pharmaceutical advances in knowledge about hormone treatments that were gained from reproductive organ cancers. Consider the Internet's digital protocols that since 1980 can speed the countless photographs, images, symbols, and words that ceaselessly flow worldwide – mostly without constraint – among people and cultures for virtual conversation. Released into the world is what we analysts might call "enactments" within a kaleidoscopic vision of a world of possibilities.

In classifying gender, by popular demand in the last couple of years, spearheaded by LGBTQ organizations, more than two options became formally available in cyberspace – on say, the dating website OKCupid from 2014,[5] or by Facebook which in 2014 around Valentine's Day added a tab for "Custom" alongside "male" and "female," with 56 gender options, including "agender," "androgyne," "pangender" and "trans person," (as well as an option for controlling who can see the customized version, thus also paradoxically exuding a mantle of privacy). In that massive world of exchange, once the "right messages reach the right people at the right time" (Biron, 2016), forms of personal address can start to become absorbed into the culture from the eye literally to word of mouth. Thence they carry to the age-old family dinner table, transforming elements of scenarios of family interaction and environment into encoded individual psychic life that results in the behavioral and attitudinal affective impacts that inform us all in everyday life. The business world of Branding and Marketing would add a great deal to psychoanalysis' grasp of how these changes have been taking hold so vividly relatively recently. Although these notions and intellectual ideas have been present for decades before this, the reification and visualization of what used to be necessary for people to conjure up only imaginatively is now vividly instantly available at a stroke of the screen. This drama helps break down cultural resistance – though it may also create waves of counter-reaction too.

Litowitz (2012), writing about children of the Internet generation, comments on the changing brain and points out that there is little information about the impact of the "bombardment of information" and its effects on "how we feel and how we relate to other people." As the Internet is "already a digitalization (1s and 0s) of a digitalization (writing) of a digitalization (speech), the effects on cognitive functioning [such as memory] are inevitable" (p. 6). She cites Brian Christian who thinks that "computers are a continuation of our age's privileging of rationality, of the dominance of left hemisphere's functions at the sacrifice of the right hemisphere's – the side specialized for analogical communication of emotions, social (facial) recognition and context." In other words, Christian is suggesting that Descartes' "cogito ergo sum" has become "scripto ergo sum" (meaning in rapid fire text messages) – "further marginalizing the relevance of feelings and relations to others." (Litowitz pp. 10, 11) To that I would add as vital "video ergo sum." The Internet empowers as never before the visual. It suggests the mantra: "If you can see it, you can have it – you can be it."

Christopher Bollas (1989), who studies "the erasure of subjectivity" has dubbed such extreme development as "normotic illness" (p. 135) – an illness which he characterizes as the polar opposite of "psychotic illness" that could be an emerging phenomenon, he thinks, reflecting his sense of the commodified lifestyles of our contemporary worlds. Even though upholding Freudian understandings of sexuality, Sylvia Bleichmar (reviewed by Barahona, 2016), understands today's problems as involving the link to the other, not sexual repression. "While repression remains essential, in her view, to healthy psychic functioning, it is the deconstruction of this link, encouraged by today's pragmatic connection to the other, that lays the groundwork for our modern anxiety. Our problem is not enjoyment as much as how we have organized this enjoyment, so that it has become structurally unsatisfactory. Thus, the link to the other, what she refers to as genitality, is being undone in today's modes of social and sexual organization and the gains made by sexual liberalization have been squandered through these new forms of desubjectivization" (p. 1167). Barahona quotes her as saying, "'When I refer to genitality, I am referring to the link with the other. It doesn't matter if its homo, or if its hetero, or with who. What matters is that it is with another human being. It would not be the same with a sheep. What matters is the capacity to love another, and an other who, paradoxically, is an other in the sense of alterity, but is also similar, not marked by an asymmetry that makes reciprocity impossible.' (p. 47)" (Barahona, p. 1167). The other's status as a whole object, as a human being, is the requirement for a true link. Genitality is less the culmination of psychosexual development than a form of organization of amorous life.

Or as psychoanalysts, we can admit simply that we do not "know" what these social changes portend. Perhaps it is premature to launch into splendid but dark concepts like the "fragmentation of contemporary consciousness" in regard to the world today or the young? We know that the brain's capacities are plastic and seemingly infinitesimal. Children's and young people's intense relationship with the digital instruments obviously must affect a new version of "normative" development. And what about creativity, however we perceive that?

The imagination, the body and multiple genders

Rachel Hurst (2015), an academic in Womens' and Gender studies from Nova Scotia, writes of what she calls "The Surface Imagination" in modern life. She discusses the fantasy that a change to the exterior will enhance the interior, or that the outside is more significant because it fashions the inside. Drawing on psychoanalysis, feminist theory, popular culture, the history of medicine, and interviews with women who have undergone cosmetic procedures, Hurst explores the tensions between the two primary surfaces of cosmetic surgery: the photograph and the skin. The photograph, an idealized surface for envisioning the effects of cosmetic surgery, allows for speculation and retouching, predictably and without pain. The skin, on the other hand, is a recalcitrant surface that records the passage of time and heals unpredictably. Psychoanalysis offers radical change from the "inside", as it were. Hurst uses cosmetic surgery as a test example about offering change from the outside – the promise of the enticements of a visual world. The photograph is an idealized surface for envisioning the effects of cosmetic surgery, allowing for speculation and retouching, predictably and *without* pain. "After" pictures appeal to the desire for transformation, and "Before" pictures tell the story of discomforts in one's own skin. I analogize Hurst's ideas about photography to the brightly lit screens of the digital world that are stared at and worked over by most human eyes and hands nowadays. If she "sees" it she may well "want it" due to the upbeat quality of the visual presentation. The material skin, on the other hand, contrasted with a static photograph, is an individual wayward surface that records feelings, sensuousness, pain, hurt and physical injury, the insults of general illness and the passage of time. And this surface biology heals unpredictably. We can consider the "skin ego," after Didier Anzieu (1974/2016), where the skin-ego is an interface between inside and outside, and is the foundation of the container/contained relationship. Hurst argues that the fantasy involved in surface imagination *can* validate a contemporary illusion that the body is mutable and controllable, and that control over one's body will permit control over one's social world and rid one of pain. I add that the contemporary world presents itself from the outside as never before, that this could all be possible. Hurst ends, though, looking at compromise and the struggle with incompleteness – a point in tune with a notion of the establishment of richer mentalization processes: "the compromise of surface imagination [is that] the result is incomplete and not totally fulfilling in contrast to the fantasized body promised by cosmetic surgery and yet it is also because of surface imagination that the imperfect results are indeed so satisfying" (p. 200). I read this (overly simply to be sure) as a style of privileging a capacity to envision and to identify by merger with a projected image, which leads to many would-be imitative actions to become the other. In turn, more gradual internal processes can be activated in such a way that individuation and agency at more complex psychic levels of integration are transformed and "owned." In psychoanalysis, in short, mentalization is usually encouraged to precede and temper action. Imitative action, though, as an initiator may have become more significant than it used to be as a leading edge to genuine life change, analogous to envisioning the perfect "after" photo that generates action in undergoing cosmetic surgery. This can be a creative leap. But the mind's processes of ongoing development need not stop there. Connections to the "before" picture evolve secondarily, as the inner dimension of the skin has been now involved in this initial leap to action – breached, ruptured, cut, and re-formed before irregular individual attempts to heal begin. The natal body once more can become encompassed within the individual's psychic sphere.

Avgi Saketopoulou in 2014 wrote about a transgender male born child who talked as if he were a conventional girl, and did not acknowledge his penis. She advises that our field treat the gender of transsexuals "not as a symptom, but as a viable subjective reality" (p. 775). Saketopoulou, while privileging the patient's wishes and subjectivity, also calls for the acknowledgement and *mourning* of the natal body in transgendered individuals who are transitioning. This child was so young the following import was not considered, but mourning the genitalia is also to mourn their human reproductive potentials. The childbearing and childproducing body once again is present in the subject matter, but still in the realm of the risk of being lost.

Sublimation: I believe that to consider these new directions of human beings in thinking and in action, it may be fruitful to re-consider the mechanism of sublimation. For Loewald (1988), sublimation is not a defense against instinctual life as Freud originally suggested, but rather reconciliation in the area of ego development, and of internalization. This way of thinking about sublimation may be useful in this day and age of actions and lived out "surface imaginations" stimulated from the visuals and aurals of the cyberspace global socialization experience – sublimations that occur in the search for fulfillment and belonging that perhaps then, in novel ways may *secondarily* become gradually inhabited as experimental action carries potential for coming into deeper contact with the inner resources of gradually increasing subtleties of feelings, body memories and interpersonally intimate sexual and procreative experiences. Loewald stresses the symbolic linkages that are retained in sublimation: "the transmutations of sublimation reveal an unfolding into differentiated elements of a oneness of instinctual-spiritual experience. But oneness stays alive as connection . . . just as the old body would be once the only one that was known for possession" (p. 13). Loewald invokes Winnicott's description of "transitional objects" and their relation to play to make this leap. For Loewald, Winnicott's descriptions (which focus on the point at which differentiation occurs), show how this *alienating* differentiation the "me and not-me" is being reversed in such a way that a "differentiated unity" is coming into being. In this being, eroticism, bodily intimacy and what he calls "spiritual intimacy" can be expressed. For Loewald the symbolism "captures separateness in the act of uniting, and unity in the act of separating" (p. 24). An apparent leap of faith, as it were, can activate transformative effects on a gradually deepening dependable inner existence. Reverse leaps seemingly can ford a chasm. Perhaps these psychic oscillations between "the self" – in its most sexual, perceptual, bodily *and* spiritual state – and "the other" could become a key to understanding how success may be achieved in the enacted arena of repossessing the body as it is transformed from one sex into another? Our theories, as they stand, might suggest failure. Much more contemplation is obviously needed to meet the contemporary psychoanalytic challenges of this modern era, so rife with change.

CASE: I finish with a case that is both old-fashioned, and new-fashioned. Given this discussion, it demonstrates to me the potential role of a creative active surface imagination in fashioning from "the outside" a life that becomes crafted (unconsciously) to offer a vivid confrontation and contrast with this patient's original and old-fashioned sense of body deficit. In turn these positively generated experiences become integrated into a richer sense of life satisfaction that tempers the original scars of incompleteness.

This is a case of a male architect in his late 30s, from South America. He was used to being in analysis, and had attended two to three times a week throughout his college years. I was his first female analyst. He wanted help with repetitive fights with male authorities at work. One day, six months into treatment, on the doorknob going out, he turned back and dropped in an off-hand way, "By the way,

I don't think I ever told you, but I have a hypospadias." There were more than two channels through his penis for urine relief, possibly a fistula, and holes on each surface where embarrassing urine squirted out when urinating. The thorough cleaning of every toilet seat, rim and bathroom floor was thus his frequent intense and secret preoccupation. He avoided public urinals as long as he could remember. He avoided the company of his father and brothers urinating in the woods on hikes. He bitterly wished he had been born with female genitals, as he would never be embarrassed in bathrooms. However, in tune with his family's highest ideals, though held distant from his body misery, he always wanted to become "a father" of a family.

The patient was cis-gendered. He had a large desktop computer at home, and spent many hours in the dark, by himself, intensely watching movies about fathers and sons, their young beautiful women, and masturbating to sons' marriages. He also used his computer to plan many tall buildings. Juan's hypospadias had never been repaired for complicated reasons, nor had he any intention now or ever of submitting himself to an uncertain and painful surgery. Previous therapists had held this goal for successful treatment. One therapist wanted to help him get over his inevitable and immense castration anxiety; and his wild and desperate competition and deep hopelessness in comparing himself when a child with his large, famous father (literally) in the urinal, when a child – now comparing himself with men, male colleagues and brothers. He said his therapists were keen to "fix" him. I took this as a cue to realize that much as he hated his flawed penis, he had no imagined sense of risking more, due to his overwhelming but inarticulate castration anxiety involved in imagining an operation. (It seemed akin to confronting "the impossible": as with a transgendered patient's declaration "I am in the wrong body".) I, like the other therapists, explored the dynamics and tried to include his attitude to the impossible, but he was adamant in his inability to think, and silent refusal to bring it up or discuss it spontaneously, thus, I guessed, risking no further damage.

Though he talked only with labor directly about his penis, never had I been privy to such an unselfconscious poetic outpouring in Juan's associative water imagery. Fountains, and rivers and brooks and unruly landscapes with torrents and trickles of sparkling water filled his associations; tinkles of droplets; white-water floods . . . his dreams, his words, the cadences of his voice in every mood and emotion were imbued with ever-flowing water. He was a hiker, mountain climber and skier who loved nature.

Juan was immensely talented in architecture. He became successful, opened his own firm and thus became the boss, and the senior man. He got married and had a boy baby. To my point about sublimation within a play space – Juan in his artistry became freed to experiment with sensations of wholeness of his body perception and a focus of his flowing powers especially through his use of two elements *external* to him. He described becoming one with his big computer – the first time I had ever heard such a thing (but not the last). The computer was vividly experienced as an extension of himself into which he poured forth his ideas and controlled the screen with his intellectual prowess and his hands that conjured the shapes and fitted the elements of his blue prints to the exciting satisfaction of his eyes and his sensibility. The work secondarily was greatly appreciated by his clients, and in turn this fed the founts of his new ideas that he then again poured into the screen, which was importantly under his control.

The second and greatest gift that he gave himself and was given to him simultaneously, in fantasy under his control was his infant son. "He was crying in the night. I went into him and put on the little nightlight. I lifted him and he was all wet. My amazing, soaked, miserable little baby boy! I put him on the changing table and stripped off the wet diaper. I had just dried him off. He stopped crying. I was kind of behind him, and was raising his bottom up to put the dry diaper under him, when a huge stream of urine flowed right out of him, arced up and *hit* me square in the face! – all over my nose and mouth and in my eyes – I began to weep and weep with joy that his stream came out with such a *power* right in my face . . . he soaked me in the pleasure of my own tears." I was crying myself as I listened to him. What a sheer *triumph* for this man . . . this son of his own making. The penis he had helped to build, his own architecture, was now asserting its deluge into the drive of his procreative creative power. Of course he was merged with the body of his son. The son was felt as a part of his own body made whole.

For this man, it was only after this deep physical and emotional experience that he was able to begin the sad work of the "before" picture – mourning his own actual genitals and the body he never had, but at the same time salvaging – as also did Danielle Quinodoz's transsexual woman the non-shame-filled value of her strong man-built shoulders – the procreative power of his otherwise flawed organ. For the first time then, he considered the risk of surgery.

Notes

1 This is the radical opposite of a Christian religious definition of belonging: from the Nicene Creed dating from 325AD: "the essence of the Father, God of God, Light of Light, very God of very God, begotten, not made, being of one substance with the Father"
2 (Except for Freud's open-minded fascinations up till then, in 1908 he radically foreclosed his search by his turnaround paper "On the Sexual Theories of Children" where he enunciated as "foundational" a physically comparative theory of psychosexuality, instead of continuing to treat each sex's development as different.)
3 The table comes from the University of Wisconsin, Milwaukee's LGBT Resource Center.
4 In 1983, a mathematician-educator, Michael Spivak, wrote an AMS-TeX manual, The Joy of TeX (1983), using E, Em, and Eir. His set was similar to Elverson's, but capitalized like one of MacKay's sets. Writing in 2006, Spivak said:[12]

> The original pronoun set was not created by me. I think I read about it in a newspaper clipping, perhaps from the Boston Globe, during the time I taught at Brandeis, and I believe it was credited to an anthropologist; later on, when I wanted to use it, I was unable to locate the source. In "The Joy of TeX", I wrote "Numerous approaches to this problem have been suggested, but one strikes me as particularly

simple and sensible." I assumed people would figure that I was using a construction I couldn't properly credit, and not consider me so immodest as to praise my own invention (though I guess that was a rather immodest assumption).

5 heteroflexible, pansexual and sapiosexual (someone who finds intelligence the sexiest thing ever). Over 20 genders?

References

Anzieu, D. (1974/2016). *The Skin-Ego*. Translated by Naomi Segal. (The History of Psychoanalysis Series). London: Karnac Books.

Balsam, R.M. (2012). *Women's Bodies in Psychoanalysis*. New York and London: Routledge.

Balsam, R.H. (2015). Oedipus Rex: Where Are We Going, Especially with Females? *Psychoanalytic Quarterly*, 84:555–588.

Barahona, R. (2016). Book Review: Las teorías sexuales en psicoanálisis: Qué permanence de ellas en la práctica actual? (Sexual Theories in Psychoanalysis: What Remains of Them in Today's Practice?). *Journal of the American Psychoanalytic Association*, 64(5):1065–1069.

Benedek, T. (1952). *Psychosexual Functions in Women*. New York: Ronald Press.

Bennett, J. (2016). She? Ze? They? What's in a Gender Pronoun Sunday Style Section: Command Z. *New York Times*, January 30, 2016.

Bibring, G.L. (1959). Some Considerations of the Psychological Processes in Pregnancy. *Psychoanalytic Study of the Child*, 14:113–121.

Biron, M. (2016). An Inside Look at Google's Marketing and Media Strategy. *DoubleClick by Google*, December 2016. www.doubleclickbygoogle.com/articles/google-marketing-digital-advertising-approach-with-doubleclick/

Bollas, C. (1989). *The Shadow of the Object*. New York: Columbia University Press.

Butler, J. (1990/2006). *Gender Trouble; Feminism and the Subversion of Identity* (Routledge Classics Volume 36). New York and London: Routledge.

Campbell, A. (2014). The Royal We and the Scottish Spider. *Wolverton Mountain*. www.wolverton-mountain.com/articles/the-royal-we.html

Chodorow, N. (1994). *Femininities, Masculinities, Sexualities: Freud and Beyond* (Blazer Lectures). Lexington: University Press of Kentucky.

Deutsch, H. (1944/1945). *The Psychology of Women*. New York: Grune & Stratton.

Fogel, G.I. (1998). Interiority and Inner Genital Space in Men: What Else Can Be Lost in Castration. *Psychoanalytic Quarterly*, 67:662–697.

Freud, S. (1905). Three Essays on the Theory of Sexuality. *Standard Edition*, 7:136–243.

Freud, S. (1908). On the Sexual Theories of Children. *Standard Edition*, 9:209–226.

Freud, S. (1923). The Ego and the Id. *Standard Edition*, 19:1–66.

Harris, A. (2004). *Gender as Soft Assembly* (Relational Perspective Book Series). London and New York: Routledge.

Hurst, R. (2015). *Surface Imaginations: Cosmetic Surgery, Photography, and Skin*. Montreal: McGill-Queen's University Press.

Kristeva, J. (2014). Reliance, or Maternal Eroticism. *Journal of the American Psychoanalytic Association*, 62:69–85.

Langer, M. (1952/1992). *Motherhood and Sexuality*, trans. N.C. Hollander. Guilford, CT: The Guilford Press.

Litowitz, B.E. (2012). Children of the Internet Generation (The Lillian Wachtel Memorial Lecture, Children's Memorial Hospital, Chicago, IL, May 3, 2011). *International Psychoanalysis*. http://internationalpsychoanalysis.net/wpcontent/uploads/2011/07/Childrens Litowitz.pdf

Loewald, H. (1988). *Sublimation: Inquiries into Theoretical Psychoanalysis*. New Haven and London: Yale University Press.

Money, John. (1988). *Gay, Straight, and In-Between: The Sexology of Erotic Orientation*. New York: Oxford University Press.

Quinodoz, D. (1998). A FE/Male Transsexual Patient in Psychoanalysis. *International Journal of Psycho-Analysis*, 79:95–111.

Raphael-Leff, J. (2015). *Dark Side of the Moon: Pregnancy, Parenting, Persecutory Anxieties*. London, England: Anna Freud Center.

Reisner, S. (2016). *Just One More Question, Couch*. http://opinionator.blogs.nytimes.com/2016/02/02/just-one-more-question/

Saketopoulou, A. (2014). Mourning the Body as Bedrock: Developmental Considerations in Treating Transexual Patients Analytically. *Journal of the American Psychoanalysis Association*, 62(5):773–806.

Spivak, M. (1983/1990). Personal Pronoun Pronouncement: Preface. *The Joy of TEX: A Gourmet Guide to Typesetting with the AMS-TEX Macro Package*. XV. Print. Providence, RI: American Mathematical Society.

Spivak, M. (2006) *Michael Spivak in an edit to a Wikipedia article*. http://En.wikipedia.org. Retrieved 2011-11-01.

Stoller, R. (1968/1994). *Sex and Gender: The Development of Masculinity and Femininity*. (Maresfield Library) London: Karnac Books.

University of Wisconsin, Milwaukee: Lesbian, Gay and Bisexual Resource Center. (2016). *Pronouns: A How-To Guide*. http://uwm.edu/lgbtrc/support/gender-pronouns/

Wang, V. (2015). Beyond Housing, Yale Explores Gender Neutrality. *Yale Daily News*, February 10, 2015.

Part II

The body in the changing family

Chapter 5

Introduction

Vaia Tsolas

Among psychoanalysts today the often silent and not so silent question of whether psychoanalysis will evolve with the needs and demands of the changing world misses the point of another vital question; will we as psychoanalysts be bold enough, as Freud did in his time, to utilize our sharp psychoanalytic tools of inquiry to theorize the changing world as a new social order that places unique challenges for the subject and the body. This book's mission is to propose that such lack of psychoanalytic presence is not only harmful to psychoanalysis as a theory and practice, but also to the society at large.

The decline of the patriarchal order, and the law of the Father as we knew it, is an undeniable fact.

> The real father ironically can be reduced to sperm . . . the global market now makes sperm an object of exchange like any other commodity. Sperm now replaces the father in multiple ways. To take a novel recent example, a laboratory at the University of Newcastle has produced mice starting only from the undifferentiated cells.
>
> (Laurent, 2009, p 110)

Technology is altering our everyday experience and beyond, erasing limitations of sex, reproduction and even the ultimate limit, that of death.

A CNN post on March 12, 2017 provided another example of an infinite number of examples, reporting that "using thousands of texts, tweets, public Facebook posts, a woman creates a digital version of her best friend after he died." She communicates with the avatar she has created based on the archive of her friend's digital life. The message here is that it is intriguing to live digitally after your death and to be able to still tweet your friends "happy birthday."

Julia Kristeva, one of the most prominent intellectuals of our times, with her interdisciplinary orientation and talent, conceptualizes the world of the millennium as a world that is hostile to differences and insists on their erasure, saying, "When the difference between man and woman is erased, lack no longer exists, death and the impossible themselves disappear."

We live in a social order where the illusion that everything is possible is sustained by technology, and it is an imperative more now than ever before to acknowledge sexual difference and to preserve it as the cornerstone of our thinking. "I propose that before advancing theories of the 'clinical analysis of the body' the psychoanalytic approach must examine the transformations of parentality to which we are witness" (See Kristeva below). We continue to use the terms *mother* and *father*, Kristeva points out in the following paper, but still we need to theorize *what is a father* and *what is a mother* today.

This section aims precisely to elaborate on the changing structure of the millennial family and its consequences for the body. The Father of Totem and Taboo that Freud proposes is a totemic father who creates a kinship system with the law of prohibition against murder and incest installing castration, and from that the binary of masculinity and femininity has descended. Marie-Hélène Brousse in her recent presentation "Identities as Politics" states that the decline of the name of the Father and with it, the social order organized by the one of exception, has transformed into a new order where we are witnessing the pluralization of the Name-of-the-Father and the new Name(s)-of-the-Father are the norms, grounded on statistics.

Juliet Mitchell, in this section, proposes that psychoanalysis in general, by focusing on the law of the Father, has neglected the law of Mother and its consequences for the social, the subject and the body. "The Law of the Mother precedes The Law of the Father: it comes as a response to the violent desires elicited when the toddler experiences a trauma on the arrival or expectation of younger siblings," Mitchell states below. The law of the mother prohibits incest and murder among siblings, and focuses on the lateral axis rather than the vertical. The body of the lateral ego is different from that of the vertical ego, and it is based on mirroring between siblings, according to Mitchell. In her paper, she elaborates on the importance of the intertwining of the lateral with vertical axis across psychosexual development.

On the other hand, building on her vast experience of working with mothers and infants, Christine Anzieu-Premmereur focuses on demonstrating ways of working clinically with defects in symbolization in young children and adults and the autistic defenses erected to deal with the underlying fragmentation. Anzieu-Premmereur elaborates on defects of adequate mirroring, and the resultant fragility of identity, which have immense consequences for the body. The clinical focus here is on the ways in which, via the analyst's desire, the analyst re-libidinalizes symbolization in a mirroring and interpreting fashion in a similar way to a good-enough-Winnicottian mother. This work, in turn, aims at building a richer preconscious that will be able to process and bind drive energy into representations.

These defects/holes in symbolization that our millennial patients bring into the consulting room can be seen more frequently now than ever before in presenting symptoms such as addictions, psychosomatic symptoms, cutting and eating disorders – symptoms that mutilate the body rather than use the body to express unconscious conflict as in hysteria. The mutilation of the body goes hand in hand with crises of identities, the byproduct of the decline of the name of the Father and its replacement by the technological fabrication of a new social order that knows no limitations. "Our ability to question the prowess of science, technics, and unpoliced freedom is placed in danger under the pressure of a compulsive fulfillment without limits, of an immediate gratification and of an absolute satisfaction," Kristeva argues below.

What is the place of the psychoanalyst in this new social order which encourages the erasure of sexual difference, limitations and otherness? It is the psychoanalyst's insistence on differences and the awareness of the new subject's psychic fragility that he/she insists on in a case by case analysis of transference-countertransference paradigms as Anzieu-Premmereur beautifully illustrates in her clinical examples. Kristeva states below that "it is this permanent dissolution-recomposition [of transference-countertransference] this affinity of life with death, of which the analyst wants to be the guarantor, that makes possible the analysis of addictions, somatizations, criminality and other borderline conditions" which she names in her other works as the new maladies of the soul.

Reference

Laurent, E. (2009). A New Love for the Father. In Kalinich, L., and Taylor, S. (eds.), *The Dead Father. A Psychoanalytic Inquiry*. London: Routledge, pp. 109–124.

Chapter 6

Introduction to "Transformations of *parentality*"

Julia Kristeva, Translated by Edward Kenny
Rosemary H. Balsam

Julia Kristeva, the acclaimed Bulgarian born French psychoanalyst, brings to her contemplation of psychic life formidable academic scholarship from linguistics, literary criticism, religion, politico-cultural analysis, philosophy, art and history. Kristeva's poetic writing about psychic life (not always easy to grasp), flows as an expression of the functioning mind within the sexed and gendered body, representing vital experiences embedded in theory – rarely so effectively rendered in modern psychoanalysis. Like her French cohort, she re-interprets Freud in constant close reading from his texts. Lacan was her early teacher. Psychoanalytically she draws additionally on Klein, Winnicott and Bion.

Roland Barthes has said of her that "'she changes the order of things' by always linking new theories or approaches to tradition (quoted in Moi, 1986, p. 1)" (Widawsky, 2014). This essay is no exception. For example, Kristeva approaches the topic not so much through the novelty of modern gender pluralities, but through the psychic evolution of social bonding, homoeroticism, "parentality" and the fragility of heterosexuality.

Kristeva has written profoundly previously about the subjectivity of the mother, including her erotism (e.g., Maternal Reliance, 2014); the prehistory of communication as examined in her theory of "semiotics"; the encoded horror of the female procreative body in the notion of "abjection" (*Powers of Horror*, 1987); the vicissitudes of development of a child cradled within the urgent sensory proximity of the embodied mother.

To these original Maternal studies, she joins the more acknowledged world of the Father, alluding to its previous exclusivity for Freud and Lacan (e.g., Tales of Love, 1983).

In joining together the spheres of Mother and Father, her focus on "parentality" involves psychic sensibilities that emanate from the primal scene that evolved haltingly, breaking the preferred social homoerotic bonds of the primal horde. Love in heterosexual terms is thus seen here as a late and fragile "achievement" that potentially initiates "the family". It is "the problem of problems".

Now enter the fractures of modern life with procreation, medicalized and technichized, and often separated from heterosexual conjugation. Kristeva offers provocatively and graphically concerns, fears and glimmering hopes for the future of generations and the future of psychoanalysis and our collective psychic existence –

> the social pact today resembles the patchwork coat of a Harlequin, the improvisations of one group borrowing from the models of the other, and vice versa, interfering, innovating, disastrous and festive, producing singularly specific *parentalities*. It is necessary to accompany each family project – adoption, filiation, etc. – with a personalized attention, case by case. As always? More than ever.

References

Kristeva, J. (1980/1982). *The Powers of Horror: An Essay on Abjection*. Translated by L.S. Roudiez. New York: Columbia University Press.

Kristeva, J. (1983/1987). *Tales of Love*. Translated by L.S. Roudiez. New York: Columbia University Press.

Kristeva, J. (2014). Reliance, or Maternal Eroticism. *Journal of the American Psychoanalytic Association*, 62:69–85.

Moi, T., ed. (1986). *The Kristeva Reader*. New York: Columbia University Press.

Widawsky, R. (2014). Julia Kristeva's Psychoanalytic Work. *Journal of the American Psychoanalytic Association*, 62:61–67.

Chapter 7

Transformations of *parentality*

Julia Kristeva, Translated by Edward Kenny

My reading of Freud leads me to the conviction that, for the founders of psychoanalysis, the *body* – far from being a solely biological fact – is a psychosomatic construction that takes form as the speaking subject emerges in its relationships with the paternal and maternal instances. As such, I propose that before advancing theories of the "clinical analysis of the body," the psychoanalytic approach must examine the transformations of *parentality* to which we are witnesses. I hope this approach to the theme that brings us together here will allow us to open it further, to examine corporality more broadly through the lens of the anxieties and dead ends encountered in our practice.

Without isolating the paternal from the maternal, we should be aware of their co-existence *from the very beginning* in the intermediary space of *parentality*, which is a thirdness introduced to the paternal and to the maternal as soon as there is father and mother.

I will briefly call to mind two pathways to introduce the logic and the depths of *parentality*:

1 The transition from the primitive horde to the family occurs through the establishment of *homoeroticism* in the heart of the social bond, which is therefore inherent in the paternal as well, as current social changes confirm; and
2 The paternal *does not ignore the genital organization of the libido*, as certain nominalist conceptions of the paternal may lead one to believe. *Heterosexuality* – in the sense of a *psychisation (an inscription in the psychosexual register) of genitality and of sexual difference including psychic bisexuality*, as well as their inscription in the social contract – is a late and fragile acquisition, and it remains still today an essential problematic, for every one of us, in *parentality*, by necessity, and more generally in the social fabric itself.

The theoretical fable

It is because the frustrated brothers kill the father of the primitive horde – the father who possesses all the women (and perhaps all the men too?) – and because the brothers create a pact among themselves that a critical moment occurs in the evolution of men. This advance in hominization requires a divergence and a displacement of the nostalgic desire of the male genitor – the one who leads the horde which is not yet a "family" – to an attraction/seduction that is directed towards . . . the other self, my brother, my twin (in the words of the famous poem by Charles Baudelaire, "mon semblable, mon frère!"). Homoeroticism is born, which, by erotizing the sameness of one's fellow man, can triumph over the killing of the father's and the usurper son's unbridled desire; homoeroticism can control the sexual cravings of men and can provide a psychic meaning to the drive (as Ferenczi describes). Monotheistic religions in particular contain and celebrate this homoeroticism: Abraham will not devour Isaac, Jesus rejoins his Father, the faithful consume the father in the ritual of Holy Communion, and so on.

It has taken millennia for the family as an alliance between two people of *different sexes* to become thinkable and to be asserted by both men and women. This transpires through the introduction of *love* in the family space: After the so-called Platonic Love of Truth & Beauty, which was the sublimation of Greek homosexuality, it is the Hebrew *Song of Songs* that advances the word of the amorous Shulamite who pines for her shepherd king – before the courtly literature, grafted with Taoist influences apparently transmitted by the Arabs, opens the way to the grand literature of the Christian West – amorous, libertine, modern and post-modern. This is borne out in the long process of the liberation of women that proceeds by the refusal of the family and of maternity before arriving at the realization that maternity contains a specific eroticism in the *reliance* of the lover-become-mother with this first other, the infant, at the crossroad of biology and meaning.

Linguistics seems to corroborate the theoretical Freudian fable of the primitive horde. In the Indo-European world, in accordance with the "elementary structures of kinship" discovered by Claude Lévi-Strauss, the term "marriage" corresponds to an alliance among men (Benveniste, *Vocabulaire des institutions indo-européennes*, 1969). The man, conqueror and barterer, makes the alliance with another man by taking his woman (his sister or daughter): *Maritare* (in Latin) means "to pair", "to conjoin"; but *marya* (in Iranian) recovers the sense of a desirous young man, a fierce and destructive warrior, while containing this pact-making aspect. The condition of the mother, who is called *matrimonium* and signifies that the woman "carried away" or "taken" by the man is destined for procreation (that is to say, to become the mother of the son of the man), appears only late in Roman law and finishes by being confounded with *maritare* without having anything in common with this term. It is only then that the meaning of marriage is modified, by adding to its role of a social alliance among men that of being the *instrument of procreation* for which the man-father remains master, while the mother is simply the worker or rather the servant, indeed the slave.

In another tradition, the Chinese ideogram 姓*xing*, which signifies name or surname, is composed of the pictogram 女*nü*, woman, to the left of the phonetic complex 生*sheng*, meaning to grow, to be born, life. In counterpoint to the Name of the Father in the West ("Le Nom du Père"), the Chinese name is the name of the wife-mother, literally: Born of the woman. The Chinese family name was, therefore, originally the name of the clan in the matrilineal epoch, a feminine name. Thus the eight great names of Chinese high patriarchal Confucian antiquity were all composed with the pictogram 女 *nü*, woman (though this did not prevent the Confucian man from binding women's feet, due their grim horror of the feminine).

As for the homoeroticism of the socialized brothers, which has managed to be legalized in the advanced democracies, I propose the hypothesis that the majority of the men and women who are currently supporting gay marriage do not do so simply because of egalitarian jurisprudence. They support it because homoerotism – legalized and dissociated from all perversion – appears to them as the double of their own "sameness," intrinsic to the social bond in its value of "equality" and to universalism itself. As such, although embattled or even discredited, Freudian analysis of the homoerotic social bond is gaining in depth and is establishing itself in popular consciousness.

Homoerotism does not scandalize me, it belongs to me; whereas homophobia mobilizes those who do not accept their own homoeroticism, e.g., skinheads, etc.

Is this to say that "gay marriage/marriage equality" marks the defeat of heterosexual marriage? I maintain that in any case this reveals its extraordinary *fragility* – which perhaps is not foreign to its seductive character – as well as *the central and inevitable role of the norm that heterosexuality continues to incarnate*: through the original fantasy of the primal scene, this fantasy persists despite the uncoupling of procreation from sexuality.

So – is there a crisis of the heterosexual couple? Let us return to this genitality that "ruptures the group bond."

Although it was cited by those who oppose the new law allowing gay marriage, there was an analysis missing from the French debate – we lacked a defense and an illustration of heterosexuality. Heterosexuality does not only reside in the anatomical difference between male and female. It also cannot be invoked as the surest and only means of transmitting life, or of guaranteeing generational memory. Heterosexuality reveals the extreme intensity of eroticism and as a result conceals an untenable fragility.

The genius of Freud was necessary to formulate that which everyone knows intimately: the procreation that haunts human beings is not a natural act and even less so is it paramount. The primal scene is the Act itself (not to be forgotten when one deduces the paternal agency from the other act, the act of the "murder of the father"), where sexual difference affirms itself in a cascade of fantasies – hotbeds for *psychisation*. Which ones? A fragility inhabits the fury of the primal scene, an original and universal fantasy if ever there is one: fusion and confusion of man and woman, exuberant loss of energies and of identities, affinity of life with death – heterosexuality is not only a discontinuity ("I am other, alone facing the other") normalized by continuity (fusion to "give" life). Heterosexuality is a transgression of identities and codes that do not proceed from fright, but from the anguish and the deathly desire carried by the promise of life through death.

Otherwise more complex than the fable of the "murder of the father," the primal scene implies two speaking sexes, whose drives have become – by dint of *refusement* (refusal/repudiation) and of *psychisation* – deathly desires, because the two speaking sexes are always already framed in the thirdness of meaning, which is that of time and/or procreation. Genitality is not really a PRINCIPIUM – We could say that parental genitality is an INITIUM, a beginning/renewable self-beginning as act of liberty. The "paternal" participates in this genital organization of the libido, as BEGINNING and SELF-BEGINNING of parents and grandparents. The paternal is the witness of the genital organization of the libido (in the unconscious of the child) as well as its carrier (in the erotism of the man).

All this occurs alongside and differently from the mother. Completely against the *institution* of the family, genitality – made theatrical by the primal scene – is the asocial face of the family. A transgression of the forbidden, sublime perturbation of obscenity, indicator of "the *antagonism* between sexed love and group bond," the coupling of man and woman ruptures the community, ". . . the race, the division of nations and the organization of societal classes, and accomplishes culturally important operations" (Freud, "Group Psychology and the Analysis of the Ego", 1921).

Because "there is no sexual relationship" (Lacan, "il n'y a pas de rapport sexuel") (would this be because the fear of the feminine haunts the *désirance* of the father?), the sexual couple perpetuates itself with the aid of the Third: "Contingent loves" ("amours contingents," Sartre and de Beauvoir); sublimations (personal opus, vocation, political engagement, trade, party, sport, hobby, community, church . . .); and at the summit, the Creator, the third person impersonal "He" with a capital H, who encapsulates, sustains and perpetuates the parental *thirdness* itself – its significance. Two times two mirror-image homosexuals wait for Godot in Beckett's play. On the other hand, the heterosexual couple (believing or not) waits expectantly for a third which it will have engendered, because the infant relinks the chain of generations: The Symbol and the Real of the symbolic transcendence which has become transgenerational transcendence. If *parentality* is not simply a factory to make citizens who are more or less superego-ridden, this is because in the untenable fantasy of the primal scene, the future ego finds the resources for its subjectification, that provide him or her a pivot of time, of its eclipses and beginnings.

Whatever the variants of the "heterosexual norm" in the eroticism of each individual – or its rejections in the erotism of diversely composed couples – the mirage of the "primal scene" as original fantasy structures the Unconscious. In agreement with Freud and differing from him, Georges Bataille reminds us of this (1957) as he writes that erotism, whether it be sacred or profane, links itself "to the zenith of procreation."

This is to say that the "processional principle" of the paternal and/or of *parentality* itself is neither an abstraction nor a jerry-rigging of "replacements" or "functions," but on the contrary is embodied in the heterosexual dyad of the two parents.

What is a father? What is a mother?

Thus situated in the light of homoeroticism prevailing in social bonds and at the zenith of an imperious and untenable heterosexuality that breaks these bonds, it is not paternity that disintegrates in our modern secularized world.

It is parentality, with heterosexuality in us, which is "the problematic part," to paraphrase Georges Bataille again. *Heterosexuality is the problem of problems*, and is in this sense the personal and universal problem *par excellence*. When the difference between man and woman is erased, lack no longer exists, death and the impossible themselves disappear, resorbed by fertility in the laboratory, the rental of the uterus, and the fabrication of "genders" by overly sympathetic gynecologists and endocrinologists. Our ability to question the prowess of science, technics, and unpoliced freedom is placed in danger under the pressure of a compulsive fulfillment without limits, of an immediate gratification and of an absolute satisfaction.

Our secularized society is the only civilization that has voted for a marriage for all (marriage equality) but does not have a discourse on *parentality*.

When the Ethics Advisory Committee will have discerned what we owe to Medicine and what could be given back to society, we will be required to respond to an unformulated question, unthought of by the lawmaker: What is a father? What is a mother?

The father: a "legal fiction" (James Joyce)? "Fulcrum, fictitious center and concrete continuation of the genealogical order" (Lacan)? Father of Law or loving father? Pure function that can be borne by my mother's temporary partner – the educator, the teacher, the professor . . . after everything, the State? I do not believe so. In elucidating the multiple facets which compose the emergence of a paternity in a time that precedes us, have we not forgotten the male body, homo- and hetero-erotic, who recognizes me and whom I recognize, and who, by force of parricide, I as a woman, daughter and spouse, can become like, though differently from him?

The father is not the *principiel* (which is to say the primary cause) because the symbolic and the genetic precede him. He is the new beginning, the *initial* (from Plato and Aristotle to Saint Augustine, Nietzsche and Heidegger, philosophy distinguishes *Principio* and *Initio*) – but we must add the specification that this INITIAL is PARENTAL, which is to say double.

What is the difference between paternal and maternal parentality? It is by the scansion (urge and repression) of his desire that the father participates in the *asocial* thirdness of the primal scene AND in the *social* thirdness of the familial superego; while it is through *reliance* that the mother imprints her mark. Through psychic bisexuality, scansion and *reliance* of the father, scansion and *reliance* of the mother: *parentality* is performed by a quartet, such that the conjunction of the two parentalities *were* that "psychical revolution of matter" (Freud, "Two Principles of Mental Functioning", 1911) where the infantile drive succeeds in making meaning in the thirdness of language and thought.

Neither modern nor traditionalist

I am not proposing to replace the paradigm of the "murder of the father" (Freud) nor the Christocentric one of the "dead father" (Lacan), which would leave only a Name or a Principle. I suggest to reconsider these paradigms in view of the "primal scene," so as to envisage the impacts of genitality and dual parentality in the construction of contemporary psychosexualities.

Thenceforth, beginning with psychic bisexuality, *the transformations of the parental "initial" are infinite*, under pressure of the evolution of technics and law.

The Freudian analyst, whether man or woman, works with a new version of the paternal: Neither totemic animal, nor Laius-Oedipus, nor Abraham-Isaac, nor Jesus with his abandoning and resuscitating father. In the love/hate of transference, the father is not only loved and hated, put to death and resuscitated, but literally *atomized* on our couches and nevertheless *incorporated* by the analysand. As in the primal scene? Perhaps, if one thinks of the explosion of identities and norms, where the coupling of man and woman ruptures the community and connects itself at the zenith of the re-birth of procreation. Transference and countertransference induce the position as well as the atomization of paternal agency.

It is this permanent dissolution-recomposition, this affinity of life with death, of which the analyst wants to be the guarantor that makes possible the analysis of addictions, somatizations, criminality and other *borderline* conditions. The subject of these "new maladies of the soul" (cf. J. Kristeva, *Les nouvelles maladies, de l'âme*, 1993) emerges with a paradoxical identity, which is not without evoking the Brownian motion of Jackson Pollock's "drippings," entitled *One* (cf., J. Kristeva, "La voie lactée de Jackson Pollock," in *Pulsions du temps*, 2013).

Where, then, has the One gone if the beginning/self-beginning is a dissemination? What happens to my body as an analyst in the process of transference and countertransference? Am I still One when I analyze or when I am the analysand? Surely yes, my identity exists ("There is a One") but remains undecidable, deprived of an immovable center and disengaged from a mortifying repetition. A bit like a piece of serialist music or an improvised dance that some underlying order nevertheless supports, in the Open. Though neither "dead father" nor "Führer," authority does not disappear in the analytic cure. Neither does it disappear in a recomposed society in the process of transformation. It is disseminated in the permanent adjustment of the two parents on this other scene of fertility – in addition to the primal scene – through a new beginning which is the action of raising/educating/transmitting-to their offspring.

In summary: If we continue to call ourselves Freudian analysts, the acknowledgment of sexual difference is the touchstone of our experience; the paternal "principle" inscribes itself in the initial of the primal scene "at the zenith of procreation;" the structuring thirdness shores up the unity of the speaking subject with its capacity for language and thought; the One disseminates itself and remakes itself continually in the postmodern universe (artificial insemination is an example among others of the dissemination of the One).

I have not forgotten marriage for all. It will not be the pious vow of a Republic cut in two, divided between the "moderns" and the "traditionalists:" the gays – the recomposed – the assisted reproductive technologies, surrogacy, etc., on one side, and those nostalgic for old norms, on the other. Rather, the social pact today resembles the patchwork coat of a Harlequin, the improvisations of one group borrowing from the models of the other, and vice versa, interfering, innovating, disastrous and festive, producing singularly specific *parentalities*. It is necessary to accompany each family project – adoption, filiation, etc. – with a personalized attention, case by case. As always? More than ever.

Between the Biblical family and the Chinese family, whose persistences are sharing out the destiny of the millennium to come, and beyond the dead ends of Islamic gangster-fundamentalism, there is no other choice for Europe and America. Without yielding to the temptation of a "politics of psychoanalysis" (which would be a negation of its deontology), psychoanalysis is perhaps alone to be capable of responding to this emergency: not the disappearance, but the dissemination of the One into incommensurable singularities. If we are persuaded of this, we will succeed in making the voice of psychoanalysis heard – a voice that is sorely lacking in our globalized world aware of its endemic crises.

Reference

Bataille, G. (1957) *L'Erotisme. Paris: Éditions de Minuit.*

Chapter 8

The sibling body-ego

Juliet Mitchell

When, in 1905, Freud introduced the all-importance of infantile sexuality on a world stage that claimed to believe in childhood innocence, he commented that everyone who looked after children knew about their sexuality, it was only the professionals who denied it. With sibling desire for sex and, even more importantly, murder, the denial is as, or more, extensive. This highly pertinent quotation from a psychologist is buried in Stephen Pinker's acclaimed *The Better Angels of our Nature*:

> Babies do not kill each other, because we do not give them access to knives and guns. The question . . . we've been trying to answer for the past thirty years is how do children learn to aggress . . . [that's] the wrong question. The right question is how do they learn not to aggress?
>
> (Tremblay, 2011, p. 483)

Pinker's popular argument is that we are becoming more peaceful; but how is this possible if throughout time and place, we have been and always will be, at times, murderous toddlers – not only in actuality as infants, but also persisting in the childish parts of our adult minds? The wrong question is still being asked. And the wrong answers are inevitably being given. We must ask: how do we learn not to aggress?

Looking laterally along a horizontal axis from the starting-point of the interaction of siblings, we can see that the mother intervenes between them making sure they do not have knives and guns, totally prohibiting the expression of any desire for murder and also (perhaps less emphatically) any expression of the type of illicit sexuality that develops into incest. I call this prohibition "The Law of the Mother" in teasing reference to Jacques Lacan's notorious "Law of the Father" in his re-reading and re-emphasising of Freud's proposal of a threat of castration if the desire for incest with the mother persists (the Oedipus complex). The Law of the Mother precedes The Law of the Father: it comes as a response to the violent desires elicited when the toddler experiences a trauma on the arrival or expectation of a younger sibling. The mother's prohibition operates only on the horizontal axis *between* her children: it says "no" first and foremost to sibling murder in the present and simultaneously to the sexual love that could become sibling incest.

This chapter addresses the topic of the psychological body. The argument's general framework is the problem addressed above: the sibling trauma and the law of the mother. In their turn these open out onto still larger issues because, following the effectiveness of the Law of the Mother on psychic life, we socialize the results along the same lines as the original prohibition on violence. We construct society by an attempt to differentiate murder from warfare; rape from marriage. Hoping these will be opposites when they are, in fact, also two sides of the same coin.

There is here an inner and an outer framework. The inner framework is the "lateral body" of the bisexual social subject. This subject is the "toddler," the child of two-to-three years who persists in all of us. The outer framework is my ongoing argument that psychoanalysis, like most of the social sciences, has privileged the vertical axis of human parent and child to the neglect of the horizontal axis of lateral relations. The inner focus and the outer one come together in the siblings.

The outer framework: siblings

As daughters and sons, children relate vertically to parents; as sisters and brothers, the same children relate *to each other* as siblings along a horizontal axis. The desires, the prohibitions against them, and, most importantly, the psychological defense mechanisms which come into play to make these desires unconscious are not the same on the two axes of verticality and horizontality. The "sibling trauma" and the "Law of the Mother" are building blocks for a proposed theory of a horizontal axis.

A "sibling trauma" is when a new baby does, or "should," arrive when the toddler who is now walking and talking is around two and a half years old (Mitchell, 2014). The only existence the toddler knows so far is being itself "the baby" of the family. With the new baby, the toddler's baby-status has been taken by another; what there was of the toddler's so-called "body-ego" has been snatched away, annihilated. If someone else is it, who is it now? At this age the body and mind are one and the same thing as they will be in all future psychosomatic conditions or aspects of psychic life more generally.

The toddler has probably rushed enthusiastically to the new baby as though this baby would be more of itself. Because it thinks it is *the same* as itself, it narcissistically loves it to excess. But the new baby (or threat of a baby) is, or would be, too much of itself, it would be the same – an annihilating replacement. So because it is *the same* (*not* as we mistakenly think, because it is different) the toddler wants to get rid of it. The result is that there is a near simultaneity of the desire for sex and for murder. This underlies the major early defense mechanisms, a vicissitude of the drive known as "reversal into the opposite and turning round upon the subject's own self" (Laplanche & Pontalis, 1973, pp. 399–400). In this, the human object becomes the human subject and the subject becomes the object, passivity becomes activity and also vice-versa. The annihilated toddler becomes the annihilator, and love turns to hate, hate to love within moments. We shall see that this is an important aspect of specifically lateral mirroring and inter-subjectivity and their bodily expression.

The prohibition on the toddler murdering the baby is stronger than the – still important – prohibition on incest. At this stage the prohibition on sexuality is on self-pleasuring, on masturbation which when shared with the sibling can develop into incest. Struggles with masturbation can continue throughout life. Melanie Klein vividly describes them becoming incest with two brothers who since infancy had had full sexual relationships: "The brothers got on very badly together . . . In their analysis, I was able to trace back their mutual sexual acts as far as the ages of about three and a half and two and a half respectively, but it is quite probable that they had begun even earlier . . . the acts . . . comprised mutual *fellatio*, masturbation and touching the anus with the fingers" (Klein, 1932, p. 113). Melanie Klein wrote this in 1932. To my mind she rightly saw the dominance of the destructive drive within the sexual fantasies or enactments. However she wrongly considered that boys who were torturing each other were in phantasy only destroying or having illicit sex with their parents. In other words, for Klein, they were experiencing an early Oedipus complex in which, while using each other, they were unconsciously imagining their father and mother – the vertical axis. The patently obvious horizontal axis is ignored.

The desires that the trauma triggers – sibling murder and sibling sex – are prohibited by the "Law of the Mother" which only operates laterally *between her children*. Forbidding incest and murder are the main prohibitions of human society that affect psychic formation; incest with the mother and the murder of the father are the Oedipus complex, the "shibboleth" of psychoanalysis which is the *sine qua non* of psychoanalytic thinking. An interest in siblings today as in the past, can be used to displace the Oedipus complex. This seems to me to be completely wrong and to damage the possibility of thinking laterally on the horizontal in tandem with the later vertical complex. What is proposed here is an addition not a substitution. However, reciprocally, the central importance of the Oedipus complex does not entail it being all there is. Classically it is argued that sisters and brothers step into the places of mother and father. The suggestion here is that the two pairs are different. In both cases murder and incest are forbidden but murdering your sibling and having incest with that same sibling is not the same as murdering your father and marrying your mother.

Siblings are forbidden to enact their desires for incest or killing earlier, before the Oedipus complex, which means that their psychological responses are more "primitive" too. Where the Law of the Father uses the threat of castration to vertically enforce the *repression* of Oedipal desires, the Law of the Mother operates horizontally between her children to threaten the withdrawal of her love and care. With this threat she aims to enforce the prohibition on her still highly dependent toddler. The toddler will use such mechanisms of defense as "dissociation," "splitting," "disavowal" and so on. This means that where the Oedipus complex with its over-riding pursuit of pleasure (the *pleasure principle*) heralds normality-neurosis, the sibling trauma forefronts earlier normality-narcissistic/psychotic states of mind. These are not repressed, they are *socialized* along with the mother's command that the infant acknowledges what constitutes reality (the *reality principle*) which she has been trying to instill since its birth.

The trauma of the "sibling trauma"

The focus here is only on the sibling situation and what the interaction of siblings opens up for our understanding of the "body-ego" in psychoanalytic thinking.

After proposing a "sibling trauma," I subsequently discovered that the "sibling trauma" found a match in Winnicott's categorical, if scattered, statements about what he calls "the separation trauma" of the two-to-three year old (see Winnicott, 1972). Winnicott's observation arose from his vast experience of babies and small children. The trauma he refers to takes place on the vertical axis between child and mother. It is the same trauma as the sibling trauma on the horizontal axis. Winnicott describes the experience of the toddler when the mother becomes preoccupied with the new baby as undoubtedly traumatic for the toddler.

Parents forget or deny that it is a trauma, often insisting either that all was perfect or that the squabbles were unimportant; that the tantrums had nothing to do with the baby whom the toddler adored. As indeed it does. Psychoanalysts can follow suit describing the toddler's experience as "a difficulty" not a trauma. It matters for psychoanalysis that this advent of the baby for the toddler is not just a varying degree of difficulty, but is categorically a trauma. Unlike a trauma, a "difficulty" does not produce unconscious effects.

A trauma brings to the surface the dangerous desire and its prohibition, both of which had been unconscious. The sibling trauma and the law of the mother are a double whammy: first the trauma of feeling annihilated because the new baby has stolen the old baby's "identity" as "baby;" then the trauma that again the toddler will not survive because the mother threatens desertion if her prohibition is not observed. The first is actual – the second a threat. I shall restrict the term "sibling trauma" and its implications to the first; but both actuality and threat need an understanding of trauma. The understanding and history of trauma as a key part of psychoanalytical theory is complex and complicated. My selective rendering is for the sibling experience.

The definition we need of trauma is this: there will be a violence from outside which breaks through our psychic protective barriers on an analogy with a physical trauma which breaks through the protective skin and muscle. Freud's crucial addition to this general understanding was that this breakthrough from outside meets an equivalent breakthrough from inside, a surge of illicit desires and their forbidding, which arise from within. Everyone has these desires which no-one is allowed. Equally important is that society is created by the prohibition on their implementation. The desires and their prohibition "break through" because both are unconscious.

The combination of an external blow and an internal danger of released prohibited desires indicates a psychogenic trauma. The trauma floods the organism with uncontrollable energy. What remains of the shattered ego tries over and over again to get a hold of and once more bind the chaotic energy so that there can be an equilibrium in which the drive to attain pleasure can once more operate. But this can fail and then what persists is the endless repetition of the ego's effort, a state of affairs that suggests there is a psychic state "beyond the pleasure principle," a situation in which either chaos and psychic fragmentation or death and stasis hold sway. Such trauma leaves no space and without space the possibility of *representing* what has happened, vanishes. This is where the traumatic possibility of abandonment opened up by the mother's law differs from the sibling trauma to which it is the response.

The prohibition of the "Law of the Mother"

The mother has been preoccupied with introducing her infant to reality; she has done so through her general authority. But a prohibition is different: the punishment for breaking the law would be fatal: I suggest it is not the same as the later *threat* of castration but that it is commensurate. As it too is only a threat, unlike with sibling trauma, there can be a response. We have now to think from the side of the woman not the man, the Law of the Mother as opposed to the Law of the Father. It is the threat of absolute loss of the mother's love and care for the infant who still, as toddler, is utterly dependent and who, as the baby whom the toddler still wants to remain, would of course be completely helpless – as when faced by death.

The "sibling trauma" is on the horizontal axis where the mother's law operates. Although "sibling" and Winnicott's stress on "separation" are different aspects of the same trauma, Winnicott's "separation trauma" on the vertical axis of parent and child has no Law attached to it. It takes place within the framework of the pre-Oedipal and the family with no prohibition, no Law, only "authority" in play.

Differently, the mother's law offers the pre-*social* infant the way to social childhood. Just as the conflict between the desire and its prohibition is responsible for the symptoms of psychic distress or ill-health, so the reasonably successful resolution of the conflict acts as a *rite of passage*. All rites of passage are heralded by trauma because one must leave an old state in order to enter a new one. Acknowledging the Law of the Mother, the traumatized toddler enters the social world that has always awaited it but that, equally, it creates anew. The a- or pre-social infant leaves the family in which its pre-Oedipal self remains and transitions to become a social child.

Only if the desires that arise are prohibited and thus their reappearance is a threat, can the trauma be what I will call "foundational." If the Law of the Mother did not elicit the threat of traumatic punishment then it could not be productive of unconscious processes. If the toddler's separation and sibling experience were only a "difficulty" then sibling relationships may be of great interest sociologically, anthropologically, psychologically, historically, and in literature and indeed in the to-and-fro of the psychoanalytic session but not for psychoanalysis as a theory as well as a practice. So far psychoanalysis recognizes only the Oedipus complex as a foundational trauma with the castration complex establishing the prohibition on maternal incest and paternal murder. Theories of the pre-Oedipal period elevate the mother but do not offer an additional foundational complex with a trauma that unleashes the desire and its prohibition. The horizontal social axis is interactive with, but different from, the vertical family. Another understanding is needed.

The pre-Oedipal infant-self on the vertical axis stays in the family as it enters the Oedipus complex. To the contrary, the toddler sibling-self *repudiates* the family: if the mother wants the new baby, the toddler will want its friend. The love between children becomes notable. The becoming social child finds a new world that has always been there. The proposal of a sibling trauma and the mother's prohibition of the desires it elicits from the toddler is not pre-Oedipal, rather it is pre-Social. The child, of course, is both.

There is thus a vertical pre-Oedipal and a horizontal pre-Social. The baby has been born not only into a family but into a social world which it must both discover as already there and also create anew for itself. Its body-ego relations belong to this process. What does this universal sibling trauma and subsequent prohibition on sibling murder and incest on the horizontal axis tell us about the body, what does the body of the "body-ego" tell us if seen along the horizontal axis of lateral relations, siblings and their heirs in cousins, affines, social sisters and brothers, friends and foe, marriage/sexual partners, enemies who yesterday were and will tomorrow, be brothers?

The inner framework: the bisexual subject

Unlike femininity and masculinity, unlike passivity and activity, indeed unlike homosexuality and heterosexuality, bisexuality is a psychoanalytic concept. Its status was assured throughout Freud's scientific writings but its initial history was entangled in one of his most important personal relations. He derived the concept from his exchanges with Wilhelm Fliess who then accused him of handing the notion to Otto Weininger who went to town with it. Never abandoning its importance in his clinical observations nor its explanatory powers, Freud did, however, worry that it had not been properly integrated into the theory of the drives: "The theory of bisexuality is still surrounded by many obscurities and we cannot but feel it as a serious impediment in psychoanalysis that it has not yet found any link with the theory of the instincts" (Freud, 1927, p. 106).

If looked at through siblings on the horizontal axis, its relation to the drives becomes clearer. My proposal is that bisexuality belongs better with the thesis of a pre-social, earlier, "sibling trauma" and a Law, an absolute prohibition emanating from the Mother. If we place it in this earlier experience it can find a place in the theory of the drives, which is, to me, still mandatory for psychoanalysis.

Today both colloquially and within psychoanalytic thinking where it plays a somewhat underground role, bisexuality is thought of primarily as an object choice – one loves or sexually desires someone of both sexes. Although it will be this, it needs to be understood first and foremost as a subject position which Freud called "a bisexual disposition" as in his statement of what psychoanalysis could contribute to the understanding of the psychology of women: "In conformity with its peculiar nature, psycho-analysis does not try to describe what a woman is – that would be a task it can scarcely perform – but sets out enquiring how she comes into being, *how a woman develops out of a child with a bisexual disposition*" (my italics) (Freud, 1933, p. 116). It is the same for the original psychic position of the man. However, it is in this essay, "Femininity" that he most clearly sets out why a girl retains more of her bisexual subject position than does the boy after the castration complex (the law of the father). We need to ask if this is the case for the social girl and boy after the earlier law of the mother. I think not.

Freud used the notion of bisexuality primarily in relation to the Oedipus complex and in particular in relation to the girl's subjectivity. Her greater bisexuality accounted for her greater predisposition to hysteria: having, like the boy, desired the mother as her first love object, the girl's Oedipus complex entails that she should instead become the love-object of her father. In hysteria, however, she protests against such a loss of her subject position. (The issue of all-important male hysteria is outside the scope of this chapter; see Mitchell, 2000.)

The horizontal perspective changes some problems. Take, for instance, the issue of "conversion hysteria" a designation of a malady that can only find an explanation with reference to the Oedipus-castration complex. There it refers to the return of repressed unconscious thoughts, or psychic conflict in the somatic. As late as *Inhibitions, Symptom and Anxiety* (Freud, 1925), Freud bemoaned that the mysterious leap of the mind into the body had not really been understood. However, seen horizontally from the position of the becoming-social toddler in what was commonly known as "infantile hysteria," there is as yet no mystery. The toddler is only on the edge of achieving metaphor – but has not as yet grasped it. Metaphor says something in terms of something else – the toddler does not yet make the transposition; nor does the hysteric – body is mind and vice versa.

Wilfred Bion had a patient who described coming into the bedroom to find her small daughter with her profiled face resting on the baby's tummy. Questioned about her posture, the little girl said she was "keeping an eye on the baby." The body acts the question. When the adult hysteric in all of us uses this part of our psyches we forget metaphor, become pre-metaphoric and have a physical pain in the neck when we are "a pain in the neck," a cramped ache in the stomach instead of "belly-aching," some posture or behavior that expresses our sexual desire and the law with which the mother has prohibited it. This can become the later expression of Oedipal thinking through the body but can be understood as also involving a regression to the pre-metaphoric toddler. The concept of a bisexual subject position is latent within this understanding of infantile conversion hysteria: a demand that might treat the toddler as an object is resisted by its insistence on its active subjecthood. The need for omnipotence that follows trauma will contribute to this. When bisexuality, as first and foremost a subject position is part of drive-theory, then its implications for the "body" of the "body-ego" can have a context. We can embed body-ego issues such as "gender," peer-mirroring and peer inter-subjectivity within bisexuality as a subject position.

Freud was excited by the paradigm shift represented by "bisexuality," which was part-and-parcel of his love for Wilhelm Fliess as it was for the ending of that relationship. Although he never agreed with what he saw as Fliess' over-emphasis on biology, bisexuality did give a biological body-emphasis to the psyche which was all-important. What must be stressed again here is that, so differently from today, it was, and should still be, primarily a subject position, not an object-choice.

For Freud bisexuality was a subject position that the vertical Oedipus-castration complex should resolve into a clear distinction between the sexes. This did not mean that bisexuality ended; indeed it plays a major role in the construction of what has come to be called "sexual difference". However, unlike "gender," "sexual difference" (Klein, 1975, p. 9), a result of the castration complex, is a non-negotiable state in which future mothers are on one side of a line and future fathers on another.

Gender and sexual difference

The future Oedipus complex which is a generic not individual matter, affects the earlier experience of the toddler and the earlier (which I claim is also generic) is delayed in some ways until later. However, if we attach bisexuality to "gender" on the horizontal axis of lateral relations as opposed to "sexual difference" on the vertical, then its place in the drive theory becomes more easily discernible and the impacts of this on the "body-ego" become importantly different. The concept of "gender" or "social sex" in its French translation was an introduction of second wave feminism and the beginning of the 1970s. A large topic, here I want only to emphasize its link to the sibling body-ego through its fundamental lateral bisexuality. The bisexual infant-toddler thinks it could be either sex but the serious problem of the new baby (the "sibling trauma") forces it to think about a *gender* distinction: the baby is either the same or a different sex from the toddler.

I would hope to keep "gender" for this horizontal relation, leaving "sexual difference" for the vertical Oedipal relation. All societies make the sex-gender distinction on birth. Behavioral distinctions and attributes will have been in place before, as well as on and after birth. Babies and infants will have had the experience of various socially ascribed gender distinctions but until the sibling trauma, they will have "had the experience but not known the meaning" of the distinction that is part of their daily life. The epistemophilic drive – a "component drive" – will become dominant as Melanie Klein illustrates from three-year-old "Fritz": "At this time there recurred repeatedly the question whether his mother, I and his sister had always been girls, whether every woman when she was little was a girl – whether he had never been a girl." The toddler's own and its playmate's body together with its gender will become a source of endless investigation, until the mother's law effects an inhibition on violent or sexual exploration.

Infantile penis-envy is matched by womb-envy and an interest in the body of the baby and the mother will shift emphatically to the body of the sibling then play-mate. This is where the notorious "penis-envy" first belongs – with the sibling and play-mate. What happens in the Oedipus complex will retrospectively affect it but penis-envy will always primarily be for a lateral relationship not for the Oedipal father of the vertical axis.

In a famous case, Winnicott heard his middle-aged, married and professionally successful, *male* patient evincing "penis-envy" (Winnicott, 1972). They came to explain it through his mother's having seen him as a girl instead of what "he was" – a boy. The penis-envying little girl whom they had discovered constituted a "foreign body" within the larger psyche. What is significant in relation to the bisexual subject under discussion is that a "foreign body" is characteristic of an unresolved trauma. The discrepancy between the world's view of this patient's male gender and his mother's contrary perspective was a traumatic experience. Indeed when Winnicott first mentions what he is hearing, his patient acknowledges it with difficulty and comments that therefore he must be mad. Winnicott, however (presumably feeling himself as the mother in the transference), points out that it is he, Winnicott, who is mad to see a penis-envying girl when it is evident that it is a man who is lying on his analytical couch.

From the viewpoint here, what is interesting is that the traumatically encapsulated imaginary little girl with penis-envy in this adult male patient of Winnicott's is two and a half years old – a toddler – *and she does not grow any older*. This means that even if the patient's mother saw him as a girl from birth onwards, the patient only found that meaningful when he became a toddler. The traumatic moment was in toddler-time. The penis-envying little girl in the man patient had all the characteristics of a toddler, such as getting attention through illness. The two and a half year old little girl was, as a "foreign object" insisting on her bisexual subjecthood. This trauma-derived penis-envy arose not from the Oedipus complex but from an obstacle to bisexual subjecthood.

If we look at the penis-envying little girl more generally from the horizontal instead of the vertical perspective, we get something additional that is rather different from our normal understanding. Instead of penis-*envy* and womb-*envy* we get what I would call penis-play and womb-play. This is transmuted to envy with the Oedipus complex – but before that, it is play. Looking from the toddler's bisexual standpoint I recall my two and a half year old daughter – a long time ago – and her very close boyfriend one hot summer's day, playing naked in a large kitchen, serving the surrounding grown-ups with tiny toy cups of tea. A wide and mischievous grin on her face, my daughter went up to her friend and delicately poised a cup of tea in the right place, saying sweetly "cup of tea, penis?" Freud's "Little Hans" likewise kindly reassured his father that he too would be able to have a baby soon and questioned about the provenance of his own many babies, he replied – "I got them from myself of course." The penis can be another playmate and the small child's imaginary babies are conceived and born both happily and parthenogenetically; penises and wombs can feed or have a drink.

But the child is also learning "reality." Knowing reality while turning what has previously been hallucinated into what can be imagined, constitutes play. The play that takes place between baby and mother as Winnicott richly describes, also occurs from as early as four months between babies; in later infancy it becomes the quite elaborate province of bisexual lateral peers in which they increasingly can be subjects and, when necessary, objects for each other. Having understood "gender" from the advent of the same or other sex sibling, they can, so to speak, add it to their bisexual subjecthood.

The body-ego of latency

While still establishing themselves clearly as independent bisexual *subjects* at the time of the sibling-separation trauma, bisexual children are asking about gender distinction. They enter the Oedipus complex knowing their gender in relation to each other. It is on this basis of "gender" that "sexual difference" will become established. We can see clearly the difference between the vertical parent-child axis of sexual difference and the inter-child horizontal axis of gender if we consider the period known as "latency."

So-called *latency* is the supposed non-sexual period between the repression of incestuous desires for the mother and the massive re-entry of sexuality when it becomes reproductive at puberty. However, if we add in the horizontal axis, latency is different. After the Law of the Mother, the social aspect of the child at around the age of three to three and a half enters what, if we are going to keep the term "latency," we will need to describe as pre-latency while the family aspect becomes obsessed with the mother and enters the Oedipus complex. After the castration complex at about the age of five or six, the family aspect child enters latency where the social aspect child is all ready and waiting in pre-latency with its own social sexual element having been already transformed into play and love with another child.

Again, psychoanalysis working only with the family aspect ignores the relationship between children. As psychoanalysts, Winnicott found latency children boring and Klein found them challengingly difficult while she hunted out their early Oedipal desires. JK Rowling explained that Harry Potter went to a boarding school so that she could omit adults from the children's lives. If we do this, then from a psychoanalytical point-of-view as well as a fictional one, latency becomes a scene of fascinating children making up plays, acting and inventing *inter alia*.

Commenting on a secretly recorded children's sleep-over discussion on a BBC4 program "A Child of Our Time" (Feb. 2013) Germaine Greer rightly exclaimed "they are wonderful – I feel I have nine new friends." Latency, of course, can also include bullying and physical fights which range from the intensely enjoyable to the very frightening – if we let them have knives and guns. Importantly, there is a clinical transference from these lateral instead of parental relations. The horizontal interaction can be a very key element of the highly creative, playful (and/or difficult) interaction of patient and therapist.

All along the horizontal spectrum, the body is as active as the mind to which it belongs. Following latency, with puberty and adolescence, we have lateral sexuality coming under the aegis of potential pregnancy and violence coming under the aegis of potential murder. The real possibility of both shifts the picture. However weak the actual mother, her law is still in place but subsumed by the Law of the Father. The attempt will be to put further emphasis on the allowances that are the inversion of the prohibitions so that with adulthood there are a range of permissible lateral relations for which marriage and war stand as exemplary. Marriage and war parade as the opposite of incest and murder – they are, in fact its other side. All relations which are not these legitimated relations of war and marriage are also lateral relationships: within war, the girl's role goes along a trajectory in which rape and murder is as prevalent as fighting.

Neither sex's gender subject position means there is an inexorable choice between same-sex and other sex subject relations as there is with "sexual difference" on the vertical. Same-sex social or sexual bonding always continues alongside other-sex relationships. Marriage has female friendship; war has male-male camaraderie as its emotional *raison d'être*.

The presence of the lateral body-ego

Both the illegal and the legitimated interactions always involve the "body-ego" as much in the "talking cure" as in the social world. In order for the transference to become usable in the clinical encounter, the patient cannot see the analyst behind the couch, but the analyst can see the patient while "listening" to the body as well as the words. The body of the lateral ego is different from that of the vertical ego. For something to be represented it has to first be missing. Vertically the words represent the missing breast or missing penis of the mother and the body echoes this missing. The lateral body of the sibling trauma is a present body.

Lacan corrected Ernest Jones' notion of aphanisis (the fading of *desire*) with his theoretical reformulation of this clinically observed phenomenon as a "fading of the *subject*." He linked this with the castration complex. The fading of the subject, rather than desire, is correct, but "sibling annihilation" on the occasion of the sibling trauma is not "fading;" we are not looking at an "absence" in the mother (the missing breast or penis) that makes the threat of castration a possibility. With the sibling trauma, children of both sexes will have felt the annihilation of their only just emergent meaningful experience of subjecthood. The overcrowding of the traumatic experience has its other side, a "white annihilation," a total emptiness which is, so-to-speak, a black hole. From now on any further trauma will reveal the marks of this annihilation. Once they have survived the annihilation, their subjecthood will be stronger but this will be experienced in their interaction with *each other* as present. The threat of her abandonment if she is not obeyed means there would be no mother. The mother as described in Freud's essay, "The Three Caskets" presents the child with the possibility of death. The "no-mother" incorporates the effects of the sibling trauma. This "presence" in the context of "absence" suggests a process of "representative presentation" rather than "representation;" rather than just a "before" metaphor we have a "beyond" such as we can find in creative art.

Lateral inter-subjectivity and mirroring

Two psychic ground-plans of all relationships are the processes of mirroring and inter-subjectivity; these will differ on the lateral and lineal.

All inter-subjectivity involves a space, in the words of group analyst Rene Kaës:

> The issue of intersubjectivity opens up a central question of psychoanalysis: it concerns the intersubjective conditions of the formation of the unconscious and of the subject of the unconscious. In these conditions, I call intersubjectivity the dynamic structure of the psychic space between two or several subjects. This space includes specific processes, formations and experiences, the effects of which have a bearing on the accession of the subjects of the unconscious, on their becoming I at the heart of the We. This definition is very far removed from a perspective that reduces intersubjectivity to interactional phenomena.
>
> (Kaës, 2006, p. 8)

This takes understanding of intersubjective space to where the "I" becomes "We." It can be used to supplement Freud's classic formulation of the "We" in the "I," the social in the individual:

> The contrast between individual psychology and social or group psychology, which at a first glance may seem to be full of significance, loses a great deal of its sharpness when it is examined more closely. It is true that individual psychology is concerned with the individual man and explores the paths by which he seeks to find satisfaction for his instinctual impulses; but only rarely and under certain exceptional conditions is individual psychology in a position to disregard the relations of this individual to others. In the individual's mental life someone else is invariably involved, as a model, as an object, as a helper, as an opponent; and so from the very first individual psychology, in this extended but entirely justifiable sense of the worlds, is at the same time social psychology as well.
>
> (Freud, 1922)

Here in Freud's account of the individual the baby takes the world into itself; in Kaes's social group understanding of intersubjectivity, the infant enters the world.

The idea of a "mirror phase" was introduced by Jaques Lacan. It indicates that the subject's subjecthood always receives its reference from elsewhere. A cat looks in a mirror and proceeds to look behind the mirror for the other cat. The human baby does not. With its carer saying to its mirror-image: "that's Jenny" or "Johnny," it perceives its flailing body with its spoon in its ear as nevertheless something whole and together. However this mirror *Gestalt* is not identical with itself; it feels all over the place but its carer refers to its co-ordinated mirror-image by its name.

Contrary to this disjunctive mirroring in which the mother/carer bestows the baby's identity on the image, sibling-sibling and child-child mirroring has no alienation. A baby, seeing its older sibling enter the room with its parents, will have eyes and excited (or fearful) body only for the sibling; wheel a baby along the street when a schoolchild dances by, and the baby is entranced. It is as though its own still helpless, uncoordinated body grows by what it looks upon: this is an early identification. The older child will have its own lively, coordinated body-subject confirmed by the baby's delight.

The intra-child inter-subjectivity partakes of this mirroring identification between two people seen as one and the same by the baby and as different by the older child. Later it turns into the "we are as one" of couples as opposed to the "we are different" of mothers and fathers. Put reductively, where the daughter and son predominantly learn they start different from their parents but "should" become the same, on the horizontal the other starts as the same as itself and struggles to become someone different.

In the early twentieth century, the psychoanalyst Charlotte Buhler observed an interaction she named as "transitivism" (Lacan elaborated the idea). In transitivism, the child hits its friend on the friend's left cheek, instantly clutching its own mirroring right cheek, exclaiming: "She hit me!" This is the sort of process that takes place in the intersubjective space between small lateral children. It never completely vanishes.

The toddler takes into its intersubjective, mirroring space its particular psychic defenses: "reversal into the opposite" – hate becomes love and hate again with lightning speed. Instead of repression, we have splitting, projection and dissociation. In all cases these narcissistic-psychotic defenses have a normative and a pathological end and everything in between. In turn this effects how we see the societies we continually recreate and which are always there. Psychic splitting becomes social splitting; there is no contradiction between the two, just a difference from the vertical aspect of human relations with which the horizontal always melds and interacts but by making its own contribution.

A recent talk by Christopher Bollas, published in *IJPA* has introduced what he calls "horizontalism" as a negative feature met with in contemporary clinical work. However, a horizontal structure is always, and always has been, and always will be, with us. This can be both negative as Bollas deplores, or positive as I argue. "Globally" we are in the throes of the third great revolution in communications: writing, printing, and now "social media." Social media privileges lateral relations – the horizontal axis. Siblings and the horizontal are benefitting from this new attention.

Freud always described the traumatic effects of the next sibling's birth. I have become convinced that he also recognized its potential theoretical importance. But this only made him *more* emphatic about the dominance of the Oedipus/castration complex and the Law of the Father. He originally insisted on the importance of infantile sexuality in a world that denied it; with sexuality and psychoanalysis more-or-less established, the repeated denial by friends and foe, shifted from the importance of sexuality to the "shibboleth" of the Oedipus complex. He saw the sibling trauma as yet another instance of the constant wish to eliminate the key role of Oedipus in human life -- an inevitable desire bound up with the very implications of the complex. Alfred Adler, one of Freud's *bete noir*, for instance, made the sibling position the only determinant of psychic life. If we see that the vertical and the horizontal axes, their similar desires and prohibitions are *distinct* ways of handling the fact that we are all "born under one law but to another bound," then we can realize that there is room for both.

References

Freud, S. (1922). Group Psychology and the Analysis of the Ego. *Standard Edition*, 18:66–144.
Freud, S. (1927). Civilization and Its Discontents. *Standard Edition*, 21:106.
Freud, S. (1933). Femininity. *Standard Edition*, 22:116.
Kaës, R. (2006). *Linking Alliances and Shared Space: Groups and the Psychoanalyst*. London: Karnac Books, p. 8.
Klein, M. (1921–1945/1975). *Love, Guilt and Reparation and Other Works*. New York: The Free Press, p. 9.
Klein, M. (1932). *The Psychoanalysis of Children*. London: Hogarth Press, p. 113.
Laplanche, J., & Pontalis, J.B. (1973). *The Language of Psychoanalysis*. London: Hogarth Press, pp. 399–400.
Mitchell, J. (2000). *Mad Men and* Medusas. London: Penguin.
Mitchell, J. (2014). Thinking Theory. In *The Psychoanalytic Study of the Child*.
Tremblay, R., in Steven Pinker. (2011). *Better Angels of Our Nature: A History of Violence and Humanity*. New York: Viking Books, p. 483.
Winnicott, D.W. (1972). *Playing and Reality*. London: Penguin.

Chapter 9

Perspectives on the body Ego and mother-infant interaction

I've got you under my skin

Christine Anzieu-Premmereur

Adults and children who feel the danger of losing the sense of themselves, of experiencing "non existing", are eager to find ways to articulate their body experiences with representations, words and thoughts. The mirroring activity of the psychoanalyst using his countertransference experience gives the difficult patients a containing frame and a capacity for associations between sensations and ideas, dreams and memories that lead to a new feeling of existence, while they can inhabit their body.

Artists already have shown the strong essential needs to create a space where they can live in their body. As in art, constructing figures of one's body and one's origins is at the core of the psychoanalytic work.

Problems in mind-body integration are key obstacles in working with difficult to reach patients. What we understand as the adult psyche in our patients has its roots in a far less differentiated bodily experience. Winnicott uses the phrase "indwelling of the psyche-soma" (Winnicott, 1960, p. 589).

Some difficult to treat patients have developed autistic defenses against overwhelming sensations, or have faced early trauma resulting in breaking the relationship with their body. Those annihilation anxieties place a strain on their ability to maintain a coherent sense of self. The nascent psyche is no longer securely connected to the physical harbor of the body. The less the libido and the sexuality are integrated into the living body, the more the destructiveness is invading the psyche.

Nina is a young woman suffering from fear of disintegration, of being frozen to death. She fights her distress by harshly mutilating her body, destroying her skin, bleeding, "Marina Abramovic's performances style" as she said, trying to make me more comfortable while reporting unbearable experiences. She remembered perceiving her mother's body as scattered pieces with no face.

When she was a child, her mother couldn't look at her, since she was a seriously depressed woman that Nina had been unable to resuscitate. She thought that if she were having a full lively body, she would lose her mother's love. Staying in an inanimate area was her compromise.

The analysis was about creating a frame where she could inhabit under my looking at her. Her chaotic experience of herself has changed for a unified and consolidated body, through representations of her body in many dreams.

The analytic work with such helpless patients is about the deep intersubjective exchange through countertransference being used to facilitate the patient's transference to her own body. Developing a capacity for representation of the sensorial turmoil, for differentiating feelings and for a creative capacity in the patient has a precondition: the relationship with her body and its generative role.

During the first sessions, Nina was losing the perception of her body's contour, with sensations of becoming a dead corpse. This experience of having no shape was associated with losing the identification with maternal figures, losing the "Body for two" that Joyce McDougall wrote about as the beginning of life (McDougall, 1980, p. 448). Nina had the fantasy that someone was getting satisfaction from her pain when she was mutilating her skin. I had to deal with a negative persecutory transference for a while, which I interpreted as her creating an Other who was permanent, before being benevolent. Finally, she could report about an imaginary body associated with vivid dreams full with sensations, using the words I had given to her when I was labeling her sensations and emotions, and talking to her mostly by metaphors.

Her first dreams were only in black and white. After she had associated my voice as enveloping her, she started to feel having a shape. Then she had volcanic experiences of desire, when drives and libido were associated in a new explosion of violent affects. "Thinking, it's in the body," she said. Articulating the body with words and representations was a big part of the analysis, finally giving her the creativity of own her body, real and imaginary, and to get the fantasy of being a source of desire for others. "I am now the captain of my body", she finally said, "for the first time I own what I do. I don't forget my actions anymore. I feel my body enveloping me as if a grandmother figure was caressing me when I need comfort".

The body is the point of origin of the ego, wrote Freud, and the Italian analyst Riccardo Lombardi calls it the subject's first vital object of reference (Freud, 1923, p. 26. Lombardi, 2010, p. 880). In treating difficult patients, we confront explosive disorganization, or non-emotionalized states, with patients seemingly deprived of life, having no "texture", who remain estranged from symbolic functioning. The most urgent clinical necessity is not anymore to reveal the unconscious, but to produce content to permit the conscious mind to function. Such defects of representation, profound splitting and incapacity to associate freely put the analyst in a painful position.

Sensory experience of the body corresponds to the beginning of early mental life's autonomous functioning and the capacity to exist as a separate subject. The body does not express unconscious repression to be interpreted in symbolic terms, but is a central driving factor of liberation from "A dark and formless infinite," as quoted by Milton and cited by Bion and Lombardi (Bion, 1970, p. 87; Lombardi, 2010, p. 882). The analyst's leading role is then to facilitate the analysand's transference onto her own body.

The use of metaphors, and the co-construction of representation are here at the core of the beginning of the analytic work. The role of the affect is then essential:

transforming physical sensations into psychic experiences cannot be done without the mediation of the feelings. The analyst, like the mother, is the first one to translate bodily feelings into emotional experience. Attraction or repulsion, love or hate, are part of the mental of the "felt self" as Frances Tustin wrote (Tustin, 1984, p. 286).

Psychoanalytic work with children shows the increase of behavioral symptoms that can be understood as a failure in the early symbolization process. Those young children lack the possibility for representation and suffer from the consequences of this inability: separation issues when the absent mother cannot be kept represented in the child's mind, sleep disorders and severe anxieties when distress cannot be organized through representation and symbolization. The creation of a psychic representation begins with body experiences in a pleasurable relationship with the object.

The early integration of a sense of oneself and the capacity for autoeroticism depend on the baby-mother dyad's creative capacity. The "being together" – by looking at each other with the right rhythm, smiling at the same time, feeling like being in the same mind – are moments that give support to the child's experiencing being oneself through body sensations.

The notion of the embodied self comes from Freud's concluding remark in the Ego and the Id: "The ego is first and foremost a bodily ego". Freud thought that the internal perceptions were primordial, as the roots of the ego (Freud, 1923, p. 26). Recently, neuroscience has offered evidence that the internal state of the body is perceived as feelings. Damasio suggested that the core of the self might be found in "primordial feelings" as a continuous background body sensation that cannot be separated from the feelings. He wrote that the bodily roots of the ego are, from the very beginning, transformed by interacting with the object.

I quote Damasio:

> The deep roots for the self are to be found in the ensemble of brain which continuously and non-consciously maintain the body within a narrow range and relative stability required for survival. These devices continually represent, non consciously, the state of the living body . . . I call the state of activity within the ensemble of such devices, the proto self, the unconscious forerunner for the levels of self which appear in our minds as the conscious protagonists of consciousness: core self and autobiographical self.
> (Damasio, 2011, p. 217)

In Freud's Project for a Scientific Psychology, the mother acts as a protective shield against stimuli, essential for maintaining the internal balance in the child's psychic functioning as it is as stimulating pleasure and desire (Freud, 1895). There is a mutual inclusion of the bodies of mother and child. An infant, under its mother's care, receives both stimulation and communication, and thus the establishment of a body-ego responds to the need for a narcissistic envelope, and creates, for the psychic apparatus, the assurance of a constant, certain, basic well-being. The body ego is at first a body in relation.

Spitz gave the mother the name "auxiliary" ego, as the symbiotic half of the mother-child unit (Spitz, 1965). The mother's body, the breast, and the milk are part of the infant's experience as his own body. The smell, the first way to recognize the mother, then looking at her face, the rhythm and the sound of her voice, the quality of her holding, her skin and the tenderness of her touching, all those sensations and perceptions are part of the infant's self. A few months later in development, the mother's hair, her nose, then the glasses, the jewelry, and her scarf are integrated into the body-ego. As detachable parts of the body they will be used eventually as transitional objects.

At first, the internal sensations are the ones that give the infant an experience of repetition and continuity: Winnicott wrote in his description of the importance of letting the infant experience the whole long process of ingestion and digestion, as a discovery of the journey of the milk inside the body, between pleasure in the mouth, warmth in the belly, then weird colicky unpleasant sensations and relaxation when expulsing the feces (Winnicott, 1964).

Babies not only need milk, but also the good soft eyes of the mother entering their eyes. The nipple in the mouth is experienced as part of the body of the infant. Sensations are integrated, introjected with the feeling of being held, when the body is not at risk of falling down while the back is supported solidly and the eyes offer a similar experience of incorporation. Drive activity and infantile sexuality can play a fundamental role only when the core of the body ego is not at risk of being disorganized by primitive agonies in a non-safe dyadic relationship. The libidinal pleasure is the essential source of energy at keeping the body ego centered and integrated, with memories of oral and anal pleasure easy to use to recreate satisfaction.

In his description of the oral cavity, Spitz has stressed the essential role of the pleasure: the libidinal cathexis of the mouth allows for the appropriation of shared bodily zones (Spitz, 1962). The primitive anxieties are bodily, as falling endlessly, being liquefying, according to Winnicott (Winnicott, 1945). When the body is held together, the psyche can be developed. The paternal quality plays an important role for the identification with a vertebral axis in the background presence. Owning of one's body, as shown in the thumb sucking, plays a vital part in the establishment of feeling a combined envelop-muscular body with a sense of strong back support as a constant maternal-paternal presence. The support of the back and of the head relates to what some adult analysts treating narcissistic disorders, like Grotstein, called "the background of primary identification", that is close to Kohut "self-object", as in Sandler's "background of safety" (Grotstein, 1980, p. 488, Kohut, 1972, p. 364, Sandler, 1960, p. 352). Bick's notion of adhesive identification refers to a state of partial fusion with the mother, a skin-to-skin sensorial modality and a primitive imitation, as described by Gaddini, a primary identification and a support for narcissism (Bick, 1968, Gaddini, 1978).

Observing a four-month-old baby, I could check about the importance of linking the right side of the body with the left side as a sense of continuity-security. The baby had been left alone and kept trying to find his mouth with his right hand. It was an extra effort and he kept failing, his hand falling back again and again.

He then attempted in vain to find his left hand. The moment the mother returned, the baby made a successful enveloping movement with his right hand grasping the left one, while looking in the mother's eyes.

The importance of the body in the process of becoming "myself" is clear when we observe pathology. In her work with autistic children, Frances Tustin described children

> who felt skinless and disembodied. The skin has been replaced by the armor of autistic practices which help to feel protected from the terror of falling, dissolving or spilling ... during therapy, the body image begins to feel more substantial and intact. They begin to feel that they have an inner structure.
> (Tustin, 1984, p.280)

This is about the importance of the gaze attention for the integration of the tactile quality of the skin, as well for the ownership of the body joints.

In its earliest days, the baby not only receives care but also gives out signals to its family circle. In the mother-child dyad he is no passive partner: he solicits as much as responds, and can withdraw as much as be neglected: exchanging looks, smiles, noises and sense-impressions. Babies have a 'bodily pre-ego' which helps them to develop as individuals; and this is based on reliable feedback from a 'twin' caregiver. Touch is the first sense to develop embryonically and thus 'the skin is the basic reference point for all the various sense data'; and because touch is the only reflexive sense – I feel myself feeling, touch myself touching – it gives rise gradually to the reflexivity of thought. The baby develops the phantasy of a 'skin common to the mother and the child, an interface with the mother on one side and the child on the other' (Anzieu, 1985, p. 44).

Schilder in his classic oeuvre, The Image and Appearance of the Human Body, stated that the schema of the body develops within the interplay of the body and the environment, by tactile, kinesthetic, visual, and vestibular impressions. If a severe imbalance between inside and peripheral sensitivity exists, the body-image formation will be seriously impaired (Schilder, 1935).

The self-boundary formation derives from touch, smell, taste, sight, and the coming of age of motor coordination, which complements the important vestibular kinesthetic positional schemata of our selves.

The importance of libidinization of the baby's body by the earliest contact with the mother has been emphasized by Willy Hoffer. The sensitive interchange not only helps differentiation and eventually separation-individuation, but also seems to be a sine-qua-none of the earliest sense of the body self as entity. This seems to be the condition on which the feeling of being alive rests (Hoffer, 1950).

At the same time the infant develops a recognition memory of the human face, by three months of age, he also shows considerable interest in moving, examining, and mouthing fingers and, slightly later, toes and feet. By the time he has developed a specific attachment to the mother at four months, the infant's behavior suggests that he has also developed a specific recognition memory of parts of his own body: he shows an increased interest in the body parts and a certain familiarity with them.

A few months later, the constructive use of aggression promotes turning passive into active and contributes to physical distancing of self and objects, and to a distinct and separate sense of self.

One of the most important consequences of the sense of self as agent is the infant's ability to internalize some of the mother's organizing patterns of behavior – her soothing activities. These internalizations eventually play a significant role in shaping the nature of the body self.

I will quote a brief clinical vignette from Margaret Mahler, that illustrates how the developing infant has comparable feelings about the self and the object world and that disturbances in one area are likely to be accompanied by disturbances in the other:

> Harriet's relationship with her narcissistic, immature, unempathic mother was poor from the beginning of her life. From as early as five months she showed little interest or curiosity in animate or inanimate objects. She was frequently observed, however, to derive pleasure from rocking herself.
>
> Harriet at six months, in contrast to her continued lack of interest in people, responded to her mirror image with great excitement and pleasure. She waved her arms, made faces, and accompanied her activity with squeaks of unmistakable joy. Nothing matched the excitement and pleasure with which she looked at her mirror image. From six to ten months, Harriet seemed to find her mirror image more reliably responsive than her detached mother. Her lack of interest in other people or things suggested that her excitement and pleasure in her mirror image did not reflect a positive relation with her mother. It seemed, instead, to be a continuation of the self-stimulation we had observed earlier.
>
> (Mahler & McDevitt, 1982, p. 843)

In Winnicott's "The precursor of the mirror is the mother's face", the mother's emotional response to her baby looking at her gives the child the sense of its own experience. "Being seen" is crucial, and the child gets the ability to recognize what it feels and to own its experience when reflected by the mother's face (Winnicott, 1971). The modern research on baby-mother's interaction in Beatrice Beebe's work has shown that the mother reflects her baby's experience not only through her looking at him, but through all the modalities of communication (Beebe, Lachmann, Markese, & Bahrick, 2012). The mirroring function is conveyed not only through the face of the mother, but her body contact and the quality of the holding that gives back to her baby the sense of what it is experiencing.

Paul is a 15-month-old tiny boy with a very unbalanced walk, confused and disconnected from others as soon as he is away from his mother's body. He doesn't talk, doesn't exchange any look with others, as if his body is not organized when his mother is not close to him. He can play only when she is attuned to him, but she is too depressed to pay attention to his needs. When I started talking to him while caressing his back, he could be reassembled, then able to walk and look for a toy. But he could interact with me and play only when leaning on his mother's body with his mouth full with a piece of bread.

> The need for a containing object would seem, in the infantile unintegrated state, to produce a frantic search for an object – a light, a voice, a smell, or other sensual object – which can hold the attention and thereby be experienced, momentarily at least, as holding the parts of the personality together. The optimal object is the nipple in the mouth, together with the holding and talking and familiar smelling mother. This containing object is experienced concretely as a skin.
>
> (Bick, 1968)

Infantile sexuality is involved in the cathexis of the object through autoerotic activities, and the process of subjectivity – being myself – is built in the mirroring relationship with the mother associated with the libidinal energy. At the same time, agencies in babies and the importance of being active helps for the development of a sense of self.

The pathological association of the limitation in the baby's capacity for keeping a representation of the mother and its violent self-soothing activities is a pattern that is found in many young children who had not been contained and couldn't find a pleasurable interaction with their caregiver. They use their body to create a sort of muscular armor, uptight body precociously independent, or some behaviors as self-stimulation in repetitive, violent ways (Anzieu-Premmereur, 2013).

The consequences of disparity between physical and emotional maternal contact have been developed in Spitz's observation of inconsistent maternal behavior in the mothers of infants who rocked. The mothers were described as alternating between outbursts of hostility and tender love toward their infants (Spitz, 1962).

Among those rocking infants, 63-percent showed developmental retardation. Spitz suggested that the sharp swings in maternal behavior made it difficult or impossible for the infants to relate to the mothers, and so their libidinal balance had moved away from normal object relations and toward an overinvestment in narcissism, which became manifest in their rocking. The rhythmic movement itself provides a physical sensation of warmth and vitality for as long as it endures. When it stops, the longing and the distress flood back, and the sadness is same as in a mourning.

Child analysts see children who have rocked for months in the first and second year, and who were brought for help later in latency around motor disturbances – tics, hyperactivity, impulsivity – and around intense fears of object loss, clearly dating from infancy.

Kernberg emphasizes that ego weakness is linked to problems in establishing object constancy in the child (Kernberg, 1985). The child who has not achieved object constancy cannot evoke the image of the mother consistently and remains perceptually reliant upon her. The child does not relate to persons as a whole, but instead in terms of part-objects, for example, the mother's breast.

Tom was a child who had tried in vain to relate to his mother's body part, the hair. He was a 14-month-old toddler with a hair pulling symptom. He moved slowly on his tiny legs, unbalanced. His parents didn't try to help. For them he was an independent difficult character, with nothing similar to them. Tom didn't smile, had a stern unemotional face. He had started pulling his hair dramatically four months ago when he was put in day care. He almost had no more hair and his skin was damaged. The parents reported that he was pulling his hair compulsively each time he was dealing with frustration.

I engaged him to play with me and he seemed to be reorganized when we exchanged some toys rolling on the floor. I played being upset with toys falling down, saying "bad toys" to explore the baby's repression of aggression, a play that he eventually repeated at home since it was a source of intense emotional discharge. I offered him to keep a small stuffed animal that he found in the bag of toys, trying to make some ritual around separation, since the parents didn't feel the need for any mediation around separation and rapprochement.

I told them that Tom being too independent concerned me. The mother picked up this understanding and started to give back the milk bottles that she had stopped, and to put him on her lap, something she never thought could be important for him. After a few sessions, interacting with Tom was pleasurable. His aggression was still low, and active only when pulling his hair. But he had mostly stopped this self-injury symptom, and began sucking his thumb.

We can understand Tom's symptom as an aggressive reaction connected with grief and rage with a series of affective frustrations in his early development, the result of feeling deserted; the child attempted to hold onto the body-self when others failed to provide emotional support, then bodily feelings were disturbed. The child learned to "lean on itself" or feel itself through self-injurious hair pulling. This deep failure of representation in some depressed parents can cause the baby to lack libidinal quality in their relationship, leaving him without any other possibility for his emotions, and excitements than to be discharged in his body.

What will be the body self-representation in babies who are facing iPads when an iPhone fascinates the caregiver? Not looking at each other, but mirroring a virtual figure always in the same mood. After a short time of pleasure and curiosity, the experience is of losing the attention; being left neglected could lead to fragmentation of the sense of being attached to one self as to the parent.

Charles was 20 months when I met him with his mother. Like all young children dealing with representation failure, he was speech delayed, never smiling nor playing (Anzieu-Premmereur, 2009).

Covered with eczema, he was running in the room, jumping and hitting his body against the wall. When I tried to intervene by talking to him, he started banging his head on the floor. His mother didn't move. She couldn't associate with any feelings. She had no word for emotions; she wanted to get some concrete advice about her son's behavior. When Charles was covered with eczema, he was calm;

when the somatic symptom was over, he was acting crazy and she couldn't contain him. I was surprised by his mother's inability to offer him a bodily relationship when he was close to her; "We are not tender people in the family," she said. Charles was strolling around the room. When he felt an emotion, mostly fear of sounds, he banged his head on the wall.

By chance, Charles pushed a small car on the floor and I started a game by exchanging the car between my feet and his feet. He stopped moving and for once was receptive. Remembering Freud's observation of the reel game of his grandson, I commented on us taking turns, getting the car, and losing it and giving it back and so on. Then I added some affects, talking about the pleasure to have the car back and the sadness when it was away. Charles looked at me intensely. He went to his mother's lap when I insisted on depressive feelings like fear of losing the car.

Listening to his mother complain about his behavior, he showed an embarrassment that I interpreted as shame. He went behind my chair to hide. I started a hide and seek game, by faking looking for him and finding him behind my back. He asked for more and began laughing. This jubilation was completely new and his mother found it touching. For the first time she had an association: she talked about the father being away for traveling and Charles having some feelings about his father's absence. This was the beginning of her having thoughts about her son.

When finally Charles developed a capacity for association through play, he didn't use his body anymore for discharge, and developed good sleep with a regular dream function. The eczema disappeared when the dreaming activity had resumed.

When a toddler is about to move, primitive bodily anxieties are revived along with the unfolding process of individuation. At the time of the achievement of sphincter control, when a sense of body boundaries is on the way, the integrity of the body as a whole is not supposed to be threatened anymore. Tantrums during diaper changes show how often toddlers experience that as a painful loss of a body part equivalent to castration. As Freud wrote, the body Ego is created by identification with the mother's body and her attentive care, by Being the breast, before Having it.

Body pleasure is one of the best sources of representation in childhood, since through autoeroticism the child can develop a figurative power. Later in life, when genital adult sexuality had been organized, the fantasy world is again supported by the quality in object relations. When the differed action (Après-Coup) gives a sexual meaning to the childhood events, the narcissistic issues that the child has faced will make the adult feel again a sense of emptiness of life. The importance of addictions that is part of the modern society seems to be associated with those early troubles.

The frenetic need to use pictures or videos on the Internet to stimulate sexual fantasies, and the intensive masturbation developed instead of a relationship with a partner, could be understood as an equivalent of the lacking of a good level of representation. Early narcissistic failures can later in life be replayed in a sexualized way, in order to get fixed. Those addictive behaviors show how the process of creating representation is damaged, and how pressing is the need for concrete bodily stimulation in the absence of an object.

Freud's discovery of the libidinal development of the child shows that orifices of the body, based on vital needs, have an erotic quality that is fundamental for the psyche. We have learned about the oral body, with impulses at absorbing and destroying, about the anal body and the playing with exchanging between internal space and outside world, the phallic body and issue of castration, and then about identification with the body of both parents. That gave us access to the notion of the fantasmatic body, of the body's image and their role in the feeling of the presence of the body.

The body remembers early experiences. Suffering, illness and loss of the body unity interfere with the building of the Ego. Pleasurable sensations can also be overwhelming, as too much stimulation or intruding interactive patterns are traumatic events. Like pain, intense sensations leave a scar in the Ego. For us, as therapists, it is important to remember the strong association between body sensation, body image and mental life. While treating adults and children, in a time of tattoos, piercings, plastic surgery, gender transformation, technology for restoring damaged bodies, it is essential to focus on the narcissistic and libidinal qualities of the body as the essential source of mental life.

I will conclude by quoting Marion Milner, about her analytic work with an artist:

> The inner conscience we have of our own body takes back the role of the external mother, in a way where we create a kind of psychic sphere from the image we have of our own body, as the only safe place to live, from which we can extend our antennas toward the world.
> (Milner, 1969, p. 272)

References

Anzieu, D. (1985/2016). *The Skin Ego*. London: Karnac Books.
Anzieu-Premmereur, C. (2009). The Dead Father Figure and the Symbolization Process. In Kalinich, L., and Taylor, S. (eds.), *The Dead Father, a Psychoanalytic Inquiry*. New York: Routledge, pp. 133–144.
Anzieu-Premmereur, C. (2013). The Process of Representation in Early Childhood. In Levine, H., Reed, G., and Scarfone, D. (eds.), *The Work of Figurability: From Unrepresented to Represented Mental States*. London: Routledge, pp. 240–254.
Beebe, B., Lachmann, F., Markese, S., & Bahrick, L. (2012). On the Origins of Disorganized Attachment and Internal Working Models: Paper I: A Dyadic Systems Approach. *Psychoanalytic Dialogues*, 22(2):253–272.
Bick, E. (1968). The Experience of the Skin in Early Object-Relations. *International Journal of Psychoanalysis*, 49(2):484–486.
Bion, W.R. (1970). Attention and Interpretation. In *Seven Servants*. New York: Aronson.
Damasio, A. (2011). A Reply to Jaak Panksepp. *Neuro-Psychoanalysis*, 13(2):217–219.

Fraiberg, S. (1987). Foreword. In *Selected Writings*. Ohio State University Press, pp. 13–28.
Freud, S. (1895). Project for a Scientific Psychology. *Standard Edition*, 1, pp. 281–391.
Freud, S. (1923). The Ego and the Id. *The Standard Edition of the Complete Psychological Works of Sigmund Freud, Volume XIX (1923–1925): The Ego and the Id and Other Works*, 1–66.
Gaddini, R. (1978). Transitional Object Origins and the Psychosomatic Symptom. *Between Reality and Fantasy: Transitional Objects and Phenomena*, 112–131.
Grotstein, J.S. (1980). A Proposed Revision of the Psychoanalytic Concept of Primitive Mental States – Part I: Introduction to a Newer Psychoanalytic Metapsychology. *Contemporary Psychoanalysis*, 16:479–546.
Hoffer, W. (1950). Development of the Body Ego. *Psychoanal. St. Child*, 5:18–23
Kernberg, O.F. (1985). *Borderline Conditions and Pathological Narcissism*. Lanham, MD: Rowman & Littlefield.
Kohut, H. (1972). Thoughts on Narcissism and Narcissistic Rage. *Psychoanalytic Study of Child*, 27:360–400.
Lombardi, R. (2009). Through the Eye of the Needle: The Unfolding of the Unconscious Body. *Journal of the American Psychoanalytic Association*, 57:61–94.
Lombardi, R. (2010). The Body Emerging from the "Neverland" of Nothingness. *Psychoanalytic Quarterly*, 79:879–909.
Mahler, M., & McDevitt, J. (1982). Thoughts on the Emergence of the Sense of Self, with Particular Emphasis on the Body Self. *Journal of the American Psychoanalytic Association*, 30:827–848.
McDougall, J. (1980). A Child is Being Eaten – I: Psychosomatic States, Anxiety Neurosis and Hysteria: A Theoretical Approach II: The Abysmal Mother and the Cork Child: A Clinical Illustration. *Contemporary Psychoanalysis*, 16:417–459.
Milner, M. (1969). The Hands of the Living God. *International Psycho-Analytical Library*, 76:1–426. London: The Hogarth Press and the Institute of Psycho-Analysis.
Sandler, J. (1960). The Background of Safety. *The International Journal of Psycho-analysis*, 41:352.
Schilder, P. (1935/1950). *The Image and Appearance of the Human Body: Studies in the Constructive Energies of the Psyche*. New York: International Universities Press.
Spitz, R.A. (1962). Autoerotism Re-examined: The Role of Early Sexual Behavior Patterns in Personality Formation. *Psychoanalytic Study of the Child*, 17:283–315.
Spitz, R.A., & Cobliner, W.G. (1965). *The First Year of Life*. New York: International Universities Press.
Tustin, F. (1984). Autistic Shapes. *International Review of Psycho-Analysis*, 11:279–290.
Tustin, F. (1990). *The Protective Shell in Children and Adults*. London: Karnac Books.
Winnicott, D.W. (1945/1975). Primitive Emotional Development. In *Trough Paediatrics to Psychoanalysis*. New York: Basic Books, pp. 145–156.
Winnicott, D.W. (1960). The Theory of the Parent-Infant Relationship. *International Journal of Psycho-Analysis*, 41:585–595.
Winnicott, D.W. (1964). Feeding the Baby. In *The Child, the Family and the Outside World*. New York: Perseus Publishing, pp. 30–57.
Winnicott, D.W. (1971). Mirror-Role of Mother and Family in Child Development. In *Playing and Reality*. London: Penguin Books, pp. 101–111.

Part III

The sexual body, the speaking body and the sick body

Chapter 10

Introduction

Maria Cristina Aguirre

In this chapter, in a very rich and comprehensive presentation of *Body and Soul: A Never Ending Story*, Paul Verhaeghe examines the different conceptions of the body referring to his careful reading of the theories of Freud and Lacan which present two different bodies.

Verhaeghe compares both theories to draw very interesting parallels; with the Mirror Stage and the Oedipal Theory there is a conception of a body as a surface, and the basis for our identity, while the theory of the drives – of Jouissance – confronts us with a body as an organism, an energy (sexuality) that needs to be discharged. He posits that one visible body of desire, the body of the hysteric dependent on the gaze of the Other and a body of the drive, or the organism, of Jouissance can be painful, and even lethal. He goes on to compare the Victorian body to our contemporary body and our contemporary Other; emphasis is no longer on repression, prohibition and guilt but in obligatory enjoyment and shame for not being "forever young and forever sexy." But his main thesis consists in highlighting what Freud and Lacan further developed, that the speaking being is forever divided since the moment of birth and nothing can heal/mend that, though contemporary psychotherapies futilely aim to do so.

To conclude, Verhaeghe posits that this Immpossibility to recover primordial loss – which can be summarized with Lacan's axiom: *"There is no sexual report"* – far from being pessimistic, has a positive twist; it opens a possibility for choice and change beyond the alienation coming from the Other.

Panos Aloupis, in an article titled "Somatic Ailment and Death Drive: Dangerous Liaisons," examines through a clinical vignette certain questions regarding the dangerous liaisons between the somatic ailment and the death drive. He examines Freud's concept of psychic trauma, and the theoretical development of Marty, founder of the Paris School of Psychosomatics who coined the term "mentalization" in order to "define a complex psychic work that is constantly nourished and animated by the effects of the drive fusion between Eros and Thanatos." In other words, the enactment of the trauma in its repetition compulsion runs the risk of breaking this fusion, freeing the destructive action of the death drive.

Aloupis presents the case of a man who presents the words, "Doctor, my heart is sick," after suffering from an arrhythmia that unpredictability led him to suffer a permanent anxiety of imminent death. Aloupis states that the heart can occupy the space both of a suffering ego and of an object that threatens psychic integrity, saying that the somatic disorder, when it concerns organs close to sensory perceptions like the heart or the skin, affects the protective shield against the manifestations of pain and morbid excitation . . . and in some cases, paradoxically, the signal distress calls on the help of the death drive.

Marina Papageorgiou's paper, "What is Alive in the Ill Body," presents the interesting clinical case study of a middle-aged man with severe diabetes and arterial disease. She reviews the literature of the principal French psychoanalysts in the field of Psychosomatics, such as Green, Marty, Fain, Smadja, David, De Muzan and Aisenstein. According to Marty, she says, most psychosomatic patients have an irregular mental functioning, and following Freud's second theory on affect, she posits that affect is a factor of trouble, organizing, disorganizing and reorganizing the mental functioning.

She argues "the somatic ailment means the failure to organize an après-coup in terms of mental defenses and psychic symptoms, involving representative repression." Her patient can represent and imagine but the representative function is disconnected from emotional investment, feelings are disembodied, suppressed or frozen. His main defense is the drastic abolition of feeling.

Making an interesting use of countertransference as an instrument to reach the patient's difficulty in associating and remembering, Papageorgiou produces positive and noteworthy effects in this complex case.

Chapter 11

Body and soul, a never-ending story

Paul Verhaeghe

Saying that the way we experience our body has changed a lot since Freud is an understatement. Ironically enough, these changes permit us to see how we are still struggling with a fundamental problem, albeit in a different way. The problem concerns our inner division and the way this division is presented and thus, experienced. The traditional view presents the body and soul as a dualism; this discourse has determined our thinking ever since this binary opposition was made. I will argue that Freud's first topology of the Conscious and the Unconscious is a much better presentation, on condition that we combine it with the drive theory; and that Lacan's further elaboration replaces this dualism by a circular but non-reciprocal dialectic.

There are many lines of approach possible to the work of Freud and Lacan. One of them differentiates between the Freud of the *Three essays on the theory of sexuality* and the accompanying drive theory on the one hand versus the Freud of the Oedipal complex on the other. The corresponding approach to Lacan's work is the Lacan of the mirror stage and the becoming of the subject versus the Lacan of the jouissance. Obviously, these different approaches to their work talk about two different bodies. The mirror stage and the Oedipal theory present the body as a surface, which is at the same time the basis for our identity. The theory of the drives and the jouissance confronts us with the body as an organism in which opposing drives set the scene. Let us take a closer look at these two bodies.

The body as a surface

In Freud's view, the Ego finds its basis in the surface of the body. This thesis appears in his 1923 paper *The Ego and the Id*. He does not elaborate this idea much, although it dovetails with his early studies on hysterical symptoms (Freud, 1978 [1893c], [1895d]). Apparently, these symptoms of pathological feeling – the patient feels too much, too little, in the wrong corporeal zone – are linked to popular representations of the body. That is: the same representations that constitute the Ego. Obviously, representations of parts of the body can have very powerful effects; they may determine functional disorders, known as conversion. The amazing thing is that the patient is not conscious of these representations. Incidentally, this effect recurs today in the empirical study of placebo effects, where we can reproduce the same finding: a presentation about our body induced by the Other may have very important effects on the body (Diederich & Goetz, 2008).

In Lacan's approach, this thesis is prominently present. In his paper on the mirror stage, he describes the origin of the *Je*, the I, in the mirror image as presented by the mother. Such an image has literally formative effects on the body, just as in the case of conversion symptoms. It presents the infant with a first identity based upon a false feeling of unity – false, firstly because of the biological immaturity of the infant, and secondly and more importantly, because of what Lacan describes as "a certain 'déhiscence' at the very heart of the organism, a primordial Discord" (Lacan, 2006 [1949], p. 78). I will return to this idea in my conclusion. On top of that, the identification with the image presented by the Other is an alienation, as it comes from the *alius*, the other. This remains the case when images are replaced by signifiers, when Lacan expands his theory of the mirror stage into the theory of the becoming of the subject in relation to the Other (Lacan, 1994 [1964]). He refers to Rimbaud: "Je est un autre", I is another, and a subject is nothing but the ever shifting product of a chain of signifiers. Our identity is a divided one. Incidentally, one of the reasons why Lacan introduced the idea of the subject – that is, of an always divided subject – is to mark the difference with the Ego, whose main function, since Freud, is to create a synthesis, although it never succeeds in doing so.

With his focus on desire, Lacan has elaborated much more the underlying dynamics, compared to Freud. We identify with the images and signifiers presented by the Other because we want to be desired by this Other. Unfortunately, we are never sure whether we succeed in doing this. What does the Other really want? This is one of the reasons why the becoming of the subject is such an endless story.

Compared to our times, we can notice an important change in this respect: today, the desire of the Other affects our bodily presentation in a totally different way compared to the time of Freud and even of Lacan. In the eye of the contemporary Other, we are never healthy or sexy or young enough. In spite of the disappearance of hysteria from the official psychiatric jargon, we are more hysterical than ever about our appearance. The desire of man is the desire of the Other; that is the motor that keeps the human theater running. Often enough, it alienates us with the contemporary version of the rosy paintings by the Viennese Gustav Klimt.

This is much less the case with the body, as it is presented in the second approach to the work of Freud and Lacan, where we are confronted with the Freudian drive and the Lacanian jouissance. Here, another Viennese artist from Freud's time comes to mind: Egon Schiele, whose paintings are a lot less rosy.

The body as an organism

In Freud's early writings, we can read about his confrontation with something that he can't even give a proper name. It has something to do with energy, it is linked to presentations, it may shift from one presentation to another or become fixed to one particular image and it comes in quantities. That is why Freud talks about his Q-hypothesis, where Qn stands for a quantity of energy (Freud, 1978 [1894a]). Soon enough, he discovers that this energy needs to be discharged, if one wants to stay healthy. Sexuality provides the easiest pathway for such a discharge, but still – most of his patients are experiencing serious troubles in that respect.

This Q-hypothesis reappears in 1905, when Freud put forward what he considered a typically psychoanalytic construct, namely the drive (*Trieb*). One of its four components is the *Drang*, the energetic pressure, that gave the drive its denomination (this explains why 'instinct' is such a poor translation of *Trieb*). This pressure starts from a *Quelle*, a source that is mysteriously located in the organism. The two other components, the aim and the object, are of a more psychological nature and, according to Freud, less important.

Originally, he is convinced that the drive has only one aim, which is to discharge its energy, the *Abreaktion*, following the so-called pleasure principle, which states that every organism prefers a constant level of tension, as close to zero as possible. This pleasure principle explains the automatic functioning of every organism. Much later, Freud will be less certain about this – there is a *jenseits*, a beyond the pleasurable discharge of the pleasure principle, where the organism prefers a rising level of tension (Freud, 1978 [1920g]). This is rather confusing, because according to the pleasure principle, this should be experienced as something painful; consequently, the pleasure principle is not the only thing that drives us. In his final attempt, Freud will put forward the all-encompassing life and death drives, each with their opposite aim.

In his own way, Lacan also struggles with the pleasure principle. Phallic pleasure is easy enough to understand; he coins it not without irony as the 'familiar' pleasure. Underneath, there is another form of jouissance at work, one that he associates throughout his work alternatively with psychosis, with the mother, with perversion, with femininity, with the mystics and finally, in his last writings, with the body as such (for an extensive discussion, see Verhaeghe, 2001a).

At the time of his seminar on ethics (i.e. 1960), the description of jouissance has something heroic. There is courage needed, he says, because it implies a transgression of the law. Much later, at the time of his *Encore* seminar (1972), Lacan presents us with a totally different reading. This other jouissance comes in eruptions and is lethal; even a primitive organism needs a defense against it in order to postpone its death. The origin of this jouissance goes back to the loss of eternal life at birth and the necessity of death for every sexualized being. Jouissance as such implies death, that is why a subject has to be happy with slivers of jouissance, with 'le plus de jouir'. That expression is difficult to translate, because of its double meaning; 'plus' means more, but 'plus de' means 'no more'. As such, jouissance is impossible for the subject (for an extensive discussion, see Verhaeghe, 2001b).

This is Lacan's version of Freud's Eros and Thanatos, and just as in the latter, it has a mythical ring. Obviously, both Freud and Lacan were struggling to understand a paradox: how is it possible that something in our body is operating *against* our body, against ourselves?

The fact that Lacan talks about the organism marks the difference with the first body, the one of the mirror stage. The second body, the organism, concerns the psychoanalytic theory on drive and enjoyment. This theory is less accepted and more difficult. Even in our contemporary analytic practice we prefer to focus on the vicissitudes of desire and the endless loops we and our patients make in that respect. Lacan explained this when he elaborated his theory on the four discourses: we prefer to focus on the upper part, where we meet the impossibility of desire, because this part protects us and keeps us away from our impotence in matters of jouissance, as presented by the lower part of every discourse (Lacan, 1991 [1969–1970]). From a Freudian metapsychological point of view, repression and the dynamic unconscious operate on the upper level. In the lower part, we are confronted with primal repression and the system Unconscious (Freud, 1978 [1915e], pp. 186–189).

Desire and jouissance

So, following Freud and Lacan, it seems as though we have two different bodies. The first one is the very visible body of desire. The second one is the body underneath, the one of the drives. In these two bodies, two different forms of pleasure are at work. The desired or desiring body is typically hysteric because of its dependence on the gaze of the Other and its need for a stage. The body as an organism is altogether different. It is the field in which the drives are operating, forcing the body towards an enjoyment that might be quite painful and even lethal.

Obviously, the desired or the desiring body is not the same as the body of jouissance. Nevertheless, there is a connection between the two, which is very aptly summarized in the Lacanian notion of the big Other. It is the big Other who mirrors the way our body should look in function of the desire of the Other. At the same time, it is the big Other who dictates how we should handle pleasure and jouissance. The contemporary big Other is quite different compared to the big Other of the Victorian era, whilst it is generally agreed upon that our body as an organism has remained more or less the same as compared to that of our forefathers.

We could say that the Freudian big Other is the Oedipal Other in overdrive. He works in overdrive, because the Victorian Other did not only prohibit incest, he prohibited almost everything sexual, especially for women. Bodies were imprisoned in their clothing, everything sensual and erotic was banned and even at a young age, the Victorians looked already old. The main thing about sex was the need for relief of tension, especially for men. In that respect, we have witnessed in our times a radical reversal. Today, the big Other is doing overtime as well, albeit in a reversed direction, as he now obliges us to present ourselves almost constantly as a possible partner for an erotic encounter. Men and women alike should work very hard to look forever young and forever sexy. Sex is no longer prohibited, on the contrary, the quest for sexual satisfaction has become obligatory, incest and pedophilia being the only taboos left. Our contemporary Super-Ego has only one imperative: Enjoy!

Strange enough, the result of this freedom is rather paradoxical. People do not experience more pleasure or jouissance today. On the contrary, the more satisfactions we experience, the less pleasurable they become. The best description of this phenomenon I have found so far is 'depressive hedonia'. The British analyst Mark Fisher explains this condition as the inability to do anything, except the pursuit of pleasure whilst having at the same time a sense that something is missing (Fisher, 2009, pp. 21–22). Notice that this change has no impact on our inner division as such. We are still divided, but the terms have changed. Enjoyment used to be forbidden, today it has become obligatory. Our Victorian ancestors used to feel guilty about their overly sex-ridden body; today, we feel ashamed, because we are never sexy enough.

In the meantime, it is obvious that the question of the body concerns our identity as well. Where am *I* in matters of desire? And is it *me* who is enjoying the effects of the drive, or something else? In order to treat these questions, I want to address what I consider the most central idea in Freud's theory, namely that there is no center, we are essentially divided.

The divided subject

When Freud started his clinical practice, one of the first things he experienced was the resistance in his patients to talk about their desires, let alone about their erotic life. He introduced the idea of *Abwehr*, defense, and explained it as a consequence of the Victorian prohibition on sexuality (Freud, 1978 [1894a]). The Victorian patients had identified far too much with the societal repression, which resulted in obsessional neurosis and hysteria. Their erotic life was crippled, there was no normal discharge possible, even their sexual representations had been moved to what Freud calls "another scene" (*Schauplatz*) in *The Interpretation of Dreams*.

Because of the defense mechanisms, the patients did not have access to their own thoughts. Consequently, they suffered from a number of symptoms in which Freud read a repressed sexuality, with quantities of energy fixed to the wrong representations. Periodically, those accumulated forces erupted in hysterical attacks. In order to prevent those attacks, the Victorian medical doctors had discovered a very effective practice. They themselves or midwifes brought their female patients to what they called a "paroxysm", thus relieving them temporarily from their tension. This was presented as a neutral medical technique for the treatment of hysteria, especially for women who suffered from hysterical attacks. What these midwifes and doctors did, was to masturbate their patients up to the point of orgasm by using the forerunners of the vibrator. This practice disappeared the moment vibrators appeared in erotic movies. It disappeared from the medical textbooks as well and was only recently rediscovered (Maines, 1999).

Freud and Breuer focused on the psychological part that caused the rise in tension, meaning the repression of the representations and the reasons for this repression. Based on the results of Breuer's hypnocathartic method, Freud helped his patients make these repressed representations conscious again, with a resulting therapeutic discharge – the *Abreaktion*. The most surprising discovery was the fact that these representations had a pathological influence on the patient while being unconscious. In his early work, he was convinced that the splitting in the psychological functioning of these patients was a pathological artifact. Normal people didn't have it. Following Breuer, his technique aimed at restoring the consciousness of the repressed sexual ideas, thus enabling his patients to have a normal *Abreaktion*.

Discharge of energy combined with consciousness is the therapeutic aim based on the initial theory; in clinical practice, this proved to be a lot more difficult. It seemed as if his patients did not want to give up their symptoms, and there was something wrong with the pleasure principle as well. Moreover, the typical splitting in their psychological functioning did not disappear, even when the therapy proved to be successful. Soon enough, Freud had to admit that his understanding was insufficient, and he formulated what proved to be the central idea of psychoanalysis: every one of us is essentially divided within and even against a part of ourselves. Throughout his work, he formulated several attempts to get hold of this inner division, with his two topologies as the most well-known: the Unconscious versus the Conscious and the Ego between the Id and the Super-Ego. The fact that he used different formulations indicates that he considered not one of them as truly satisfactory. In the post-Freudian era, the focus will shift towards other things, and the psychology of today has almost forgotten Freud's starting point, i.e. the splitting.

In my introduction, I argued that there are two different bodies. The division between them mirrors the inner division of the subject. The body as desired by the Other confronts us with the demand of this Other. The other body, the one as an enjoying organism confronts us with the drives.

The first division is easy to understand, it is the one between the Freudian Super-Ego or the Lacanian Other on the one hand, and the Ego or the I ('le je') on the other hand. The second division is more difficult to understand, especially in our times, where the prohibition on enjoyment has been reversed as represented in the Victorian era. In both cases, one of the best descriptions Freud gave of this division and its effects still applies: "a drive appears to us as a concept on the border between the mental and the somatic, as a measure of the demand made upon the mind for work in consequence of its connection with the body" (Freud, 1978 [1915c], pp. 121–122). Obviously, this demand is never fully met; as such, it is yet another illustration of our division.

Body and soul versus consciousness and the unconscious

By itself, Freud's idea of the division is not new. On the contrary, it is not too difficult to recognize in it the classic body and soul dichotomy. It goes back at least to the ancient Greeks with Pythagoras and his expression about 'soma sèma' – the body is a grave for the soul – and of course to Plato. The moral undertone was present right from the start and the traditional Western religions will endorse this tone exponentially. The soul is eternal; it is a part of God in ourselves. The body is its temporary temple, but it is a bad one, as it is a source of sinful desires. These ideas combined with the moral appreciation determined the start of modern science as well, e.g. in the radical dualism of Descartes, with the body as the *res extensa*, the soul as the *res cogitans*. Thus, modern science inherited the idea that thinking is immaterial, in contrast to our bodily substance.

Until today, the combined effects of religion and early science determine our way of understanding ourselves, especially through their impact on the Western educational system. The body is studied in medical school, the soul in the departments of theology, philosophy and more recently, psychology. In this way, our educational system endorses the original dualism, with a predictable result that both sides have been fighting each other ever since. At the start, the scholars of the soul had the winning hand, whereas the body was left to the barber-surgeon. Today, the medical class is on top, with psychologists struggling to better their position by identifying with the enemy – neuropsychology is the new fashion and clinical psychologists are fighting for the right to prescribe medication.

In my reading, Freud's theory might present us with a different understanding of this dualism. Firstly, it doesn't run any longer between body and soul. Especially with his introduction of the system Unconscious, Freud introduced a paradigmatic shift in the comprehension of our dualism. In 1917, he wrote to Georg Groddeck that "the unconscious is the proper mediator between the somatic and the mental, perhaps the long-sought 'missing link'" (Groddeck, 1977, p. 38). Secondly, it has to do with our identity, because this division has an ontological ring to it. Thirdly, it determines our way of thinking about health and illness, about normality and psychopathology. Following from that, it determines the goal of therapy. These three issues are part of a larger whole – it is almost impossible to discuss them separately.

Health versus illness

Our conception about health and illness implies the way we conceive treatment. A first paradigm on health goes back to Louis Pasteur: illness is caused by an external cause, an attack coming from the outside by parasites or viruses. They attack my body that defends itself by using an army of white-colored soldiers to fight them. This presents us with a reassuring world view: us, the goodies, against them, the baddies. The discovery of auto-immune diseases dismissed this reasoning. Some part of myself can turn against me, the enemy has always been within the walls.

The same evolution can be seen in Freud. Originally, he coined the repressed presentations as *Fremdkörper* (foreign bodies), the medical denomination for viruses, because he was convinced that they originated in external traumatic events. Already at the time of his *Studies on Hysteria*, he had to admit that this was not necessarily the case, and that these presentations were part of ourselves, albeit a part against which the dominant ego had developed a defense (Freud, 1895d, p. 290). This obliged Freud to reconsider his ideas on the etiology, more specifically his theory on trauma.

A second paradigm about health and illness is based on the idea of homeostasis. In this line of thought, illness is a consequence of the loss of an inner equilibrium. In Freud's time, this equilibrium had to do with energy and tension, either in terms of too much or not enough. Treatment aimed at reducing the surplus or supplementing the lack (e.g. the difference between mania and melancholia). Symptoms are failed attempts of the body to restore the balance.

This paradigm can be found in Freud as well. The ideal homeostasis presents a constant low level of tension that is held in balance by sexual discharge. Such a discharge is experienced as pleasurable, hence our natural propensity towards it – this is how the pleasure principle works. Neurotic symptoms are failed attempts at discharge, and the treatment aims at restoring the normal safety valves.

Just as happened in medicine, Freud combined the two paradigms. Unconscious thoughts operate as *Fremdkörper* against the better part of our Ego. The treatment aims at making them conscious again, via the free association and the interpretation. Once they are conscious, a correct discharge of their energy becomes possible. In this way, the therapy heals the divided Ego of the patient and restores the homeostasis at the same time.

On paper, this sounds fine; the only drawback is that it doesn't work. In spite of all his therapeutic efforts, Freud had to conclude that it is impossible to mend or heal the inner division, and that obliged him to reconsider the aim of the treatment. Obviously, there is another motive at work, besides the pleasure principle. Before going into that, it is worthwhile to focus on a rather unexpected quality of this medically inspired approach. In spite of its scientific appearance, it has a very strong moral underpinning. The first paradigm about health describes the pathogenic external elements as parasites, viruses – i.e. they are the evil invaders. This evil quality becomes personal in the second paradigm, the one about homeostasis, where it is believed that the loss of the somatic equilibrium is a consequence of an unhealthy life full of excesses. In this reasoning, health and illness receive a moral quality. Being healthy is a consequence of a good character, a reward for a virtuous and sober life. Being ill is a consequence of a bad character, a righteous punishment for a sinful and lecherous life. Illness is an inherently just punishment.

The good, the bad and the mute

This moral underpinning is present in Freud as well. Repressed representations are repressed by the dominant part in the Ego because they are immoral and hence, incompatible with the reigning thoughts. They are reprehensible and bad because they have everything to do with the lower passions of the body against which the higher part of the psyche should resist. The same reasoning goes for the loss of the equilibrium. Neurosis is a consequence of an immoral sexual life, meaning a lack of normal discharge combined with unhealthy forms, with masturbation as the most detrimental practice during the Victorian era. This moral tone becomes obvious in Freud's reformulation of the treatment aim. I will argue that it has important implications on our sense of identity as well.

The new aim of the treatment is that the patient does get access to his repressed thoughts in order to master the underlying impulses. In the case-study known as Little Hans, Freud writes:

> "Analysis replaces the process of repression . . . by a temperate and purposeful control on the part of the highest agencies of the mind. *In a word, analysis replaces repression by condemnation.*"
>
> (Freud, 1978 [1909b], p. 145, his italics).

Obviously, at that time, the aim of Freudian analysis was highly moralistic. The irony is that this aim can be reversed, whilst keeping the moralistic tone. In the wake of Freud, several of his followers took the opposite view: the repressed thoughts are not immoral, it is their repression that is wrong. Wilhelm Reich, especially, held a strong plea for a liberated sexuality with as much orgasmic discharge as possible; the psychoanalytic cure should free the patient of his unjustified sense of guilt.

The net result is that the treatment confronts us with a hitherto unknown part of ourselves that we are not that happy with. It is generally accepted that a psychoanalytic cure leads to a better insight in ourselves, that it enhances our self-knowledge. This is true, but only up to a certain point. A closer look at this process reveals that this self-knowledge focuses on the *bad* part of ourselves, the part that we did not want to know about. The repressed thoughts are repressed because they concern a sexuality that we did not or could not acknowledge as 'ours'. The psychoanalytic cure bypasses our resistance and confronts us with our inner self, be it the immoral side of it.

Because of this focus, there is always a risk that the psychoanalytic cure turns into a typically obsessional neurotic mirror palace, where the obsessional ego is forever chasing his bad mirror image without ever getting hold of it. In this respect, the net result of a psychoanalytic treatment is a confrontation with the immoral part of our identity, with the aim of controlling it. It reminds me of a cartoon in *The New Yorker* of many years ago. Says one father to another father: "I don't know what to do with our son, he is too old for a good beating and too young for psychoanalysis".

This point of view can be reversed in its opposite as well, without losing its moralistic tone, just as I argued concerning repression and condemnation. In the late seventies, during the heyday of psychotherapy, one of the central ideas was that deep in ourselves, we are truly good, but alas, our authentic true self has been buried under a totally alienated bad self. In this reasoning, the aim of psychotherapy is to liberate the real me which is a good me, etc.

My argument is that this bad (or good) part is not the Unconscious. The division between moral and immoral is a typical effect of our consciousness. The Unconscious is unconscious, i.e. mute.

Division as the human condition

It is obvious that the two different ways of thinking about health and illness are still a product of a moralistic reading of the body and soul dualism, in which one of the two gets a privileged position. Such a reading misses the point of what is truly innovative in Freud. He presented us with a new perspective on ourselves, i.e., *we are essentially divided*. Lacan adds that there is no such thing as an original or authentic self, there is only an original division resulting in a divided subject (Verhaeghe, 1998).

The traditional dualism has saddled us with a negative image of ourselves. Freud's interpretation and especially his first topology can offer us a more neutral reading. This is much less the case with the second topology, where the moralistic tone is inherently present. His presentation of the Unconscious and the Conscious is an important alternative to the Cartesian dualism. In this respect, Freud is closer to Spinoza than to Descartes. Freud's first descriptions of unconscious processes highlight a material aspect which he tries to understand in terms of energy. Conscious thinking comes later in our development, and often enough this thinking presents a wrong interpretation of what is felt.

We have to wait until the metapsychological papers before Freud returns to this idea. Repression is 'after repression' and concerns the 'dynamic Unconscious', where repressed ideas can be made conscious again. The core of the Unconscious (the 'system Unconscious') is not a product of after repression. The system Unconscious is the result of so-called primal repression which is not a repression at all but a fixation: original quanta of affect energy remain in their original form because the translation process into words failed. The reason for this failure is not very clear, but, says Freud, it must be quite analogous to what happened during a trauma (Freud, 1978 [1911c], pp. 67–68; 1978 [1915d], p. 148; 1978 [1926d], p. 94).

In my reading: the human being is driven by underlying energetic processes, 'affects', operating in a dialectical process of charge and discharge. If discharge is thwarted, this leads to pathology. One of the evolutionary developed ways of discharge is to associate these affects to 'Vorstellungen', to signifiers; at that point, affects are turned into conscious emotions and talking is an evolutionary advanced way of discharge. Some of the original affects are not translated and keep their original status.

The kernel of the Unconscious is indeed ... unconscious. Lacan (1994 [1964]) comes to the same conclusion in the first chapter of seminar XI, where he studies the Unconscious as the first of the four fundamental concepts of psychoanalysis. The Unconscious points to a process that never happened, to a failure that keeps insisting. In Freudian terms: a failure of bridging the gap between the original affects and the system of representations. The many different denominations used by Lacan indicate the sheer impossibility to signify this insisting factor: the Real, the other jouissance, the object small *a* – ever so many indications for an energetic force beyond the signifier. This force is the fourth fundamental concept, i.e. the drives. The conscious experience of these processes might be either pleasurable or painful, but our cognitive and conscious understanding of them is never total and often misses the point. There remains a division between unconscious affects and consciousness.

Because they are what drive us, we have a need to understand them, that is: a need to control them. At that point we meet the effect of the upper side of our division, where the conscious Ego operates. I am consciously aware of an unknown force at work in me, and that scares me. Hence my never-ending attempt to master it, meaning to master 'myself', i.e. a part of myself that operates as an external element. Drive is translated into desire, desire is entered in our moral system, to control means to condemn or to give in. To be myself is to master myself; in Lacan's wording, with its double orthography: 'm'être à moi-même', to belong to myself, is 'maître à moi-même', to be a master of myself (Lacan, 1991, p. 178). The idea of self-control is deeply inscribed in our psychological history, especially as it keeps producing its own failure. For Freud, the original failure to translate part of the drive energy into words cannot be undone. For Lacan, the Symbolic is the 'not all' and a part of the Real remains real. The attempt to master psychologically and morally this unknown force is at the same time a denial of our division.

Contemporary cognitive psychology and psychotherapy are in many respects the most recent manifestations of this denial and the attempt at mastery, often joined by the work of philosophers such as D. Dennett and neurologists like A. Damasio. In their reasoning, there must be a kind of continuum between the conscious and the unconscious, the main problem being the 'emergence' of consciousness. Here we can see the radical difference with a psychoanalytic reading of our division, based on a different ontology. Let us not forget that at the time of the *Studies on Hysteria*, Freud considered the splitting in two different psychological groups as a pathological artefact. Normal people did not have it, and normal psychological functioning is based on the pleasure principle. It did not take long before Freud had to acknowledge something altogether different. Every human being is divided, and the pleasure principle explains our functioning only up to a certain point. In one of his very last papers he recognizes the splitting as a normal characteristic of the ego (Freud, 1978 [1940e]).

Eros, Thanatos and 'Triebmischung' (fusion of drives)

A division between an originally unconscious energy or affect and a verbalized version of it under the form of conscious emotions dovetails with our intimate experience: something that drives us, escapes us. This reasoning is clinically useful as well – there is more and more evidence that 'repressed emotions' belong to the causal factors of several diseases (Thomas & Greenstreet, 1973). But a description is not an explanation. Freud and Lacan tried to reach a deeper understanding. Both of them left the original dualism for a more complicated view and ended with axiomatic statements.

In one of his first attempts to understand the inner division, Freud opposed the ego-drives with their aim of self-preservation, to the sexual drives, that don't care about self-preservation (Freud, 1978 [1910i], p. 214). When he discovered that the ego may function as a sexual object for itself, he had to abandon this opposition (Freud, 1978 [1914c]). Many years later, he presented another far more complex couple: Thanatos, the death drive versus Eros, the life drive. Both have a goal that is directly the opposite of the other's. The Eros drive aims at fusion, and hence at the continuation of life; the Thanatos drive aims at deconstruction, and hence at death. The underlying processes concern the rise and fall of energy levels. Falling apart is an effect of the ultimate discharge, meaning that death with its zero level of energy is the final pleasure. Fusion based on Eros implies ever higher levels of tension, something that should be painful but provides another form of enjoyment as well. The two of them operate together in a strange system of checks and balances, a *Triebmischung* (fusion of the drives). Obviously, the pleasure principle is not the only principle at work and Freud concludes that pleasure is the most difficult problem in psychology.

In his turn, Lacan rewords the same dichotomy. Phallic enjoyment operates within the pleasure principle and provides us with an always limited and thus safe enjoyment, but there is another one at work as well. In his attempts to understand this other jouissance, he associates it at different moments of his work with different impersonations of the Other, be it the devouring mother, the psychotic, the mystic, the woman who does not exist, and finally with the body as an organism (see Verhaeghe, 2001b). One thing remains clear: the jouissance beyond the pleasure principle amounts to an unlimited enjoyment of the organism, at the subject's expense.

In his attempt to understand how this jouissance operates, Lacan comes up with his own axiomatic formulation. We are endlessly driven because of a primordial loss that can never be mended. At birth, half of an original whole is lost (the part of the fertilized egg that becomes the placenta; half of the chromosomes) and that lost part flies away. This lost part is eternal life; its loss is inevitable because of the very nature of sexual reproduction (Lacan, 2006 [1964]), pp. 718–718).

Lacan does not give much information, but it is plausible that he refers to the major difference between sexual and non-sexual reproduction. The latter happens by mitosis, which produces two perfect copies of the original cell; the former happens by meiosis, thus losing half of the original two cells (half of the chromosomes) and thereby creating something new. At the same time, this new organism loses the possibility of eternal life. From that moment onwards, an endless attempt starts to regain what was lost. This is what Lacan understands as the aim of the drive: to restore the original loss (Lacan, 2006 [1964], p. 720). Here, he joins

Freud in his reading of Plato: the aim of the drive is to return to an original state (Freud, 1920g, pp. 57–58) as described by Aristophanes and his parable in the *Symposium* (the original double-backed creatures were cut in two by Zeus, each one looking for their lost half ever since).

In my reading, this is the axiomatic explanation for what the young Lacan described as "a certain 'déhiscence' at the very heart of the organism, a primordial Discord" (Lacan, 2006 [1949], p. 78). This is the mixed division at work in me, obliging me to do something with it, forever balancing between the need for fusion and the urge to split. The net result is an endless dialectical endeavor to reach an impossible whole.

From dualism to a circular but non-reciprocal dialectic

The real organism functions as the original cause, in the sense that it contains a primal loss. Which loss? The loss of eternal life, which paradoxically enough is lost at the moment of birth as a sexed being (Lacan, 1994 [1964], p. 205). In order to explain this, Lacan constructed the myth of a lamella flying away at birth (Lacan, 2006 [1964], pp. 717–718). This lamella stands for the life instinct, and the myth mimics a biological fact. Non-sexual reproduction implies in principle the possibility of eternal life (cf. single-celled organisms and clones), whilst sexual reproduction installs a necessary death of the individual. In the latter case, each sexed organism tries to undo this loss, and wants to return to the former state of being. This was already with Freud the basic characteristic of the drive, here to be read as Eros and Thanatos. At this stage, we are talking about the drive as such, preceding the evolution into component drives, meaning phallic drives.

Thus considered, the first level of what will turn out to be a circular but non-reciprocal dialectic starts at the appearance of individual life and the simultaneous loss of eternal life. The opening of the evolutionary gate for sexually differentiated lifeforms implies the closure of eternal life for every sexual organism. The attempt to return goes via sexual reproduction, which means that as a return to eternal life, it is a failure for the individual. From that moment onwards, a non-reciprocal although circular relationship will continue on different levels, each time with the same effect. That is to say: the process doesn't manage to mend the loss; on the contrary, it endorses the loss, albeit on another level.

The next level in the attempt to regain what is lost, brings the formation of the I via the primary identification of the mirror stage. The newborn acquires a first identity through the unified image of his body coming to him from the mirror Other; at the same time this 'I' loses the real of its body, on top of the preceding loss of eternal life. Consequently, this 'I' will try to join its body again (see Descartes' 'Je pense, donc je suis'), giving rise to the classic dualism between body and mind.

This leads to the next level, that of the advent of the lacanian subject. The 'I' attempts to fuse with the (m)Other, in order to recapture its body and to be *m'être/*

maître à moi-même, to belong to myself, to be master of myself (Lacan, 1991, p. 178). Instead of regaining its body, the I disappears and the subject enters the scene as a divided product of the signifiers that cannot meet the desire of the Other.

Continuing this series, we arrive at a fourth level wherein the divided subject tries to become whole again by joining the other sex. This is what the Oedipus complex does, in its own peculiar way – that is, by interpreting the original loss in terms of castration. The phallic interpretation will be applied retroactively to all preceding levels, meaning that each loss is read in a phallic way. Gender identity is the final stage of this circular but non-reciprocal relationship. The original gap between life and death, between the body and the I, between the subject and the Other is reproduced and worked over in the gap between man and woman. Moreover, this repetition produces the same effect: if the aim of the relationship is to become whole again, then failure is inevitable: "There is no such a thing as a sexual relationship".

The negativity of this conclusion hinders us in seeing its positive side: "It is always about the subject as indeterminated." (Lacan, 1994 [1964], p. 26). The thesis that our identity is symbolically undetermined opens a possibility for choice and change, beyond the alienation coming from the Other.

References

Diederich, N., & Goetz, C. (2008). The Placebo Treatments in Neurosciences: New Insights from Clinical and Neuroimaging Studies. *Neurology*, 71:677–684.

Fisher, M. (2009). *Capitalist Realism: Is There No Alternative?* Winchester and Washington: Zero Books.

Freud, S. (1978 [1893c]). Some Points for a Comparative Study of Organic and Hysterical Motor Paralyses. *The Standard Edition of the Complete Psychological Works of Sigmund Freud*. I: pp. 155–172. London: The Hogarth Press.

Freud, S. (1978 [1894a]). The Neuro-Psychoses of Defence. *The Standard Edition of the Complete Psychological Works of Sigmund Freud*. III: pp. 41–61. London: The Hogarth Press.

Freud, S., & Breuer, J. (1978 [1895d]). Studies on hysteria. T*he Standard Edition of the Complete Psychological Works of Sigmund Freud*, 2, pp. 1–306. London: The Hogarth Press.

Freud, S. (1978 [1909b]). Analysis of a Phobia in a Five-Year Old Boy. *The Standard Edition of the Complete Psychological Works of Sigmund Freud*. X: pp. 1–149. London: The Hogarth Press.

Freud, S. (1978 [1910i]). The Psycho-Analytic View of Psychogenic Disturbance of Vision. *The Standard Edition of the Complete Psychological Works of Sigmund Freud*. XI: pp. 211–218. London: The Hogarth Press.

Freud, S. (1978 [1911c]). Psycho-Analytic Notes on an Autobiographical Account of a Case of Paranoia (Dementia Paranoides). *The Standard Edition of the Complete Psychological Works of Sigmund Freud*. XII: pp. 3–82. London: The Hogarth Press.

Freud, S. (1978 [1914c]). On Narcissism: An Introduction. *The Standard Edition of the Complete Psychological Works of Sigmund Freud*. XIV: pp. 67–102. London: The Hogarth Press.

Freud, S. (1978 [1915c]). Instincts and Their Vicissitudes. *The Standard Edition of the Complete Psychological Works of Sigmund Freud.* XIV: pp. 109–140. London: The Hogarth Press.

Freud, S. (1978 [1915d]). Repression. *The Standard Edition of the Complete Psychological Works of Sigmund Freud.* XIV: pp. 141–158. London: The Hogarth Press.

Freud, S. (1978 [1915e]. The Unconscious. *The Standard Edition of the Complete Psychological Works of Sigmund Freud.* XIV: pp. 159–215. London: The Hogarth Press.

Freud, S. (1978 [1920g]). Beyond the Pleasure Principle. *The Standard Edition of the Complete Psychological Works of Sigmund Freud.* XVIII: pp. 7–64. London: The Hogarth Press.

Freud, S. (1978 [1926d]). Inhibitions, Symptoms and Anxiety. *The Standard Edition of the Complete Psychological Works of Sigmund Freud.* XX: pp. 75–175. London: The Hogarth Press.

Freud, S. (1978 [1940e]). Splitting of the Ego in the Process of Defence. *The Standard Edition of the Complete Psychological Works of Sigmund Freud.* XXIII: pp. 271–278. London: The Hogarth Press.

Freud, S., & Breuer, J. (1978 [1895d]). Studies on Hysteria. *The Standard Edition of the Complete Psychological Works of Sigmund Freud.* II. London: The Hogarth Press, pp. I–XXX, 1–335.

Groddeck, G. (1977). *The Meaning of Illness.* London: The Institute of Psycho-Analysis & The Hogarth Press.

Lacan, J. (2006) [1949]. The Mirror Stage as Formative of the Function of the I. In Fink, B. (trans.), in collaboration with H. Fink and R. Grigg, *Écrits: The First Complete Edition in English.* New York and London: W. W. Norton & Company, pp. 75–81.

Lacan, J. (2006) [1964]). Position of the Unconscious. In Fink, B. (trans.), in collaboration with H. Fink and R. Grigg, *Écrits: The First Complete Edition in English.* New York and London: W. W. Norton & Company, pp. 703–721.

Lacan, J. (1991 [1969–1970]). *Le Séminaire, livre XVII, L'Envers de la psychanalyse* (texte établi par J.A. Miller). Paris: Seuil.

Lacan, J. (1994 [1964]). *The Four Fundamental Concepts of Psychoanalysis.* Edited by J.-A. Miller and translated by A. Sheridan. London: Penguin Books.

Maines, R. (1999). *The Technology of Orgasm: "Hysteria", the Vibrator and Women's Sexual Satisfaction.* Baltimore and London: The Johns Hopkins University Press.

Thomas, C., & Greenstreet, R. (1973). Psychobiological Characteristics in Youth as Predictors of Five Disease States: Suicide, Mental Illness, Hypertension, Coronary Heart Disease and Tumor. *Johns Hopkins Medical Journal,* 132(1) (January):16–43.

Verhaeghe, P. (1998). Causation and Destitution of a Pre-ontological Non-entity: On the Lacanian Subject. In Nobus, D. (ed.), *Key Concepts of Lacanian Psychoanalysis.* London: Rebus Press, pp. 164–189.

Verhaeghe, P. (2001a). Subject and Body: Lacan's Struggle with the Real. In Verhaeghe, P. (ed.), *Beyond Gender: From Subject to Drive.* New York: Other Press, pp. 65–97.

Verhaeghe, P. (2001b). Mind Your Body. Lacan's Answer to a Classical Deadlock. In P. Verhaeghe (ed.), *Beyond Gender: From Subject to Drive.* New York: Other Press, pp. 99–132.

Chapter 12

Somatic ailment and death drive

Dangerous liaisons

Panos Aloupis

At the very beginning, I would like to head my text with a quotation from a letter Freud sent to his friend Oscar Pfister in 1930, about the controversy his notion of the death drive had provoked:

> "The death instinct is not a requirement of my heart, it seems to me to be only an inevitable assumption on both biological and psychological grounds."
> (Meng and Freud, 1963, p. 132)

Viewed in this light, psychoanalytical psychosomatics studies the path from instinct to drive, from the soma to the body.

Trauma and death drive

There is a concept, absent in the title I have chosen, which is at the crossroads of my clinical and theoretical questions, the concept of psychic trauma. The somatic disorder constitutes of its own a trauma, insofar as the person is subjected psychically to an aggression which actively invades the psychic space, requiring adjustments and readjustments for which the subject may not be ready or adequately equipped to face. The aggression might provoke, in return, aggressiveness and destructiveness, which for want of appropriate psychic means is able to result in drive defusion and the prominent action of the unbound death drive.

Freud, very early, on the basis of the clinical study of hysteria, referred to the notion of psychic trauma:

> "If the subject is unable or unwilling to get rid of this surplus, the memory of the impression attains the importance of a trauma and becomes the cause of permanent hysterical symptoms."
> (1893c, p. 170)

The excitation here finds itself in the center of his questioning, settling the psychic in the body. Besides, the hysterical symptom makes use of the erotic body as if the matter at issue were the somatic ailment.

After having introduced the first drive theory and having defined both the narcissistic and object poles, Freud, in the middle of the First World War, notes:

> Indeed, the term traumatic has no other sense than an economic one. We apply it to an experience which within a short period of time presents the mind with an increase of stimulus too powerful to be dealt with or worked off in the normal way, and this must result in permanent disturbances of the manner in which the energy operates.
>
> (1916–1917a, p. 274)

The trauma is perceived like a disturbance of economic energetic order and this point of view will result later in the article "*The economic problem of masochism*" (1924c) in which the latter is directly linked to the vicissitudes of trauma.

Just after the War, Freud points out an important note of remarkable consequences:

> We have a perfect right to describe repression, which lies at the basis of every neurosis, as a reaction to a trauma, – as an elementary traumatic neurosis.
>
> (1919d, p. 209)

In fact, a perception strikes the psychic apparatus that for its own reasons is not willing to accept it. Faced with this elementary traumatic situation, the repression represents a compromising solution, enlisting the psychosexuality and the drive representatives.

For the infant, this virtual instant of primitive anxiety may take place when faced with either the absence or the presence of a psychically non-responding object. This is an ordinary situation, which according to the tribulations of the primary object relation, may prove to become traumatic, when the permanence of the object is not sufficiently guaranteed, within a cathexis experienced as failing, unforeseeable, lacking in certain precious repairing qualities.

In my opinion, the term 'impingement', introduced by D.W. Winnicott, describes perfectly this elementary traumatic situation. In his definition of primary maternal preoccupation, he notes simply: "The first ego organization comes from the experience of threats of annihilation, which do not lead to annihilation and from which repeatedly there is *recovery*." (1956, p. 303, italics original).

If this fails, the reactions to the trauma are inscribed more solidly within and their repetitiveness often results in the representation of a not surviving object. The human being, during his lifetime, will be threatened by the aggression of traumatic shocks that the psyche cannot integrate and metabolize. When it is a question of a psychic apparatus naturally oriented towards denial, animated by archaic projective mechanisms, foreclosure and abreactive regression, it will use radical means in order to get rid of the traumatic effects. Maybe the most radical one is the deathly silence, "nothing happened, nothing is happening".

Last but not least, because of the development in the human being of a psychic apparatus that thinks and speaks, the psychic inscription of the trauma takes place almost in the same way regardless of whether the source is external or internal. Freud, in his last, never completed work, "*An outline of Psycho-analysis*" notes: "(In the circumstances of a feeble ego) instinctual demands from within no less than excitations from the external world operate as 'traumas'" (1940a, p. 184).

The trauma takes the form of an actual psychic element, as an external event or as a subjective reading of conflicting perceptions, insofar as working through is not efficient enough to face the surplus of excitation in order to transform the experienced fact to a psychic drive representative. The Freudian instinct, both integrating factor of the psychic apparatus and representative of the soma, particularly through excitation and affect, determines the role of the otherness played by the body like a force imposed on the psyche. It is easy to imagine that in the case of a somatic ailment and disease, actively imposed and to which the human being is subjected, the psychic apparatus feels constrained to an active reaction with the aim of repairing the wounds. This active motion often gets the death drive prominently involved.

Otherwise, if aggressiveness or activity are forbidden, inhibited or suppressed, a state of shock invades the psyche, a sign of radical helplessness; the traumatized psychic apparatus, resigned and impotent, feels unable to react, even with illusion or denial. André Green, talking about operatory somatic patients, has written: "Being nothing in order not to stop being there" (2007, p. 48). In this case, we are far away from the repetition of the traumatic scene as an attempt of active control. The subject here tragically repeats the traumatic state as an actual fact with the stunning effects of physical and psychical paralysis.

Aggressiveness, displeasure, active object avoiding, regressive turning round, evacuating discharge, de-cathexis of the object and of the object relation (disobjectalization for Green) are possible facets of a destructiveness desperately seeking a balance, even if it should be deadly. If there is a death narcissism, if there is a death masochism, there is equally a death peace. This psychic state, radical with regard to withdrawal and dangerous with regard to survival, was clinically defined by Pierre Marty, founder of the Paris School of Psychosomatics, in the form of essential depression.

> [F]ollowing the break of a first emotional tie, a chain reaction gradually leads to the rupture of every emotional tie. What we witness then is a general de-cathexis of all libidinal areas. Such a progressive and deep destruction produces a particular state which I have termed "essential depression". It is essential because it contains the very essence of depression, namely the general disappearance of libidinal tension uncompensated by any positive economic counterpart.
>
> (Marty, 1968, p. 246)

For Marty, it is not a state of post-traumatic psychoneurosis, since the defense mechanisms do not refer to a classical neurotic organization. However, the clinical description of operational functioning, "The patient loses interest in life which seems empty to him" (Marty, 1968), accurately recalls the paralyzed, shocked and stunned person in a sort of permanent post-traumatic situation.

Indeed, what kind of dangerous liaisons may the body carry on with the psyche? Freud, working on anxiety and excitation, since 1894 in Draft E, associated the anxiety neurosis, precursor of the actual neuroses, to the existence of a failing, insufficient connection: "for several reasons the psychic linkage offered to (physical tension) remains insufficient, a *sexual affect* cannot be formed because there is something lacking in the psychic determinants" (1894, pp. 78–79, italics original). Where the somatic was, psychic does not appear.

In his Introductory Lecture about "*The common neurotic state*" Freud asserts:

> the sexual function is not a purely psychic thing any more than it is a purely somatic one. It influences bodily and mental life alike. If in the symptoms of the psychoneuroses we have become acquainted with manifestations of disturbances in the *psychical* operation of the sexual function, we shall not be surprised to find in the 'actual' neuroses the direct *somatic* consequences of sexual disturbances.
>
> (1916–1917a, pp. 386–387)

In this sense, the enactment runs the risk of affecting the somatic field for want of adequate psychosexual paths. These paths progressively construct the "representational network" which is able to work through the existing signifying chains and incessantly to create new ones. Marty invented the term mentalization in order to define this complex psychic work that is constantly nourished and animated by the effects of the drive fusion between Eros and Thanatos. The enactment of the trauma in its repetition compulsion essentially runs the risk of breaking this fusion, freeing in this way the destructive action of the death drive. In short, in a psychic apparatus failing in sufficient means of defense to metabolize the traumatic shock, either permanently or accidentally, the body is indeed in danger.

Clinical vignette

I have chosen for my case presentation a man suffering from heart disease. The heart is an odd organ; because of its particular place in the body, it has obtained a highly significant sense for human culture. We could assert the same thing for the skin and the eyes; they accompany us in our everyday life and their expressiveness implies a relation of immediacy with the psychic apparatus. The heartbeat, its reactivity and the way in which one's heart is present belong inevitably to the experience of our existence. For a human being, the heartbeat is part of subjective integrity in the same way that a representation refers to an internal object, the existence of which the psyche does not doubt. On the contrary, a suffering heart is quickly perceived as mad, weird and unforeseeable, often resulting in a psychosomatic context where it becomes for the psyche a foreign object, whose madness attacks and persecutes it.

The heart, either in hypochondriacal anxiety or in somatic disorder, may occupy the mental space both of a suffering ego and of an object that threatens psychic integrity. In this case, it is paradoxically experienced like an external-dangerously-internal object whose beating attacks the bodily boundaries.

Richard was sent to me by his cardiologist and his very first words were: *"Doctor, my heart is sick."* He started by enumerating his health problems, dwelling on the episodes of arrhythmia at length. Their unpredictability led him to suffer permanent anxiety of imminent death. *"I am not living, I am surviving."* He considered himself *"an accomplished and happy man"* until a severe problem occurred making him say that since then his life had been divided in two parts, before and after the attack. *"I was sitting in my study reading the newspaper, my wife was preparing the dinner and kids were in the living room. Suddenly I felt a sort of faintness, almost under my skin, but I said nothing. It lasted perhaps only one minute and then something strange, like an enormous wave, overwhelmed me. I just had time to get up, I took two or three steps and then . . . a strong impression of emptying, emptying myself . . . I was told it was a dissection of the arteries."* He fell into a coma, stayed in hospital for a long time and gradually went back to life discovering again shades of hope and pleasure.

Richard invested therapy with a certain distrust, associated to curiosity that sustained the regularity in his sessions. At the beginning, I paid attention to the storytelling of a happy childhood. His parents loved him and he mentioned sometimes with a light smile of beatitude that they treated him *"like His Majesty the Baby"*. Our sessions were often intersected by medical examinations, physical reviews and episodes of arrhythmia, experienced in a context of traumatizing preoccupation. As soon as his heart started beating irregularly, anxiety invaded him and the body broke down with a feeling of annihilation. *"The shock is coming again!"* he said.

The ups-and-downs of his cardiac disorders and his anxiety were giving a certain rhythm to our sessions and coloring my countertransference cathexis and preoccupation. However, the discovery of a psychic life, that he had never taken enough time to think about in the past, met my own interest and gave rise to a feeling of tenderness responding to his unconscious infantile demand. I learned quickly that the "episode of dissection" occurred two years after an early retirement. *"I was young . . . and I am feeling always young."* In spite of the persistence of his health problems, he kept on taking care of his looks and seemed surprised by the idea of the approach of old age and its dangers. He was afraid of dying because of his heart, but definitely not of his age. He experienced retirement as a narcissistic humiliation, a violent stop to his active life. Work and family activities had fully filled a program of life that loathed void.

In the frame of the happiness of being an only son, during the first period of therapy two loving and fragile parental figures appeared: a demanding and rigid father and a hypochondriacal and highly anxious mother. In this context, we may suggest that for the ideal ego of 'His majesty the Baby' it was difficult to give access to an ideal of ego, carrying out a project of life subjectively assumed.

His father's death at the end of his adolescence pushed him violently into the vicissitudes of an adult life for which he did not have enough time to ask himself if he felt ready. He started working hard and got married to a young woman he worked with. One year after, a little son was born and two years later his wife abandoned both of them and disappeared forever. He went back to live with his mother and a new life began.

"*Dragged by a group of friends*" he lived for four years an experience of adolescence, filled with pleasure, alcohol and sex. During a session, after a remark of mine about a link between the pleasure of 'His Majesty the Baby' and the adolescent debaucheries of that period, he answered spontaneously: "*I was shooting pleasure like a junky.*" This phrase came back several times in our sessions, pointing at a feeling of nostalgia, probably functioning as a manic defense, in relation to a pleasure he was unable to find again after the "dissection": before and after the catastrophe.

This phase of exhilaration of the senses stopped when he met his second wife, with whom he established a new family and started a new career; both offered him serenity and satisfaction. Two points seemed important for better understanding the circumstances of his life before the severe somatic disorder and his habitual way of psychic functioning. The first point concerned a conflict with his son from his first marriage. His son had set up house in the same city and they met for a drink. After the father complained about their relationship, the son reacted violently, reproaching him for his absence and abandonment. Bitterly astonished, he substituted sadness for a feeling of embarrassment and apprehension. The second point concerned his wife's role by his side. During our sessions, we realized together the anaclitic character of this relation. Since his retiring and particularly after the manifestations of cardiac arrhythmia, his way of being alone and of taking care of himself and his activities became problematic. "*I don't miss my work, I'm missing the contact with the others.*" In fact, his dependence was experienced as diffuse anxiety with displeasure and fear, often associated with hypochondriacal preoccupations and thoughts of impotence and helplessness.

The heart and the death drive

In listening to the story of Richard, of his past, of his way of cathecting his object relations and his therapy, I heard a thread of essential depression. Let's return to Marty for whom this psychic state takes hold when traumatic events disorganize some major psychic functions that are overwhelmed by the trauma and unable to work it through (Marty, 1980, p. 59). The phase of insidious libidinal negativity, before the somatic disorder arrived, made me think that it occurred in the context of a progressive de-cathexis of life.

The frequent repetition of the figure of 'His Majesty the Baby' drew my attention in the same way because negation points out something which cannot be repressed once and for all. My listening to the psychic solution after the abandonment and the loss of his first wife, in resonance with the defensive reaction following the quarrel with the son, led me to a hypothesis of an ideal ego that had been progressively constructed and functioned as an antidepressant and antitraumatic remedy. On the one hand, Richard nourished his anticathexis with a manic defense that supported his advancement in life, and on the other hand he used psychically the death drive's action to inhibit the object aggression and to calm the pain of the narcissistic wound.

Claude Smadja in a paper on "*Mourning, melancholy and somatization*" notes: "The ego tries to avoid the pain of an object loss by erasing the psychic pain apparatus" and he defines: "the process of disobjectalization that underlies the drives of destructiveness and death as the ultimate mean of survival" (2013, p. 22).

In the course of our sessions, I had the impression of a man who since his childhood had built a relatively sufficient strategy against the traumatic perception of the object relation. This subjective attitude had allowed him to lean in an anaclitic way on objects which ensured for him the permanence of psychic integrity. Eventually, this way of functioning could have carried on without particular modifications, as many patients and other people we encounter let us guess. However, the emptying of his psychic investments and the vicissitudes of his object relations probably confronted him with impasses, where the regressive immediacy of a somatic solution gradually dug its path. In Richard's case, the ailment of the psychosomatic disorder, going also by the rules of the soma, affected the functioning of the heart. When faced with an unforeseeable heart, the calm becomes an insoluble dilemma. Claude Smadja, in the same paper, notices the following: "It is remarkable that we find, most frequently, in the state of somatization neither affect of psychic pain nor evident loss of the patient's interest for the world" (2013, p. 12).

Richard survived by means of an ideal ego that on the one hand is exciting at an autoerotic level and on the other hand is calming against psychic pain. I think that this functioning helped him to overcome traumatic events, even the somatic episode of "dissection," by all appearances, but it proved to be insufficient particularly after the manifestation of arrhythmias and their morbid effects. He told me often how he had succeeded in investing some physical and sublimatory activities, but the appearance of the cardiac disorders with their consequences of hospital admissions, of surgical interventions and frequent reviews caught up with him, not allowing him to have rest and recovery.

Let's evoke here a question of Michel Fain, one of the founders of the Parisian Institute of Psychosomatics, on the subject of psychosomatic object relations:

"Generally they prove to be unsuitable to operate a narcissistic regression that the manifestation of an illness demands. Instead of this regression the search for a recipe with calming effect comes forward. What are we doing in this case?"

(1993, p. 66)

Indeed, what are we doing (and what is the patient doing) when there are cardiac disorders with a dangerously excited and exciting heart and with a psyche used to having access to calming strategies by means of the death drive? In case "The death drive would not act in silence, but in order to restore silence" (1993, p. 61), anxiety becomes central, like an alarm signal that rings in an unpredictable and mad way, whereas anxiety and the heartbeat lose their quality of protection and prevention.

For Richard, his effort to neutralize the pain was in vain and became a nightmarish dilemma, insofar as the heart's silence was linked to death. For M. Fain, the failure of the calming process to tone down the effects of a morbid excitation results in "the traumatic reality's return from within which the process had until then contained" (1993, p. 65). I think that my patient found himself in an intolerable situation, since on the one hand he carried on psychically using the death drive's effects with a calming aim and on the other hand he was constantly listening to his heart, whose silence or over-excitation were perceived as a risk of imminent death. This situation could be seen as an example of pathological primary maternal preoccupation, where the mother is replaced by the madly worried patient and the child is replaced by the dangerously ill heart (and the body).

Richard continued his therapy, becoming increasingly interested in his own life. He discovered a different way of being in contact with his son and his wife. He started feeling less threatened by his son's aggressiveness, absence or sadness and less dependent on his wife's presence. His heart took also another place; it became mostly a suffering organ essentially looked after by the medical team. In my view, he discovered a new balance in his life that negotiated the distance with the object differently than as usual. In this context, he planned to settle indefinitely in their country house and started to look after it, spending much of his time there. This country house was located at a reasonable distance between his daughter's house and a good hospital.

During this period of preparations, of changes and of the end of treatment, he brought the following dream:

> It's dark . . . I'm leaving my place for a walk. I am alone and start walking. The city is not dark, there are the night lights and in front of me the main arteries are well lit, open . . . I walked for a long time, as if I was discovering the city again. I was so happy!

When I pointed out *"the main arteries?"* he smiled and easily assented. This dream accompanied our last period of treatment and he ended the last session saying: *"The arteries are not blocked now . . . I can be alone and happy to be alone!"*

Conclusion

Before I conclude, I would like to return to an important point, the point concerning the distance with the object, significantly useful for the analytical treatment and essential for the treatment of psychosomatic patients. For Winnicott, the space between the mother and the infant after his birth is seen like a substance progressively filled with objects and phenomena being part both of the infant and the environment (1988). This remark is highly interesting in the frame of treatments of patients with somatic ailments, and particularly when the suffering organ is treated and experienced psychically both as internal and external object. These patients are inclined to create in the transference-countertransference setting the same object relation. We are led to work through the distance with the object in order to lighten the narcissistic object's weight and to offer them a less risky object relation. Within this space, the mechanism of projection constitutes at the same time a useful and dangerous ingredient, because the attacking elements contain the risk of destabilizing the balance of distance, which is constantly unconsciously negotiated between the analyst and the patient. The therapist should take into account the effects of the death drive, facilitated by projective identification, in order to evaluate the danger it represents, but also its stratagems, adjustments and its role in the psychic conflict. Marty, in his paper *"The narcissistic difficulties presented to the observer by the psychosomatic problem"* has a wise remark: "Whatever it is, psychosomatics evokes the effective self-destruction and this is a reason . . . why the observer may be troubled as far as his most profound depth" (2010, p. 360).

This is a remark that concerns both of the actors.

Marty wrote about the mothering function of the therapist (1976, p. 122) with the aim of describing the cautious steps the analyst faced with patients who run the risk of falling ill physically. From another perspective, Winnicott introduced the term of the good enough mother sketching the profile of a mother who looks after her child's wounds. Both of them approached the question of the function of care in the human being and especially in the psychoanalytical setting. The somatic disorder when it concerns mostly organs close to sensory perceptions, like the heart or the skin for example, affects the protective shield against the manifestations of pain and morbid excitation. Sometimes imperceptibly, sometimes suddenly and violently, the distance with the object breaks and then paradoxically the signal distress calls on the help of the death drive as the appropriate fireman to put out the trauma's fire.

References

Fain, M. (1993). Spéculations métapsychologiques sur les procédés autocalmants. *Revue Française de Psychosomatique*, 4:59–67.

Freud, S. (1893c). Some Points for a Comparative Study of Organic and Hysterical Motor Paralyses. *Standard Edition*, 1(1966):180–172.

Freud, S. (1894). Draft E: How Anxiety Originates, June 6, 1894. In *The Complete Letters of Sigmund Freud to Wilhelm Fliess*, 1887–1904, Belknap Press (1986), pp. 78–83.

Freud, S. (1915–1917). Introductory Lectures on Psycho-analysis. *Standard Edition*, 16 (1963).

Freud S. (1916-17a [1915-17]) *Introductory lectures on psycho-analysis, Standard Edition*, 16 (1963).

Freud, S. (1919d). Introduction to Psycho-Analysis and the War Neuroses. *Standard Edition*, 17(1955):207–210.

Freud, S. (1924c). The Economic Problem of Masochism. *Standard Edition*, 19 (1961):159–170.

Freud, S. (1930). Letter to Oscar Pfister. In Meng, H., and Freud, E.L. (eds.), *The International Psychoanalytic Library*, New York: Basic Books, pp. 132–134.

Freud, S. (1940a/1938). An Outline of Psycho-analysis. *Standard Edition*, 23(1964):144–207.

Green, A. (2007). Pulsions de destruction et maladies somatiques. *Revue Française de Psychosomatique*, 32:45–70.

Marty, P. (2010). The Narcissistic Difficulties Presented to the Observer by the Psychosomatic Problem. *International Journal of Psycho-Analysis*. 91(2):347–60.

Marty, P. (1968). A Major Process of Somatization: The Progressive Disorganization. *International Journal of Psycho-Analysis*, 49:246–249.

Marty, P. (1976). *Les mouvements individuels de vie et de mort*. Paris: Payot.

Marty, P. (1980). *L'ordre psychosomatique*. Paris: Payot.

Meng H. Freud E.L. (1963) *Psychoanalysis and faith. The letters of Sigmund Freud and Oscar Pfister*, London, The Hogarth Press.

Smadja, C. (2013). Deuil, mélancolie et somatisation. *Revue Française de Psychosomatique*, 44:7–24.

Winnicott, D.W. (1956). Primary Maternal Preoccupation. In *Through Paediatrics to Psychoanalysis*. London: Tavistock Publication, pp. 299–305.

Winnicott, D.W. (1988). *Human Nature*. London: The Winnicott Trust.

Chapter 13

What is alive in the ill body?
Affect and representation in psychosomatics

Marina Papageorgiou

"Affect is a look on a moved body," says André Green in his major work "Le discours vivant," (1973, p. 228), where he places affect at the core of mental functioning of psychoanalytic thinking, in opposition to the views of structuralism and Lacan's theory that gave priority to the signifier and the language as a rather homogeneous structure.

Green prefers the term of discourse as a moving construction made from heterogeneous materials, that involves the affect "as signifier in the flesh and the flesh of the signifier". His theory recovers the essential parts of Freud's theory of the drive as a concept between psyche and soma, stressing two psychic representatives of the somatic instincts: the affect-representative and the representation-representative which become efficient delegates after having accomplished specific work required by the soma upon the mind.

Green believes that the quality of mental functioning, quite singular for each person, depends on the success and failures of this movement that aims to transform the somatic excitation in a body animated by the drives. The first Freudian topography sets out the concept of affect as opposed to representation. In his initial theory of drive, Freud separated the quota of affect from the ideational representation or object representation. He shows how each of these elements follows specific vicissitudes. Affect may be subject to three vicissitudes: repression, transformation into anxiety and transformation into another affect. The repression and the transformation of the affect into anxiety, particularly into diffuse anxiety, marks for Freud the functioning in actual neurosis. This conception was also taken up by Ferenczi (1955) in his description of organ neurosis, and later by Alexander (1950), who made it the theoretical and doctrinal linchpin of his psychodynamic description of psychosomatic illness.

Freud (1916) gave a definition of psychosomatic illness "as something highly composite, including at the first place particular motor innervations or discharges and secondly certain feelings: the latter are of two kinds – perceptions of the motor actions that have occurred and the direct feelings of pleasure and unpleasure which give the affect its key note". In Freud's conception, there is a somatopsychic structure of the affect. He added two poles to this structure, one somatic and one psychic, one resulting from its integration in psychic formations and the other from its dispersion in different somatic modes of the functioning. The factor that will play a major role in the choice of destination is the quality of the structure of the Ego. Freud (1926) distinguished two types of anxiety, one as the consequence of the traumatic factor associated with actual neurosis, and the other as a signal-alarm announcing the reappearance of such a factor that is the mental functioning of the neuropsychosis of defense.

Freud differentiated the perceptions of the motor actions from direct feelings of pleasure and unpleasure. According to Green (1999), this is related to the unconscious level of the affects. Green then formulates a new theory of affect as an unconscious phenomenon, articulated with later theoretical developments in Freud's thought, as in the unconscious feeling of guiltiness, and the unconscious aspect of the Ego.

In the second topography, a new metapsychological conception of affect forced itself upon Freud; he no longer saw it as a first element opposable to representation, but as a second element arising from an initial drive state that Freud calls the psychical representative of the drive. Green (1999) has shown that in the second topography, affect and representation may be said to be undifferentiated at the beginning of psychic life. Green prefers the term representative-affect, which describes a qualitative mixture of a quota of affect and the future representative – representation, meaning a psychic force in movement, distinguished from the representation. Following this approach, the nature of the representation is double: an economic quantity coming from the inner body, and a symbolic quality articulated with the action of the external object and the language. This way to view links between the first (P-Cs, Pcs, Uncs) and the second topography (Id, Ego, Super-ego) aims to put together the question of the sense and the mnemonic prints, or the structure, and the one of the force of the drives.

The new conception of affect, including the second drive theory, allows for a complex theoretical approach to most severe forms of psychosomatic illness. The term of "progressive disorganization" created by Marty (1967) involves the erring of psychical formations which concerns both the affective dimension and the representative one. Thus, affect and representation undergo the same vicissitude: a process of a radical negativation and disqualification.

The term alexithymia, proposed by Sifneos and Nehmia (1970), describes the inability to identify feelings. The word comes from Greek words; lexis and thymos, literally meaning "no words for feelings". This describes a deficit or a failure of the representative mental function.

There is also another hypothesis for this etymology: the root alexi, which means to defend or to protect from, and thymos, meaning being emotional proof, or to be protected from feelings with the resulting etymological hypothesis stressing the drastic repression of the affect. The two etymologies seem to correspond with the two major concepts of Marty's (1968) Psychosomatics theory of the operational thought (concrete thinking) and the essential depression.

Pierre Marty and the Paris school of Psychosomatics have rejected Alexander's approach because of the underlined dual psyche-soma, elaborating an original and rigorous conception of the processes of somatization which rests on two parts: the psychoanalytic evaluation of the mental functioning, and the economic dimension of the relations between the mind and the somatic systems. The quality of the affect of anxiety (automatic and diffuse or neurotical, object-related) is associated with the quality of mental functioning. According to Marty (1968), most psychosomatic patients have irregular mental functioning.

Claude Smadja (2005) developed a theory on "the silence in psychosomatic praxis" that describes the operational state as a singular disturbance of thinking when it has been evacuated of affects. Because of the initial traumatic situation of the state of phagocytosis of the child's id by the mother's ego, the child is prohibited from experiencing his or her own affects that could represent a threat to the mother's psychic life. Those children often become "good" or "well-behaved" children that don't worry their mother. This creates a subjective psychic space of blank. The child operates a denial of a somatic frontier of his mind concerning primary affective and instinctual reality. This negative hallucination of affect, or this denial of internal perceptions of bodily origins, causes an ego split. For these patients, body care represents a search for calm, not for pleasure. During the analytic treatment, when facing silence, the analyst experiences as countertransference reaction a rich representational activity about the affects that are lacking in the patient.

For Christian David (1970, 1985), a French analyst close to Marty, the affect's representing is a particular quality of knowledge about the object's action and movement in the sense of a transformation, quite independent on the representation and the work of figurability. In other words, the affect is a cause of trouble, disorganizing and reorganizing the mental functioning. In psychosomatics, "the shared affect", according to C. Parat (1995), is the part of a particular quality of the positive transference that makes possible the patient's identification to the analyst's investment in mental functioning.

Marilia Aisenstein (2010) has developed an original conception of the specific countertransference reaction in the analyst's mind and body during the analytical work with a somatic patient. A clinical case will illustrate those theories:

"Name, profession, register number." David introduced himself in that way in our preliminary session. He is a handsome 40-year-old man, elegant and sporty looking, with a military look. He agreed to see me "by duty", when his doctor told him he had an illness that could become worse if he is depressed or anxious, and also because she knows a good friend of his, a woman who cares and is concerned about David, who is very surprised to learn that friends are worrying about him, because he doesn't feel sad. He suffers from a rather severe diabetes and arterial disease, but for him there is no emotional reason linked to this. He is used to the physical symptoms: neuropathic pains of toes and fingers, fainting or tiredness, and once a transient stroke attack. He also does not ask for help, always taking care and responsibility for himself. The disease started six months after he got his "first commandment", as a chief director of an important industrial firm in Shangai. It was a serious challenge for him, as he was young and unexperienced but he accepted the position without a second thought.

"By duty," I asked?

"No doubt, renounce was not an option," he said.

David is a gifted engineer, a brilliant man who graduated from Polytechnic School like his father. After studying in France, he spent some years at MIT in the United States, where he earned a Ph.D in Physics on steel resilience. He also did research in France and then moved all over the world as an expert consultant. David talks little about his personal emotional life. He has been married and divorced twice, "it is not important for the CV", and "fortunately he has no children", he would not like to "give a bad seed" to transmit his illness. He has no childhood memories before the age of seven, when his father became the director of the largest oil group in Africa, where the rest of the family, including a four-year old sister moved, sending David to an English-speaking boarding school in Switzerland. David did not see his family for a year, and after that met with them only once or twice a year, until the age of 17, when he was admitted in preparatory classes for Polytechnic School. He has no feelings about this long separation; it was his parents' decision, there is nothing to say. Maybe he feels bitter but he is not angry. He does not complain. He learned to be desire-proof and pain-proof, to be resistant. As a fire fighter, he has extinguished feelings, extinguished memories.

Speaking about fire, David mentions that he has no memories from his childhood except for a very blurred image of the opera, "a very strange Russian opera, with a complicated and mysterious plot and dramatic reversal of fortune". But he forgot the name of the opera. The Queen of Spades, I thought.

I consider this association of mine as the first print of countertransference. This female figure of cards that represents a maternal imago of Destiny, who inspired Pouchkine's novel and Tschaikovski's opera, will appear later in the analytic work with David. He preferred a setting twice a week face to face, that seems to him as a "reasonable pleasure", and a "reasonable engagement in therapy" that limits the danger to suffer if we have to be separated. Besides, a classic analytic setting on the couch seems very difficult for him, because of his need to control the object's relation and contain his own temper.

He is a warm and well-mannered person, and he describes himself as a very loyal and reliable man, liked by his colleagues and his teachers. This is the part of a direct conscious identification to his father. He would like to be different from him and to be able to make his own choices, but they are like twins, born on the same day! This is a joke, meaning the same birthday, but it seems to me that being a fake copy of his father is the only way for David to feel in touch with his father. I imagine his father as a very silent and phlegmatic man, an idealized, distant father, with whom it is difficult to be in conflict.

As does his father, David loves literature and music, he plays alto and is very fond of good food. He could have been a conductor or a chef, but he prefers the solitude of chamber music.

Sublimation is an essential defense mechanism for David. Sublimated objects are more reliable and secure for his narcissism than love or hate object relations that can be deceiving or lost. It also appears that David fights against any kind of attachment because he is afraid of getting addicted like a junky or a tramp.

So, the diagnosis of diabetes sounded as a fatal verdict because of the permanent medical control, diet restrictions and the dependency on insulin injections. For about three years David had been very depressed and had developed extremely dangerous and self-destructive addictions: sugar, fat, alcohol, smoking, sex with prostitutes, gambling. In that way he wanted to defy his destiny, to change the cards. He didn't want to make money, not even gambling by passion or getting strong feelings, he is too wise for this, as he said. It was a desperate hope to have a chance, to feel lucky once in his lifetime. Winner gets it all, David tried to turn his loss into a win. Game of life or game of love?

At this moment in therapy, I understood that David's somatic disorder appeared during his first divorce proceeding. However, he insisted on denying the emotional or conflicted impact of his decision to separate from his wife. One day he saw her giving a "burning look" to a man, a friend of his. It was just a look, but David immediately guessed his wife's desire for this man and their love affair. His first thought was to keep cool and avoid scandal. He always had been a gentleman, and this time he felt he had to protect his wife from dishonor, and to protect the two lovers from his own anger. Although he "felt an explosion within", an "earthquake", he had to keep still, to not disturb the right order by containing his emotion and "freezing his feelings". He tried to delete from his mind this unbearable and ridiculous "show", and at the same time he said to himself that "he had to get into the fire like a fireproof robot", like an "oven dish". The importance of sensoriality in David's discourse shows the degree of deconstruction of the affect's quality. David used his addictions as a kind of self-soothing procedure, a particular anti-traumatic defense system, both fragile and non-neurotic, described by psychosomaticians Smadja (1993), Szwec (1993). Several repetitive behaviors involve motor functions and/or sensory perceptions that aim to control levels of excitation which cannot be bound by psychical means belonging to this category. Since the methods employed are not suitable for the kind of discharge that leads to satisfaction, they simply bring about a return to a state of calm. David seeks not for a pleasure but for calm.

"To save, to protect" is the motto of the Marines. This is David's favorite expression concerning his internal affective statement when he was faced with a very violent and unexpected Oedipus conflict that arose suddenly, like a malicious trick of the Queen of Spades. Not prepared by a neurotic castration anxiety and unable to be in conflict, David tried to extinguish the traumatic excitation of the burning Oedipal scene.

His somatic disorganization emerges from the affective charge of the primal scene, as it appears as an après-coup of the first traumatic separation from the parents, which cannot be represented or transformed in mental defenses.

Destiny also strikes twice. Sometime after the diabetes diagnosis, David's little sister, a brilliant young architect, had a serious car accident that left her paralyzed.

She had always been the mother's favorite and David loved her very much, never was he jealous. After the accident, she became the most important thing in the world to her parents; her mother arranged a special room in the family house and changed her professional and personal life in order to look after her daughter. But she had never asked David about his own health problems. David had to be a good son, a good brother and a good soldier.

"Semper Fi" is another motto of the Marines. David has an excessive masochistic investment in suffering as if it is the only way to be faithful to family values and ideals. His mother is a very demanding perfectionist, issued from an aristocratic family, who devoted herself to her husband's career. She participated in humanitarian associations in Africa, taking care of orphans, but was insensitive to her son's life. At the time of his therapy, David had a fantasy about his father who looks to him like a "giant with feet on clay". The father came from a very rigorous Jewish family which converted to Protestantism. He seemed as solid as a rock, but after his daughter's accident he was broken, looking like a wise and obedient little boy, subject to his mother's orders.

This image showed a particular aspect of transference. David trusted me, but he was vigilant. Behind a permanent idealization of paternal transference, I felt a negative maternal one. Each time a triangulation appeared, he either refuted my interpretation or was absent in next session. His associations were quite rich and interesting but they were disconnected from any emotional investment; feelings were disembodied, suppressed or "frozen". David said he didn't have dreams, but had a sensation of nightmares without image. He also observed, with a very acute perception, all things in my office and spoke a lot about them during session: He is wondering about my mental functioning and my capacity to remember what he says or keep him in memory from one session to another.

"Who commands here? The analyst or the patient?" he asks.

He wonders how I can record his thoughts in my mind and recall them without deforming his ideas, and how I keep my files without forgetting him for real. On the other hand, he is convinced that the analyst does not have real feelings. I must not have my own feelings, I have just to be a mirror that reflects exactly what he feels.

What is shown in this mirror? Does this mirror reflect the otherness? The desire for a rival that cannot be represented? I think it is a rather narcissistic mirror in which David searches to fight against a mother's face and mother's look that cannot be able to recognize the drive body of the infant. In this way, David tries to negate the affective component of the drive that he considers a dangerous threat. He tries to anesthetize the living body in order to make it painless, to reduce it to a silent picture. In David's mental functioning, the main defense is the drastic abolition of the affect.

One day after a session, after David had left, I suddenly felt very sad, as if my office was getting silent and empty. David left behind him the impression of a very painful and dense absence. At that moment I probably felt the sadness that had failed to be felt by his mother or himself when the parents left him alone in the boarding school. The failure of his mother's affective investment, that Marty and Fain call maternal function, had been registered as the negative of the missing print.

Is it an unconscious affect or a split affect? J. McDougall calls it the foreclosure of the affect.

According to Green, "The affect is a psychic event in movement waiting to be configurated, to take shape" (Green, 1985, p. 779). In other words, it is something that really took place in the past, but the patient cannot feel it as real, so this feeling has to be embodied by the analyst and therefore, it becomes an intelligible form that can be represented by the patient. I should add that I consider countertransference as a psychic phenomenon belonging to the analysand, but it takes place and becomes alive in the body of the analyst. With neurotic patients, that underlies the analyst's reveries and fantasies, as with Bion's (1962) capacity to dream. With psychosomatic patients, the countertransference is often expressed by bodily, sometimes somatic symptoms felt by the analyst in relation to an alarming anxiety or distress and other affects of suffering that cannot be felt as a real experience by the patient.

Concerning my countertransference, at this moment I was saying that David uses a paradox: he struggles to keep alive the warm flame of the object investment while he has to freeze the burning pain of the object loss. He searches for ways to represent the possibility of staying present in my mind out of the sessions, but when during the session we get too close to the wound, he says to me, quite mysteriously: "You are at Seychelles while I'm in Siberia".

Does Seychelles mean Paradise's lost? Does he use suffering to refer to the cold Siberian exiles as a masochistic way to avoid punishment and the loss of the object love? The sensoriality of the contrast in this metaphor is relevant. His view and his touch began to be damaged because of the diabetes, which is a real prejudice for his sensual feelings and sex relations. At this period, David met a woman, and for the first time he thought that he could fall in love. This was complicated, because she lived in another country and seemed to be a very independent woman. David missed her and was anxious about his body integrity, he was afraid of having a stroke. The castration anxiety made him think about his "emotional amputation" as he said, and his compulsive need to test his resistance.

He was wondering if there was a causal relation between his childhood and his illness and he wanted to know more about the mental functioning of his parents. They are very charming and really warm with their friends, but they are incapable of tenderness with their children or with each other. This time he accepted my interpretation of his own masochistic attitude that aimed to protect himself from pain making him insensitive.

In the next session, after Christmas holiday, David was very anxious and described his neuropathic pains and dysesthesia, like burning and biting. He talked about a conflict at his job and a scientific award ceremony. The winner was a young researcher, ambitious and brilliant. His colleagues were very envious but the young man was not attacked by the malicious arrows of his enemies, because of his mother's presence. She was standing beside her son as a protective shield.

Then David talked about his own father's aging and weakness. He looked like a disabled helpless child depending on mother's care. It is unbearable to him, it reminds him of an old teacher, who was very gentle and passive towards the young students. He would prefer to have a very severe father, a battering father, rather than a nourishing father. He gets upset thinking that his father doesn't dare to speak aloud in the presence of women. Next, he had an association with his own passivity comparing himself with the figure of San Sebastian pierced by arrows. He saw this statue during a journey in Italy with his girlfriend and he thought that it must be terribly painful to be pierced by arrows.

I thought that it was the first time that David had a symbolic figure of his painful and ill body, pierced by insulin injections, like a torture. "You are searching for a shield that protects your pains" I said. He was very touched and answered:

> My illness is my bad half, my dark side, and I cannot deal with this. I wish my mother could see my suffering and watch me, but she had always expected me to be brilliant. In spite of my studies in the U.S., and all my background she still doubts my knowledge of English. My father wanted to give me a perfect education but I felt completely abandoned in the boarding school. Nobody cared about me.

As David talked about his job, I was listening in a floating attention and at this moment I had a fantasy, a memory of the Snow Queen from the Andersen's Tales; that was my favorite fairy tale when I was a child. I was fascinated by the little girl who searched for her best friend, a boy that had been kidnapped by the Snow Queen and locked in the ice castle. When she found him, the boy looked like an ice statue that had completely lost his memory. Then she cried and her warm tears revived the boy. His heart and his body were frozen, but he was still alive.

David's warm voice takes me back from my own reverie and regression. I am hearing that he says: "Maybe there is a way to stay alive and faithful also . . . like Michel Stroggoff, do you remember this novel?" I responded, saying, "He sacrificed himself in order to save the little Czar, because of his love of this child. He has to be a protective shield." "But Stroggoff lost his vision, didn't he?" asked David. "He was blinded by the burning sword, but I forgot the end of the story. I'm sure you know better; I trust your memory."

I am very astonished by the quality of regression and dreaming for both of us in this session. I said to David: "You wish you could trust me as a loving father that protects his son. You would like to show to your father your courage, your love and your faithfulness to him when you were a child, and you endured exile and suffering without complaining, without crying", I added, "But Stroggof saved his eyes, thanks to his tears." David was moved. He had forgotten this detail of the story. He said, "Tears mean that my body is still alive, like my feelings. When

I was four or five, my father read a story every evening before I went to bed. We were very close to each other; at the boarding school everything changed."

My interpretation aimed to transform his passive masochistic submission to the mother's Ideal Ego and conformism into a possibility to share a paternal Superego love. Some years later, David was very surprised to discover two family secrets. His father's family had been traumatized by a violent conflict between two brothers that pushed one of them to kill himself. His mother's little sister was considered the black sheep that dishonored her family because of adultery and an illegitimate child.

When childhood memories appeared in therapy, David remembered he was frightened from a sudden fire in a wood while on a walk with his grandmother who pushed his little sister in the baby carriage. The affect can be reborn from ashes and revive the flame of desire and the demand of the drive body upon the mind for psychic work. What is alive in the ill body looks like a seed of fire, in greek *sperma pyròs*. In Homer's (1924) Fifth Rhapsody of Odysseus, Ulysses is completely alone after the wreck of his boat and the loss of all his companions. The story puts the hero between two islands and between two times, the time of the epic story and the time of Ulysses' own memories and thoughts about what happens. He is hopeless and doesn't know whether he is going to be dead or back home. He has two images: In the first he gets a view of the earth after a terrible tempest and he feels very happy. He compares his emotion with the happiness of the children who see their father coming back to life after a long disease. Then, in the second image, Ulysses is preparing to go to sleep. He covers himself with foliage and branches, and then he buries a lighted torch under the ashes, in order to save a seed of fire, for not having to search for one elsewhere. In this way, he keeps always alive that it could be extinguished. And also, he puts in a safe place, takes care of and cherishes a piece of seed that could breed new objects.

References

Aisenstein, M. (2010). "Les exigences de la représentation", Rapport au 70ème Congrès des psychanalystes de langue française "Entre Psyché et soma ". *Revue Française de Psychanalyse*, XXVI(5):1367–1392.

Alexander, F. (1950). *Psychosomatic Medicine: Its principles and applications*. New York: Norton.

Bion, W. (1962). *Learning from Experience*. Portsmouth, NH: Heinemann.

David, C. (1970). Affect, travail et signification, intervention sur A. Green, L'affect. Rapport sur le XXXème Congrès de psychanalyse des langues romaines, *Revue Française de Psychanalyse*, 5–6:1191–1202.

David, C. (1985). A propos de la représentante de l'affect. *Revue Française de Psychanalyse*, 49(3):797–823.

Ferenczi, S. (1955). Organ neuroses and their treatment. In *Final Contributions to the Problems and Methods of Psychoanalysis* (pp. 22–28). London: Hogarth.

Freud, S. (1915). The Unconscious. In *The Standard Edition of On the History of the Psycho-Analytic Movement, Papers on Metapsychology and Other Works (1914–1916)*, XIV: pp. 159–215. London: Hogarth.

Freud, S. (1916). Introductory Lectures on Psychoanalysis. In *The Standard Edition*, XVI: pp. 1–240. London: Hogarth.
Freud, S. (1926). Inhibitions, Symptoms and Anxiety. In *The Standard Edition*, XX: pp. 75–175. London: Hogarth.
Green, A. (1973/1999). *Le discours vivant*. Paris: Presses Universitaires de France. (1999, *The Fabric of the Affect in Psychoanalytic Discourse*). Translated by Alan Sheridan. London and New York: Routledge New Library of Psychoanalysis.
Green, A. (1985). Reflexions libres sur la représentation de l'affect. *Revue Française de Psychanalyse*, XLIX (3):773–788.
Green, A. (1999). In Discriminating and Not Discriminating Between Affect and Representation. In *The Fabric of Psychoanalytic Discourse* (pp. 292–315). London: Routledge.
Homère. (1989). *L'Odyssée, Chant V. 490*. Paris: Belles Lettres.
Marty, P. (1968). A major process of somatization: The progressive disorganization. *International Journal of Psychoanalysis*, 49:246–249.
Nahmias, J., & Sifneos, P. (1970). Affect and fantasy in patients with psychosomatic disorders. In O.W. Hill, (dir.), *Modern Trends in Psychosomatic Medicine* (p. 126). Boston, Butterworth.
Parat, C. (1995). *L'affect partagé*. Paris: Presses Universitaires de France.
Smadja, C. (1993). A propos des proceeds autocalmants du moi. *Revue Française de Psychosomatique*, 4:9–26.
Smadja, C. (2005/2010). La place de l'affect dans l'économie psychosomatique. In *L'affect, Monographies de La Revue Française de Psychanalyse*. Paris: Presses Universitaires de France. Translated in 2010. The place of affect in the psychosomatic economy. In Aisentein, M. and Rappoport de Aisemberg, E. (eds.), *Psychosomatics Today*. London: Karnac books.
Szwec, G. (1993). Les procédés autocalmants par la recheche de l'excitation. Les galériens volontaires. *Revue Française de Psychomatique*, 4:27–50.

Part IV

Sex, gender and infantile sexuality

Chapter 14

Introduction

Christine Anzieu-Premmereur

The chapters in this section show the role of infantile sexuality in the construction of identity, gender and the "mental" body.

According to Freud, the concept of drive refers to a need in the organism that pushes toward a specific action in order to obtain satisfaction. Drive is a notion connected to a quantity of tension, and a quality associated with anatomical zones at the service of satisfaction, with the help of the object. Therefore, infantile sexuality has a much wider scope than does genital, due to the variability of the sources, aims and objects.

Hallucination of the satisfaction when the object is absent or lost occurs by the means of auto eroticism: this is the emergence of fantasying. This marks the qualitative excitation of an erotogenic zone in the body and the origin of fantasy, when the object of satisfaction – the breast – is taken up into a fantasy. The seductive part of the object also plays its role.

Dominique Scarfone makes a powerful discussion of Freud's affirmation that the psyche is embodied, by showing how the sensations experienced after the trauma of amputation of a limb are connected with the mind thinking and feeling as if the body were intact. If hallucinating an absent part of the body as real can occur as a perception, this means the Body Ego, or the Body Psyche, is a unit. But, as Freud warned us, "psyche is extended, knows nothing about it".

Psychoanalysts listen to psychic life and could forget about its embodiment. Referring to the painful experience of loss and mourning, Scarfone gives amazing examples of a method to alleviate the pain after the loss of a limb, with the visual illusion of actively controlling the missing limb. Pain cannot be repressed, writes Scarfone, and we know how the return of the repressed in the psyche can cause psychic pain – the painful phantom limb is a psychic reality. Scarfone makes a remarkable association with the fetish, when the "absent" part of the body that has to be hallucinated is the female phallus and his elaboration on Freud, along with Laplanche, states that infants, no matter how active they are, remain unprepared and helpless to deal with repressed Infantile sexuality (the Sexual for Laplanche) embedded in the adult messages.

This book benefits greatly from Patricia Gherovici's clinical work with gender issues. She gives an interesting history, starting with Freud and other sexologists, to introduce the complexity of the relation to the body in some patients, when embodiment doesn't play its function to unify anatomy and psyche. Gender affirming surgery, she says comes as the consequence of an identification with a body that is different from the one given at birth – almost as if the enveloping body can be changed like clothes.

Gherovici writes that the sex-gender binary is ending, since we are living in a time that allows gender mutability associated with a large spectrum of sexualities. As in Lacan's mirror stage, the body is a fiction created by identification. The complex process of embodiment doesn't lead always to a unified harmonious body Ego. The interplay between Id and idealization leads the subject to alienation towards his image, in an illusion of wholeness. Some feel trapped in a body they don't experience as theirs; the body is like a vacant wrapping system that modern hormonal and surgical medicine can change. Plastic sexuality is then claimed as a new value. Gherovici traces the limits between anatomic transformation, reproduction, kinship and denial of mortality that analysts face now with their patients. Her Lacanian understanding leads her to point out the fundamental lack in the subject as constitutive of human beings. By showing the case of an alcoholic patient experiencing the body as flesh, as an "envelope", moving from female to male, she demonstrates that obtaining a sexual orientation requires the acceptance of a primal loss.

Infantile sexuality and its constant pressure for satisfaction is at the core of Vaia Tsolas's chapter on the repudiation of femininity – how to leave behind during development the pre-genital mother, the one associated with anal issues and harsh superego.

Tsolas describes two very touching and difficult cases of female patients whose maternal superego has limited their libidinal energy, with a return into the body as a non-symbolized defectiveness; these two women experienced their bodies as sources of narcissistic injury and humiliation, as they struggled with archaic maternal figures and severe bodily symptoms. One patient suffered from vaginismus associated with a masochistic relationship to men, in a sort of sacrifice of her female body due to unconscious loyalty to her father. When the penis represents the maternal phallus, and is associated with destructiveness, penetration is intolerable and the female genitals are a source of anxiety and disgust. Sacrificing genital sexuality then becomes idealized.

The second case shows how the paternal function is at the center of resolving conflicts of the anal phase, leading to the development of the later and mature superego. It tells of a very successful woman who came from an immigrant poor family, which, during her childhood, was often fraught with fighting stemming from matters of jealousy. As a result, she developed as a "tomboy". Analysis helped her regain some of her femininity, and she later married and had children. Ten years later, however, she returned to therapy with resumed feelings of being aggressive, masculine and defective, resulting in an experience of unhappiness as a punishment. When her father was diagnosed with cancer, she lost her sense of stability and in turn was diagnosed with terminal cancer, leading her to believe she had to pay with her life for betraying her mother during childhood. Tsolas describes how she maintained a solid frame to continue therapy while dealing with a difficult countertransference. In women, changing from the maternal object to a paternal one faces the meeting with the early anal superego and the repudiation of femininity.

In short, the body of the drives has to be revived in the consulting room, as these papers show. As Scarfone reminded us, using Laplanche's theory on the Sexual, human beings are helpless at the beginning of their lives, so they must manage infantile sexuality as aroused by adult enigmatic messages.

Chapter 15

Foreign bodies
The body-psyche and its phantoms

Dominique Scarfone

Psychoanalysis emerged from the practice and the thinking of a neurologist, yet it is clearly not neurology. Nor, in my opinion, is there any hope for a seamless synthesis between neuroscience and psychoanalysis, their respective objects and methods being totally different. Psychoanalysis, however, is a peculiar discipline: it is first and foremost a *praxis* whose specific field is constantly in need of being reinstated. The foundational gesture delineating the analytic space needs to be repeated with every session. In terms of its theory, psychoanalysis must also continually reinstate what one could call its "operational closure" (Varela, 1979), i.e. its semi-permeable borders with neighboring disciplines such as biology, philosophy, anthropology, linguistics, etc. The borders must remain semi-permeable because psychoanalysis needs to be constantly informed of everything human all the while it must remain capable of preserving the original stance of its *praxis* and its unique method of accessing the unconscious.

As J.-B. Pontalis wrote:

> Psychoanalytic language often presents a metaphoric character, marked by anthropomorphisms (e.g.: Id, Superego) or by explicit references to non-psychological domains (neurophysiology, biology, mythology). Such metaphorical character has a specific value in psychoanalysis and is not reducible to simply offering images to *illustrate* notions . . . The diversity of the idioms employed should not be understood simply as a diversity in operational models. It reflects the impossibility of a unified language given the very nature of the object to be apprehended.
>
> (Pontalis, 1967, my translation)

In this sense, the language of psychoanalysis occupies a wide semantic spectrum that is both specific to its method of investigation and imposed by the heterogeneous nature of the objects under study. Though this can be a source of misunderstandings, it also gives psychoanalysis its unique heuristic value. Psychoanalysis, indeed, is particularly apt at describing additional folds in the already complex human phenomena. These folds are necessarily heterogeneous, reflecting the complexity and ambiguity of the human being. But psychoanalysis cannot simply make its own the discrete notions of its neighbors. Its semi-permeable border necessarily transforms any foreign concept imported within its domain, so one soon realizes that psychoanalysis cannot but work in its own way and at a specific level of discourse. Hence, if its language may at times seem close to, say, the biological idiom, it is because the ambiguity lies with the human soul itself; a soul that for psychoanalysis is necessarily embodied.

The continued interest for other disciplines not only makes us look beyond the borders of our own, but is by the same token a way of putting our psychoanalytic concepts to a sort of "resonance test," a way of probing even further their meaning and value by confronting them with those of other fields. Thus, while entertaining no hope or wish for a synthesis, I believe it is both possible and useful to start from an apparently pure neurological fact and nevertheless discern a kind of movement similar to those with which we were made familiar by the psychoanalytic endeavor. With this objective in mind, and in line with the "spectral" nature of our discipline, I was brought to ask myself a number of questions such as the following: What is there in common between a phantom pain, a repetitive utterance in aphasia, a fetish and a post-traumatic state? In what way do these phenomena regard the life of the Body-Psyche? How do they relate to Freud's assertion: "Psyche is extended," or, more plainly, "Psyche is embodied"?

Phantom limbs, phantom pain

Speaking of "spectral," let us turn our attention to the work of a well-known American neurologist, V.S. Ramachandran, on the phenomenon of phantom limbs and more precisely on phantom pain, i.e. a pain that persists after the loss of a limb, accidentally or through surgery (Ramachandran, 1998; Ramachandran & Blakeslee, 1999).

If one needed an additional argument to support the view that the psyche is embodied, phantom pain offers a most convincing one. For while the body-part itself has vanished, its pain is nonetheless real. One could of course wonder whether such painful experience is psychic at all; could it not be deemed a very basic physical phenomenon, especially considering that intense pain actually paralyses psychic functions? My answer is that, on the contrary, this situation is exemplary in that it actually allows for a better understanding of what the notion of embodiment of the psyche is really about. A pain persisting in the absence of the limb in which it is felt; what better illustration of the inseparability of body and psyche? Except that the dual denomination "body" and "psyche" can be misleading if it suggests a physical/psychological dichotomy or a mixture thereof. The body-psyche we speak of rather engages a single subject and its world. Merleau-Ponty is here a most valuable guide, remarking that a phantom limb is to be conceived as neither a neuronal trace nor a representation of the missing part:

> The phenomenon, disfigured by both physiological and psychological explanations, can on the contrary be understood in the perspective of being-in-the-world. What in us refuses the mutilation and the deficiency is an 'I' engaged in a certain physical and inter-human world, an I that keeps reaching for its

world in spite of deficiencies and amputations and that to this extent does not *de jure* recognize them.

(Merleau-Ponty, 1945, pp. 96–97, my translation)

It ensues that the living body-psyche, in spite of the hyphen at once separating and uniting the two terms, is actually a single entity possessing – and engaged in – its own specific world. Consider the famous maxim written by Freud a few weeks before his death: "Psyche is extended; knows nothing about it" (Freud, 1939).

For one thing, the statement could seem a bit paradoxical: as much as it asserts the embodiment of the psyche, this rather radical sentence seems to draw a watertight barrier of unconsciousness – one is tempted to say: "a barrier of repression" – between the psyche and its body. But what the notion of embodiment-with-unconsciousness offers is rather, in my view, a *caveat* against the illusion of a conscious access to the physiological body, precisely because there is no actual separation to be found between what are actually two aspects of a single entity. If a repression is to be posited, it is precisely the one happening *within* the body-psyche unit and which yields the notion of a separation. Our daily parlance and pre-reflexive impressions refer to such a separation, one which may have some practical advantages in the sense that ignoring the materiality of the body, i.e. the third person point of view on our embodiment, is probably the best way for achieving a unitary presence to the world. We believe our mind "commands" our body, hence the impression of being a subject, from which the illusion of an abstract – i.e. disembodied – subjectivity ensues. But what we feel to be something *substantially* distinct (the famous Cartesian duality of *res extensa* and *res cogitans*) is in fact a distinctive mode of functioning. Psychoanalytic practice and theory, in line with other disciplines, teaches us indeed that an "operational closure," analog to the one invoked earlier (Varela, 1979), operates in delimiting what, for lack of another word, we keep calling the body-psyche. The operational closure institutes not a difference in substance, but a specific set of internal rules, different from the ones reigning at the physiological level. Thus the body we have access to as psychoanalysts is always already a psychical body, not to be mistaken for the body studied by biologists or, more generally, from a third-person point of view. From a psychological standpoint, however, we can say that psychic functioning does not readily acknowledge its embodiment.

Yet, the story is not that simple. While Freud's maxim of 1939 seems without appeal in terms of the psyche's unconsciousness regarding the body, this late view of Freud's had been in fact already mitigated some 44 years earlier, in the *Project* (Freud, 1895), where he wrote: "Pain sets the ϕ as well as the ψ system in motion, there is no obstacle to its conduction, it is the most imperative of all processes" (Freud, 1895, p. 307).

This means that pain takes exception to the notion of a watertight unconsciousness of the psyche regarding its embodiment, and this, remarkably, is also in line with what Freud theorized about the drives. So, to the question: "Is pain physical or psychical?" the plain answer is that it is both, or better, that in the logic expounded above, the question is not well put, in the sense that what is "psychical" is always already "physical" and *vice versa*. In this regard, pain is a good starting point since, as Freud clearly suggests in the *Project*, it seems to transfix the psyche and to impose on it the tragic experience of its bodily substrate. But there is more. For one thing, the psychic paralysis caused by physical pain is not different from the paralysis that follows, for instance, the sudden experience of losing a loved one, until, that is, a process of mourning takes effect; nor is it different from the paralysis caused by other sudden, unforeseen traumatic events.

The unitary physical-psychic status of pain related to loss is, in my view, even more strongly supported by Ramachandran's invention of a method and a tool for alleviating a phantom pain, a procedure in which it is difficult indeed to tell the physical and the psychical apart. The tool consists of a wooden box with an open top and side, divided in two halves by a partition that is covered on both sides by a mirror. The subject experiencing a phantom pain in, for instance, a missing hand, is asked to insert his intact limb in one part of the box while the amputated limb is inserted in the other compartment. The subject is then asked to look through the open top and into the mirror reflecting the intact hand. In this way the subject actually "sees the phantom"; he is given the illusion of seeing his painful amputated limb whole again. Ramachandran thereupon instructs the subject to accomplish certain maneuvers, according to the nature of the pain. For instance, if the subject feels a pain caused by the fingernails being planted in the palm of the missing hand due to a phantom clenched fist (as the real one was just before its accidental amputation), he is instructed to clench his real fist and look at its image in the mirror while he then slowly opens the hand. What the subject then sees in the mirror is the opening of the *missing* hand and this illusion is quite effective in suppressing the phantom pain. Thanks to such a contraption, the body-psyche (Ramachandran would probably say: "the brain") is indeed informed that the painful hand is there again and moreover that it can be opened. Such vivid information is sufficient to suppress the pain, at least momentarily.

In Ramachandran's neurological view, the persistence of pain in a missing body-part is due to the fact that the sensory cortex cannot get *new inputs* from the part in question. It therefore remains fixated to the last feedback it got just before the tragic accident. In the absence of a new feedback, the motor cortex keeps "contracting" the concerned muscles, thereby maintaining active, by association, the mnemic image of pain associated with the contraction and the planted fingernails, thus keeping the pain real and present (Ramachandran & Blakeslee, 1999, pp. 53–54).

This is not the place to discuss the epistemological questions this original and important discovery entails. For the purpose I am pursuing, I wish to stress the fact that the phantom pain corresponds to the last "cortical/psychical" image that was formed just before the trauma, an image which persists in spite – or perhaps because – of the novel anatomical situation. I also wish to underscore the fact that in Ramachandran's technique, it is not simply a matter of seeing the missing hand whole again: the patient has to see it opening by his active will. This means that it is a matter of making *active* the hand that was *passively* lost. Indeed, the neural "freeze-frame" situation that seems to cause the pain mainly concerns the motor traces as they persist "clenching" the fist and lack the relaxing feedback. So that while the subject can visually test the reality of the amputation, he cannot put this information to any use until all of the concerned memory traces can be modified or overwritten, as it were, by a new *active* engagement in that reality. The *motor* traces, indeed, were "frozen" in the last state they were in just prior to the loss of the hand and need to be reactivated.

This is congruent with a capital difference Marie Leclaire and I have established between what is usually called reality testing and a preliminary phase to it that we dubbed "actuality testing" (Leclaire & Scarfone, 2000). Reality testing is the final result of a more complex process that involves unconscious mechanisms. Most important among these is the summoning of motor memory traces thanks to which the hallucinatory phenomena can be inhibited and the way cleared for the distinction between a perception and a memory trace.

In the case of the phantom pain, the "actuality" of the painful limb contradicts the "testing of reality" operating through perception. This problem is due to the impossibility for the subject to activate and implement the motor memory traces. While the pain is, in a way, a hallucination, the painful experience is nevertheless real; it is *psychically real*, or, as Leclaire and I prefer to say, *psychically actual*. It is "actual" in the sense that it is now trapped in a frozen time frame, "actual time," as I came to call it (Scarfone, 2015).

Merleau-Ponty can here again help us clarify the issue. In discussing the phantom limb phenomenon, he finds it comparable to the phenomenon of repression, by which the subject:

> remains blocked in his attempt [to accomplish a desire] and spends his energy in endlessly trying to accomplish it in spirit. The passage of time does not carry away the impossible projects; it does not seal off the traumatic experience, the subject remaining open to the same impossible future, if not in his explicit thoughts at least in his actual being. One present among all presents thus acquires an exceptional value, displacing the others and voiding them of their value of authentic presents.
> (Merleau-Ponty, *op. cit.*, p. 98, my translation)

This is an important aspect of the problem, shedding light on the fact that even as the motor traces can be activated thanks to Ramachandran's box, pain relief *is only temporary*. The exercise must be repeated over and over. The motor traces may well be summoned, the "time trap" is still in place; the mere activation of the physiological substrate apparently failed to achieve a new state where a one-handed subject and his corresponding world effectively replace the two-handed ones. In other words, an effective process of mourning has not yet happened through which the amputated subject might finally and truly recognize himself as such. One could even wonder – from a strictly theoretical point of view, which may or may not be corroborated by the actual clinical experience – if using Ramachandran's box is not, at least in the beginnings, caught in a paradox, as it works on two sides of the problem at once. On the one side, it helps the subject experience the actual release feed-back, thus alleviating the pain, but it also keeps present the visual image of what is really the missing limb, thus confirming what one could call the "two-handed being-in-the-world". This view seems to fit well with another of Ramachandran's own observations. Among patients he visited in an Indian leprosarium, the persons who lost their limbs *gradually* did not experience phantom limbs, a fact on which the author emits the following hypothesis:

> "Perhaps the *gradual* loss of the limb or the simultaneous presence of progressive nerve damage caused by the leprosy bacterium is somehow critical. This might allow their brains to readjust their body image to match reality."
> (Ramachandran & Blakeslee, 1999, p. 58)

This hypothesis is highly congruent, I believe, with the notion of a genuine mourning process where the "two-handed being-in-the-world," something more encompassing than the "body image," is gradually modified to account for the new situation. A situation in which there is no ground for asking if a physical or psychical fact is involved, since it is, as we already saw, a unitary reality, one which in Freudian terms we call "psychic reality".

Phantom pain and psychic reality

All too frequently – perhaps because physical pain is not usually involved – psychic reality is referred to in terms of some not-so-real, subjective psychological state. Ordinarily indeed, one psychical reality is superseded by another, in a fluid process of overwriting or transcription. This is what Freud had posited regarding memory traces and their vicissitudes in a letter to Wilhelm Fliess. Freud equated a failure in this process of transcription to what, clinically, we call repression (Freud, 1896, p. 208). So, to go back to Ramachandran's example, the motor image of the clenched fist in the amputated hand cannot be overwritten, and we saw that Merleau-Ponty thinks that a phantom limb phenomenon amounts to a form of repression. Now this is highly interesting from a metapsychological point of view since it sheds light on two important pillars of the Freudian theory: repression and the drives.

On the one hand, as Freud duly noted in his metapsychological paper "Repression," *pain cannot be repressed* (Freud, 1915, p. 146). Pain is then a most precious negative case regarding repression, allowing us to gain a better understanding of the phenomenon. Let us retain the idea that repression is a failure of transcription or of overwriting. Let us also consider that in the same paper, Freud refers to pain by calling it a "pseudo-instinct" (Freud, 1915) – or, in a more contemporary translation, a *pseudo-drive* (*Pseudotriebe*). If we now remember that repression and the drives are dialectically bound together, and that the return of the repressed is defended against by the Ego because it causes psychic pain, then we have a good illustration of how the repressed is a psychic reality just as much as the painful phantom clenched fist. The difference between the pain in a phantom limb and its psychic equivalent in other clinical circumstances is that in the latter case the psyche may summon supplementary defense mechanisms, displacements and symptom-formations that are not at the disposal of the amputated subject – at least not for what regards the pain.

The drives, on the other hand, are also not repressible in themselves: all repression can do is separate their two psychic "representatives," i.e. disconnect a representation from its quantum of affect, thereby rendering it ineffective at the level of consciousness. But the repressed always strides to make a comeback, endowed as it is by an "upward drive" as Freud still remarked in one of his late writings (Freud, 1937b, p. 266). The upward drive, that is, the tendency to spring back in search of expression, precisely reflects the relative failure of the "overwriting" that we could also call a failure of "translation," "transcription" or simply "elaboration." What could not be successfully transcribed and elaborated in a more opportune version thereof – stays behind in a repressed state, but this state has nothing passive about it. It behaves as an irritation that tries to make its way upward in a drive-like fashion. When the psyche is sound enough, it can defend against this revenant by wrapping it in new shrouds (substitutive ideas, conversion, displacement of affect), but when this is impossible, the return of the repressed takes other forms, not unlike the phantom pain in a missing limb: for instance, compulsive thinking and delusions, hallucinations or straight painful affect as in melancholic depression, down to blunt somatic pain and illness. Hence, the picture emerges of a true dialectical relationship between repression and the drives, in that the repressed behaves exactly like a drive. If we now wish to avoid a metaphysical conception of the drives, we'd better heed Merleau-Ponty's lesson in avoiding the "psychological vs. physiological" sort of explanation (see above) and simply consider that if it behaves like a drive then it *is* a drive.

What the phantom limb and its pain helps us understand better is that, since psyche is by definition embodied, psychic reality is just as "actual" and effective as material reality. In the experience of phantom pain, indeed, body and psyche appear inextricably interwoven, transfixed in an eternal painful present by the persistence of the configuration which was active at the time of the accident, and the same logic applies to the sort of pain that results from the irritative spine of the repressed a.k.a. the drives.

The aphasic's last words

In his book *On Aphasia* (1891), Freud cites an observation made by Hughlings Jackson regarding a peculiar phenomenon: immediately after a cerebral stroke that causes motor aphasia, patients may still have at their disposal, beyond "yes" and "no", some residue of speech which "frequently consists of a vigorous curse"

(p. 61) and of which Jackson says that "even in normal persons such an utterance belongs to the emotional and not to the intellectual language" (*loc. cit.*). In other cases, however, it is not a curse, but, surprisingly, a "phrase of special significance" bearing a seemingly intellectual content that one would have expected to be lost. The explanation of such persistence is that "these utterances are the last words produced by the speech apparatus before injury or even at a time when there already existed an awareness of the impending disability" (pp. 61–62).

A parallel can obviously be drawn with the phenomenon of phantom pain: from a neurological point of view, in both cases, there is a persistence of a residual motor image after a tragic loss of a limb or of a function, a loss happening suddenly and finding the subject unprepared. In motor aphasia, then, it is as though the speaking body-psyche was left hanging on to the last mnemic image available, a "stump of language" as it were, pursuing a semblance of activity but whose stereotyped repetition indicates that it is not real language after all. Ramachandran's neurological hypothesis probably still applies: no new motor commands can be produced, this time because of damage to the neural tissue itself. The difference with phantom pain is that in the latter the painful *sensory* mnemic image seems to prevail, while in aphasia it is the *motor* image. These are, indeed, the last respective productions before the tragic loss. We have seen that motor traces are involved in phantom limbs and they certainly are concerned in aphasia; in both cases they are stuck in repetition. In aphasia too, the residual speech elements lack the capacity to be followed by other sentences, and are therefore incapable of "becoming." But it is not only sentences that are prevented from becoming, it is the whole speaking subject, who is just as inextricably woven with language as it is with its body-psyche.

Kurt Goldstein, quoted by Merleau-Ponty (1945), wrote that "[a]s soon as Man uses language to establish a living relationship with himself or his fellow human beings, language is no longer an instrument, *it is no longer a means, it is a manifestation, a revelation of the intimate being and of the psychic bond that links to the world and to mankind*" (p. 229, my translation, italics in the original).

The amputation of language occurring in aphasia is therefore even more fundamental than the one that leads to phantom limbs. The "stumps" of language cannot even be compensated by phantom sentences. We have mentioned this phenomenon, however, as it illustrates once again the organism's emergency reaction to a sudden loss, in the form of a repetition compulsion that manifests the residual effort at "manifestation," to use Goldstein's term. It also serves to introduce the next phenomenon.

The "choice" of a fetish

The Dutch psychoanalyst Maurits Katan was able, many years ago, to establish a strong parallelism between Freud's report on the Jacksonian persistence phenomenon in aphasia and another fact, this time described from a strictly psychoanalytic point of view: the mechanism of the choice of a fetish (Katan, 1969).

In his paper "Fetishism" of 1927, Freud proposes indeed that such "choice" can, in many cases, be explained by the circumstances in which the fetishist-to-be was brought to contemplate, in sheer horror, the female genital organs:

> One would expect that the organs or objects chosen as substitutes for the absent female phallus would be such as appear as symbols of the penis... This may happen often enough, but is certainly not a deciding factor. It seems rather that when the fetish is instituted some process occurs which reminds one of the stopping of memory in traumatic amnesia. As in this latter case, the subject's interest comes to a halt half-way, as it were; it is as though the last impression before the uncanny and traumatic one is retained as a fetish. Thus the foot or shoe owes its preference as fetish – or a part of it – to the circumstance that the inquisitive boy peered at the woman's genitals from below, from her legs up.
>
> (Freud, 1927, p. 155)

We can see how this mechanism of election of a fetish, though not universal, perfectly coincides with the course of events in the formation of the aphasic's speech residues or of phantom pain in an absent limb. What is remarkable is that in the fetishist too, the problem is one of "disappearance" or "amputation," utterly imaginary as they may be. Moreover, the fetishist too, finds a "solution" resembling that of a phantom limb, only in reverse: a prosthesis, a concrete artifact destined to seal off the disavowal of the absence of penis. The fetishist's situation is thus a mirror image of the true phantom limb: the loss is in this case imaginary and the solution is concrete; yet it attests in its own way the embodiment of the fetishist's psyche, compelled as it is to find a material replacement for the "missing" body-part. And here again there is an attempt at transforming the *passive* condition of unpreparedness into activity.

Unpreparedness, and therefore surprise, are indeed eminently at work in the fetishist's traumatic experience. Paralyzed by the unexpected horrific sight, the body-psyche of the fetishist finds itself entrapped in a loop of repetition, forming a stereotyped scene similar to that of the aphasic repeating the last phrase uttered before the cerebral accident. The fetishist, however, goes one step further: in finding a prosthetic solution to what he views as the "mutilated" female genitals, he is able to fixate the horror in a scenography that enables him to perform sexually. The fetishist's prosthesis thereby achieves a result resembling, all other things being equal, the one obtained by the perception of an intact limb in Ramachandran's box! And in both cases, should it be noted, it is a matter of reestablishing the integrity of the narcissistic body image.

Post-traumatic states

In many ways, what I have described until now strongly resonates with the theory of trauma formulated by Freud in *Beyond the Pleasure Principle* (Freud, 1919), where unpreparedness indeed plays a decisive role. In this important work – usually presented as a major turn in his thinking – Freud's ideas were nevertheless in a clear continuity with the so-called "physicalists" whom he so much admired and learned from in the 1890s. More precisely, this is an application of the Helmholtzian model of the brain-mind. In this model, indeed, the brain-mind, as an "Helmholtzian machine," is devoted to keeping the level of free energy at its lowest; in psychological terms this amounts to being prepared so as to avoid surprises (Friston, 2010).

Unpreparedness means that the whole system is in danger of being overwhelmed by the high level of free energy involved in a traumatic experience. Regardless of the sort of trauma – whether cerebral, as in aphasia; physical, as in limb amputation; or perceptual, as in fetishism – the same laws seem to apply: the energy of the impact must somehow be bound. So, it's all very natural to see Freud, in his landmark writing of 1919, identify binding as the fundamental task of the psychic apparatus (Freud, *op. cit*. p. 30).

The phenomena I have examined above allow us to establish yet another connection with the theory of trauma, this time regarding the repetition compulsion. In post-traumatic states, indeed, the form taken by repetition will also depend on the last scene perceived before the horror. As for the role eventually attributable to the repetition compulsion, one can easily converge with Freud's idea that it constitutes the psyche's attempt at regaining mastery over the course of events rather than being irremediably overcome by the magnitude of the surprise. It is as though the body-psyche tried to "rewind" the sequence of events in order to be prepared, this time around, when the unavoidable happens. For when some preparation is possible, in thought or in action, the psyche, though bathing in anxiety, is spared the traumatic paralysis of its functions, and preserves its capacity to evolve and adapt to new situations rather than become captive of repetition.

Thus, the 1919 theory of trauma makes its own contribution to the thesis that psyche is embodied. Actually, all versions of the theory of trauma, including the early one formulated around the genesis of hysteria, have in common the view that trauma triggers an effort at elaboration that will eventually abort to various degrees. The major difference between the earlier and the later theory is that in the later version, just as in the cases examined above, the process of retroactive elaboration (*après-coup* or *Nachträglichkeit*) is impeded by the post-traumatic state of shock. In all cases, however, it is the body-psyche's narcissistic image of integrity that ends up shattered. A definite parallelism exists also between the various alleviating strategies that can be found, be it the invention of the mirror-box for making the absent limb visible and active again, or the institution of a fetish as a way of reestablishing the imaginary integrity of the female body. At any rate, repetition is never absent: the aphasic patient repeats the same pseudo-words while the fetishist must repeat the same scenario over and over, and Ramachandran's mirror-box must be used time and again, as the pain tends to come back, at least until a method is hopefully found favoring the gradual modification of the subject's mode of being-in-the-world and the genuine mourning of the lost limb.

A general view

Spectacular as they may be, the traumas we have examined here are but special cases in which a body-psyche stumbles upon some major obstacle that impedes its normal functioning, preventing the accomplishment of its basic task: binding the energy, avoiding surprise. It is however important to remind that, for one thing, in the well-established Freudian tradition, cases such as these operate as magnifying glasses helping to delineate more ordinary, "normal" processes. Secondly, that the description of normal processes themselves eventually reaches a point beyond which no new elements can be found.

In one of his late papers, Freud referred to such a final obstacle as the "biological bedrock" which, according to him, translates psychologically into the "repudiation of femininity" in both genders. It is there that he invokes the now notorious "envy of penis" in females, while in males he infers the refusal of passivity, namely the passivity towards another male (Freud, 1937a, p. 250 ff.). Against Freud, I suggest that the so-called "repudiation of femininity" has little to do with the stereotyped socially determined picture of the feminine to which he refers, and that *in both genders*, what is at work is a repudiation of the *primal passivity* due to the primacy of the other, in the sense expounded by the philosopher Emmanuel Levinas. In his view indeed, to be human is to be inescapably exposed to – as well as obsessed, besieged and even persecuted by – the other human (Levinas, 1978).

For us psychoanalysts, this fundamental passivity is redolent of the infantile state of *Hilflösigkeit (helplessness)* that Freud invoked in the Project of 1895. A notion that is today revoked by many, in view of the discovery that even neonates are, behaviorally, anything but passive. If, however, we examine the infantile situation from another angle, we find, following Laplanche, that in spite of its active engagement with the helpful other (*Nebenmensch*) – and in fact *because* of such engagement – the *infans* is indeed in a state of inherent primal passivity. For no matter how active the infant may be within the scene of attachment, it is all the same passively submitted to the impact of what Laplanche, in his theory of generalized seduction, dubbed the repressed *Sexual*, whose disturbing effects travel embedded in the adult's well-meaning messages; an enigmatic payload for which the child has no code of translation (Laplanche, 2011). Therefore, while the mechanisms of attachment operate within a relatively symmetrical relationship where both the *infans* and the caretaker are *active* partners, the *Sexual* within the adult's messages necessarily finds the *infans* in a state of unpreparedness. Actually, the adult himself is normally unaware of the sexual dimension of his communication. The child is then passively exposed to an unavoidable, though attenuated, form of trauma that will eventually entail a primal fixation, a primordial split within the body-psyche: a split we call primal repression, instantiating the systemic differences in the body-psyche between unconscious and preconscious-conscious processes.

It is remarkable, however, that while the *infans* is a subject who cannot speak – this is the literal meaning of *in-fans* – and could therefore be assimilated to the *a-phasic* patient, its actual trajectory in response to the trauma is the exact opposite of that of the aphasic. If all goes well, the inescapable trauma of seduction shall elicit in him active processes of translation and overwriting, partly successful and partly failed, but which end up yielding the unique individual complexion of its body-psyche. In an optimal situation, far from becoming entrapped in stereotypic repetition, the *infans* will on the contrary start producing its personal idiom. What matters, then, is if the *infans* is allowed, or not, to evolve towards such a favorable outcome. More precisely, the question is if the adult's message – necessarily contaminated by the repressed sexuality of the emitter – will implant itself at the surface of the infant's body-psyche as a relatively benign though constant irritation, triggering differentiation and evolution – this is Laplanche's "implantation" – or if the relationship between adult and infant is such that the former's message actually penetrates and invades the infant's internal space, paralyzing the normal processes of differentiation and individuation – Laplanche's "intromission" (Laplanche, 1990). In other words, will the impact of the other be seminal or will it cause a massive impingement not unlike the major traumas we have examined earlier? It is a question regarding the possibility for the psyche of the infant to come into being through its own autonomous "operational closure." A closure whose end-result is a *subject*, i.e. a thinking and speaking center of action. In the best case scenario, this subject's psyche will be able to work under the auspices of the pleasure principle, keeping clear, as much as possible, of pain and trauma.

The irony is that in the most favorable cases, the subject's psyche will reach a state where it can be forgetful of its embodied nature. Yet, the encounter with the other's *Sexual* will have implanted in the infant's body-psyche the seeds of the sexual drives, i.e. a now internal source of irritation and potential pain. The sexual *drives* – contrary to the sexual *instincts* that show up at puberty – are therefore not biologically inborn, as Freud thought; their sources are rather the residues of the infant's (partially failed) translations of the enigmatic messages of the Other (Laplanche, 1987). And it is mainly *this* aspect of its embodiment – the pregenital sexual drives – that the psyche will egregiously manage to ignore, with variable results. Pushing the metaphor a bit, such repression of the drives could be seen as a kind of self-amputation, entailing, in return, its own sort of phantoms: the unconscious or pre-conscious phantasies that the body-psyche will be brought to construct.

So much so that, when a psychoanalyst offers to listen to a subject who struggles to (not) know what ails him, she is engaging the analysand in a process somewhat comparable to Ramachandran's mirror-box. By asking the analysand to speak freely, she invites the highly complex, internal – embodied – phantasy formations to come out through the thin slit of the spoken language so that they may get back to him through the sensory channels, as if they came from the outside (Freud, 1923). In this way the repudiated formations can in part be re-appropriated through the active re-elaboration of what is made actual and visible within the analytic space, mainly in the transference. But let me be clear that the analyst is no mirror, no more than interpretation is meant to be a fetishistic prosthesis. When such is the case, it is, I suppose, because the words were not yet found that could instantiate in the psychic landscape a vanishing point of tolerable incompleteness; a capacity for mourning and for accepting the inescapable passivity; an acceptance through which otherness can be welcome, this time as a source of inspiration instead of an illusory prosthetic totality.

References

Freud, S. (1891/1953). *On Aphasia: A Critical Study*. Translated by E. Stengel. New York: International University Press.
Freud, S. (1895). The Project for a Scientific Psychology. In *The Standard Edition of the Complete Psychological Works of Sigmund Freud*. I: pp. 283–397. London: The Hogarth Press and the Institute of Psychoanalysis (hereafter *Standard Edition*).
Freud, S. (1896/1985). Letter of December 6, 1896. In *The Complete Letters of S. Freud to W. Fliess*. Translated and edited by J.M. Masson. Cambridge, MA and London, UK: Harvard University Press, pp. 207–209.
Freud, S. (1915). Repression. *Standard Edition*, XIV:143–158.
Freud, S. (1919). Beyond the Pleasure Principle. *Standard Edition*, XVIII:3–64.
Freud, S. (1923). The Ego and the Id. *Standard Edition*, XIX:3–66.
Freud, S. (1927). Fetishism. *Standard Edition*, XXI:149–157.
Freud, S. (1937a). Analysis Terminable and Interminable. *Standard Edition*, XXIII:211–253.
Freud, S. (1937b). Constructions in Analysis. *Standard Edition*, XXIII:257–269.
Freud, S. (1939). Findings, Ideas, Problems. *Standard Edition*, XXIII:299–300.
Friston, K. (2010). The Free-Energy Principle: A Unified Brain Theory? *Nature Reviews Neuroscience*, 11(February 2010):127–138. doi:10.1038/nrn2787.
Katan, M. (1969). The Link Between Freud's Works on Aphasia, Fetishism and Constructions in Analysis. *International Journal of Psycho-Analysis*, 50:547–553.
Laplanche, J. (1987/2016). *New Foundations for Psychoanalysis*. (Jonatahan House, Transl.) New York: The Unconscious in Translation.
Laplanche, J. (1990/1999). Implantation, Intromission. In Fletcher, J. (ed.), *Essays on Otherness*. London and New York: Routledge, pp. 136–139.
Laplanche, J. (2011). *Freud and the Sexual*. New York: The Unconscious in Translation.
Leclaire, M., & Scarfone, D. (2000). Vers une conception unitaire de l'épreuve de réalité. *Revue Française de Psychanalyse*, LXX(3), pp. 885–912.
Levinas, E. (1978). *Autrement qu'être ou au-delà de l'essence*. La Haie: Martinus Nijhoff.
Merleau-Ponty, M. (1945). *Phénoménologie de la perception*. Paris: Gallimard, Collection "Tel".
Pontalis, J.-B. (1967). Question de mots. In *Après Freud*. Paris: Gallimard, Coll. Tel, pp. 157–178.
Ramachandran, V.S. (1998). The Perception of Phantom Limbs; The D.O. Hebb Lecture. *Brain*, 121:1603–1630.
Ramachandran, V.S., & Blakeslee, S. (1999). *Phantoms in the Brain: Probing the Mysteries of the Human Mind*. New York: Harper & Collins.
Scarfone, D. (2015). *The Unpast: The Actual Unconscious*. New York: The Unconscious in Translation.
Varela, F.J. (1979). *Principles of Biological Autonomy*. New York: Elsevier North-Holland.

Chapter 16

Botched bodies

Inventing gender and constructing sex

Patricia Gherovici

When in 2010, inspired by my clinical practice, I published *Please Select Your Gender: From the Invention of Hysteria to the Democratizing of Transgenderism*, I had in mind a book in which I could explore what I had learnt about sexual identity from analysands who identified as trans.

One of my aims was also to critique the gender/sex divide in view of Jacques Lacan's account of sexual difference. Back in 2010, I could not foresee the trans wave that then swept away pop culture's imagination, engulfed psychiatric and psychoanalytic practices and became a tsunami. In the post-gender era, many were left behind amidst the ruins of the old binary.

My new work aims at assessing the gains, the new trends, and the concepts necessary to make sense of what has happened. However, despite the increasing, even obsessive, media presence of transgender people, the transgender community continues to be an understudied population, no matter which discipline is framing the work. This situation is even more pronounced in the psychoanalytic field.

Botched encounters

One has to acknowledge that psychoanalysis has bungled, mismanaged, and mishandled the approach to non-normative expressions of gender and sexuality, missing uniquely promising opportunities. However, this pattern of misrecognition should not be blamed on psychoanalysis itself, at least in so far as Freud is concerned.

One may remember that in the early days of psychoanalysis, Freud worked with sexologists like Magnus Hirschfeld, the so-called Dr. Einstein of Sex, who founded the world's first sexual research institute in Berlin; he was a pioneering researcher, clinician, and activist, a key figure in the early days of psychoanalysis. Indeed, he was one of the six founders of the pioneering Berlin Psychoanalytic Society.

Freud and Hirschfeld collaborated closely. While Freud contributed articles to his journals, Hirschfeld took a serious interest and an active role in the psychoanalytic movement. In August 1908, Hirschfeld co-founded with Karl Abraham the

Berlin Psychoanalytic Society (Gay, 1998, p. 141). In 1911, during the third international Weimar congress of psychoanalysts, Freud greeted Hirschfeld warmly as an honored guest, calling him a "Berlin authority on homosexuality" (Bullough, 1994, p. 64). However, even with this official recognition, Hirschfeld abruptly left the Berlin Psychoanalytic Society because it seems that Jung objected to his homosexuality (Bullough, 1994, p. 141).

Hirschfeld's departure deeply embittered Freud, who saw his advocacy of homosexual rights as a positive development. From the beginning, Freud encouraged Abraham to work with Hirschfeld (Gay, 1998, p. 181).

It is about time to address this botched relationship and take up again a debate that was cut short by the widening distance between psychoanalysis and the then emerging clinic of transsexualism. Thus, one can say that psychoanalysis has a sex problem in more than one sense.

Transgender activists and scholars have been wary of psychoanalysis with good reasons. In both subtle and brutal ways, psychoanalysis has a history of coercive hetero-normatization and pathologization of non-normative sexualities and genders, but my contention is that such homophobic and transphobic history was founded on a biased and selective interpretation of Freud's texts. If many normative theories about sex and gender claim to derive from Freudian psychoanalysis, in fact nothing could be farther from what we can observe today in the clinical practice.

Body trouble

I discovered something that I found important about the body in my psychoanalytic practice when working with analysands identifying as trans who have a complex relation to their bodies. Some will say that they are in a body of the wrong (opposite) sex, making explicit the fact that we all need to establish some kind of relation to our bodies. Others do not want to align their bodies within the male/female binary and prefer to place themselves somewhere in-between.

I am not arguing here that there is something specific in trans bodies as opposed to normative gendered bodies, but rather that the trans experience shows us the disjunction between how subjects experience their bodies and the given corporeal contours of their flesh. Such a disjunction is not pathological but universal, I would claim, adding that there has to be a process of embodiment at play for everyone in order to bridge the gap between "body" and "soul."

Indeed, who has not been confronted with the challenges of embodying carnal reality, of fleshing out subjectivity? Adolescence presents us with many cases in which we see growing teenagers devote excessive energy in an effort to imaginarize their changing bodies, in fact because they want to embody their flesh. The time adolescents spend in front of mirrors or taking selfies stresses the importance of the libidinal investment in the specular identifications; these identifications support the body as a whole, let them inhabit their bodies because they help the image dress the flesh. Let us note that what is pursued in a gender reassignment or gender confirmation is not just an anatomical change but a different embodiment. Here is why sex reassignment is now called gender *affirming* surgery, which means the ratification of an experience.

This process has been well described by Janet Mock, a journalist and trans activist; Mock calls it "realness": "To embody 'realness,'" Mock explains, "enables trans women to enter spaces with a lower risk of being rebutted or questioned, policed or attacked. 'Realness' is a pathway to survival" (Mock, 2014, p. 116).

Mock explains further: "I am a trans woman of color, and that identity has enabled me to be truer to myself, offering me an anchor from which I can uplift my visible blackness, my often invisible trans womanhood, my little-talked-about native Hawaiian heritage, and the many iterations of womanhood they combine" (249).

Therefore, Realness is not "passing," neither is it "conforming." Can this concept help us make sense of what took place in the public gender transition of Caitlyn Jenner? Recall that when Jenner's gender change became official in a *Vanity Fair* cover captioned "Call me Caitlyn," Jenner tweeted "I'm so happy after such a long struggle to be living my true self." What "truth" is it that holds self and body together? What makes the body and the perception of the self cohere? What makes a body more or less authentic to the self it contains and expresses?

In the case of the protagonist of the 2015 film *The Danish Girl*, what achieves coherence is nothing else than the controversial and often contested phallus that puts body and self in antagonistic tension. In the movie, just before Lilli Elbe is about to undergo a sex change surgery never attempted before, she responds to warnings about the dangers involved by telling the surgeon: "This is not my body. I have to let it go." Lilli lets go of the penis but the removal of this organ makes her whole body go. Genitals and body appear conflated. Combining natural and logical necessity, the organ becomes an *organon*, an instrument, a means of reasoning or a system of logic.

Is it possible to assume a sexual position as man, woman, or anything else without relying on the phallus as in the case of Lilli? In real life, Lilli Elbe died in 1931, during an experimental attempt to transplant a uterus. She was in love and wanted to have children. Einar Wegener was a Danish painter who had been married but felt she was a woman trapped in a man's body. Wegener consulted many doctors, including a close friend of Eugen Steinach. According to the bisexuality theories of the time, Wegener's treatment consisted of the removal of testicles under the supervision of pioneer sexologist Hirschfeld; this was followed by an ovarian transplant to stimulate the feminine side to help Lilli Elbe to come into being. Lilli Elbe died a year later, during one of several surgeries, possibly a vaginoplasty or even a uterus transplant. One should not take Lilli Elbe's operation as purely experimental; since 2014 the Swedish University of Gothenberg has performed nine uterus transplants, achieving five pregnancies and four live births. In February of 2016, the Cleveland Clinic performed the nation's first uterus transplant on a 26-year-old Texan woman born without a uterus. Eventually the operation failed due to a fungal infection, but the results were promising.

My position, as a clinician practicing in the United States, takes some distance from the thesis defended by most Lacanian psychoanalysts who classify transgender patients in pathologies like psychosis. I also differ from the Queer doxa and find myself at odds with current popular ideas on sex and gender prevailing in American culture today. What I know is that there is a lot to learn in our practice and that there is room for innovation if we listen to transsexuals. The couch functions like a window through which we can see how new things arrive, how they happen differently in our society and thus affect cis patients and trans patients alike. What we can learn about sex and gender from transgender helps reorient our practice and improve it.

The sex-gender binary is ending. Big, rapid changes are taking place in societal attitudes towards sex and gender. Gone is the pink and blue color partition in big-box store sections for toys, bedding, home decor, and entertainment. For younger generations who have never known a life without the Internet, like the cohort of 12-to-19-year-olds of the Post-Millennial or Generation Z, the lines between male and female have become blurred. Boys can wear dresses and look virile and sexy. Gender is blended and no longer considered a determination mandated at birth but rather a choice. To change metaphors, I could say that the wall between the binary of the sexes has known the fate of the Berlin Wall. We are still picking up its pieces and examining them. The transgender experience, which challenges traditional ways of thinking about sex and gender embodiment, is acquiring more and more visibility and losing its former exceptionality. Gender mutability has entered the quotidian vernacular for good, at least since the public transition of pop star and patriarch of the reality TV Kardashian clan, Caitlyn Jenner.

Gender in the blender

Reflecting this trend towards gender fluidity, the popular social networking website Facebook introduced a while ago an assortment of at least 58 gender options for its US users. Of course the selection moves away from the old-fashioned binary of male or female. Besides adding the option of keeping one's gender private, the platform offers a wide variety of gender identity choices. Following the success of this customized gender feature, UK users were offered an even more inclusive list covering 71 gender choices. Despite their nuances, none of the options has to do with sexuality. The comprehensive list is not about whom you go to bed with, but rather who you go to bed as. Its semantic excess gestures in the direction of a surplus of being that defies categorization. This expanded gender nomenclature proves that at least for the over 2 billion people who use Facebook, gender is no longer a binary but a spectrum. The menu of options in gender expression continues being rewritten. What we are dealing with is what Sally Hines (2007, p. 81) calls a "linguistical queering of gender" or, as Susan Stryker explains (2006), "a heteroglossic outpouring of gender positions from which to speak" (p. 11).

As for sexuality, one also finds an extensive glossary, with another spectrum of labels continuously changing and growing. Alfred Kinsey's mid-20th-century idea, which caused such a scandal in his time, that in human sexuality orientation could be gauged in a scale of zero to six, with intermediary shades between heterosexual and homosexual, appears today as a quaint oversimplification. For instance, the internet dating site OKCupid (3.5 million users) offers 12 categories for sexual orientation (besides gay, straight or bisexual, the list includes asexual, demisexual, heteroflexible, homoflexible, pansexual, queer, questioning, and sapiosexual for those who consider intelligence the most important sexual trait) but OKCupid is not as inclusive as Facebook when dealing with gender; it lists 22 options.

Despite the proliferation and the atomization of choices, being a man, a woman, or anything else altogether, is one of the many possibilities of misfire. In sexual matters of identity or object choice, no one is ever up to snuff. There is always a mismatch, something that does not work. The psychoanalyst Jacques Lacan summed it up in the formula: "There is not such a thing as a sexual relation" ("*Il n'y a pas de rapport sexuel*"). Of course, he did not mean that people do not engage in sex, or fall in love, or assume more or a less precariously sexual identity, but rather there is something constitutively out-of-synch and inherently incommensurable, even incompatible, in human sexuality. Between man and woman, and between men and men, and between women and women, there is nothing but difference. All combinations are possible but there is no reciprocal standard.

One of the truths the transgender phenomenon illustrates is that body and gender consistency is a fiction that is assumed through identification (Salamon, 2010). It is absurd to ascribe to anatomy the role of normalizer in a type of sexuality by focusing on the genitals or on a single prescribed act, as classical psychoanalysis has traditionally done. This normalizing role has been effectively challenged by transsexual discourse and practices.

Sexual identity issues revolve around a particular body, a body one is not born into but one that one becomes. Today we see patients in our practices who tell us that the sex they were assigned at birth does not align with the gender they identify with. They question and prove then, in matters of gender, anatomy is not destiny, that they have a peculiar kind of body that unfolds like an envelope emptied of its contents.

We learn that to have a body entails a complex process of embodiment. Some analysands who embarked on a journey of transformation between genders, however, expressed that the voyage does not end in the bodily transformation. Something else is needed for that process of embodiment to be successful. We are seeing more and more patients who do not think that they are in the wrong body but feel that the gender binary male-female does not fit them. Their identity is "non-binary" or "agender" – they do not identify as either male or female. They are careful about using language – instead of the pronouns "he" and "she," these analysands refer to themselves using the pronoun "they," which already exists in the dictionary, or employ new gender-neutral pronouns like ze, hir, xe, ou, ey. And, even when they may not want to change genders, they may take hormones to redistribute muscle and change the way their voice sounds, precisely to inhabit a space in-between traditional genders.

Having a relation to one's own body as foreign is a possibility which is expressed by the verb "to have" that we use for the body: one has one's own body, one is not one's body in any degree.

Here, we should go beyond the model of imaginary identification as developed by Lacan's Mirror Stage in order to understand the issues around embodiment in gender transition. Most commentators tend to stop at this point. This is the case of an author as gifted as Jay Prosser. The Mirror Stage, Lacan hypothesized, is a stage that infants pass through in which the external image of the body (reflected in a mirror or represented by the loving gaze of the main caregiver, often the mother) is internalized as a unified body. This image, which will become the "I," is an idealized imago and will be the blueprint for emerging perceptions of self-hood. It anticipates a bodily perception of unity that does not correspond with the infant's real neurological immaturity and vulnerability. It also creates an ideal of perfection that the subject will always strive to achieve. Here we can see how the Ego is dependent on an external object with which the infant identifies, how it is produced in alienation, that is, as other, as an illusion of reciprocity and a promise of wholeness, when the real experience of the body is fragmented because at this early stage the infant cannot even control its bodily movements.

In the Mirror Stage, the subject becomes an "I" in anticipation and alienated from itself. The dual relation of the body to the Ego, which is at the basis of the body image, Lacan hypothesized, was quite different in the case of an artist like James Joyce, and it did not involve identification with an image but with writing. His Ego was supported by his art (See Morel, 2003).

When Lacan turned his attention to Joyce's art, he also discovered a new relation to the body. He observed that Joyce had a peculiar body, one that could fall, slip away, like an open envelope letting go of its contents. Lacan focused on a passage of *A Portrait of the Artist as a Young Man* (Joyce, 1992), when Stephen remembers a moment of rage at his schoolmates that suddenly fades away: He feels his anger falling from him "as easily as a fruit is divested of its soft ripe peel" (p. 87). For Lacan (2005), such a transformation of anger was curious and revealing. It could be generalized as encompassing a Joycean body, a body that could fall from one's self, like a wrapping that does not fully hold up (p. 149). In Joyce's case, it was writing that would "hold" the body.

The image of the body as a vacant shell, as an enclosure oppressing the self, is a recurrent theme in sex change autobiographical narratives. Raymond Thompson (1995), a trans-man, poignantly describes this experience of the body as feeling like an ill-adjusted container, one from which he needed to escape and be free.

The sex change appears as the only possible escape from the confines of excessive *jouissance*: "I was trapped inside a living chamber of horrors" (Griggs, 1998,

p. 88). Lewins (1995) expanded this notion: "In the case of transsexuals locked inside a prison of flesh and blood, there is a constant ache for emancipation" (p. 14). The body is experienced as a burdensome exterior layer often worn like an ill-fitting piece of clothing one is impatient to shed. This is how Leslie Feinberg (1980) describes it: "I think how nice it would be to unzip my body from forehead to navel and go on vacation. But there is no escaping it, I would have to pack myself along" (p. 20). Jan Morris (1986) reiterates a similar wish when she writes: "All I wanted was liberation, or reconciliation – to live as myself, to clothe myself in a more proper body, and achieve Identity at last" (p. 104). Morris refers to her former body as an oppressive outer layer in which the real being, the true self, was locked; the urge to break free from it is pressing: "If I were trapped in that cage again nothing would keep me from my goal . . . not even the prospect of death itself" (p. 169).

The transgender experience proves that there is nothing natural that would direct us to the opposite sex. Sexual identity is a secondary nature. Since the unconscious has no representation of masculinity or femininity, we cannot speak with certainty in terms of sexual identity of being a man or a woman, but only of happy uncertainties.

The sex/gender divide is a historical development due to the development of sex change medical technology (Hausman, 1995). Prior to the introduction of "gender" in 20th-century discourse as a signifier of "social sex," "sex" was a signifier encoding both biological and social categories (p. 75). The concept of psychosocial gender identity had been invented by John Money in the 1950s and had ideological consequences. When "gender" was seen as "core gender identity," gender was separated from the body; it became an inner "psychological" experience at times in discordance with sex, as the biological substratum; the psychic gender became detachable from the materiality of the body. Judith Butler and Anne Fausto-Sterling have persuasively argued that sex and gender are discursively imposed norms that somehow create the body.

Let us see how this might work in the clinical practice. One of my patients, a trans man, told me recently, "Transitioning is complicated. It is the most amazing and horrific experience one can go through." He added, "This chance of being who you are, of having your body match how you feel is amazing but can also be horrifying. You do not really know what is going to happen." He paused, smiled, and nodding in astonishment, continued: "When I started my transition 10 years ago, I did not know what was going to happen. It was a harrowing experience. Now it may be more common. There are kids who start transitioning at age 17, 18. I am 35. I do not know what it would have been if I had transitioned earlier, at age 18 or 20."

I noticed surprise in his face:

> But I have to tell you, I have friends of friends who identify as women, who transitioned at 18, took T, had mastectomies, and now they are feminine, oh, very feminine, they say: "I had to become a man to know I wasn't one." My process was so intense, so internal, so agonizing. I did not know how to think

about it. I thought I was going mad, I felt sick, alone, isolated. It was the transformation of the whole of adolescence in just a couple of months.

I've heard this kind of narrative a lot in my experience. It's a rather common account in our practice, even if it seems exceptional by the public. Remember when, in 2014, Angelina Jolie candidly disclosed that she carried a rare genetic mutation, which predisposed her to reproductive cancers? The public was shocked. Facing the prospect of staring down cancer, haunted by the fear of death, she decided to have a preventive double mastectomy.

Angelina Jolie made a choice to amputate healthy body parts with the hope that she would steer clear of her genetic destiny. She took control of her body. Jolie has undergone surgery to reconstruct her breasts with implants. Soon, she'll lack hormone-producing ovaries. Will she not be the same as many transsexual women? Is Jolie's sexual identity really the sum of her body parts? Are any of our sexual identities really the sum of our body parts?

Sexual identity cannot be determined by quantities of hormones or the artful work of a surgeon with a scalpel. There's a lesson to be learned from Angelina Jolie's story: sexual identity transcends anatomy while it remains a mystery.

Can we understand the transformation of Angelina Jolie – her mastectomy and subsequent reconstructive surgery – and that of my analysand in the same context? Are both transformations "plastic"?

"Plastic sexuality," a concept developed in 1992 by sociologist Anthony Giddens, refers to the malleability of erotic expression in terms of both individual choice and social norms. "Fixed sexuality," on the other hand, refers to the modernity – it stands in contrast with the binaries of heterosexual or homosexual, marital (legitimate) or extramarital (illegitimate), committed or promiscuous, and "normal" (coital) or "perverse" (anal, autoerotic, sadomasochistic). For Giddens, effective contraception in tandem with the social and economic independence achieved by women has "liberated" men from the constraints of traditional gender expectations; "plastic sexuality," for Giddens, is a result of this shift. He writes:

> Plastic sexuality is decentered sexuality, freed from the needs of reproduction. It has its origins in the tendency, initiated somewhere in the late eighteenth century, strictly to limit family size; but it becomes further developed as the result of the spread of modern contraception and new reproductive technologies. Plastic sexuality . . . frees sexuality from the rule of the phallus.
> (p. 2)

Thus, Giddens claims that plastic sexuality represents a shift in value. Sex is no longer a means to an end – it involves more than reproduction, kinship, and generational continuity. Neither is sex still bound with death – today, women rarely die during childbirth.

Brazilian women, in fact, set out to erase any trace of childbirth and lactation altogether. Alexander Edmonds (2010) observed the cultural prevalence of plastic surgery in Brazil, where across social classes, in glitzy clinics and in free public hospitals, Brazilians are lining up to get surgery, or "plastica," as it's called there. Brazilian women want a body that looks young and toned, not a body that looks worn of sexual reproduction. Fundamentally perhaps, these women want to deny their own mortality – "I know full well that I am mortal, but . . ."

AIDS, though, reintroduces the connection between sex and death, Giddens notes (p. 27). Indeed, AIDS forces us to rethink sexuality because, as Tim Dean has shown, it can lead to an exchange of life for sex – a dramatic, literal relationship between the two emerges (pp. 20–21). This relationship is a complex one. Here, I will focus on the "return" of the death drive because I see such a drive as a limit to the plastic promise. One remembers Butler's conception of gender as performative, as a promise of endless plasticity. Isn't the transsexual the most radical example of the "plastic" drive, or, as Hegel would suggest, our desire to work against nature?

Let us return to the clinic. Another analysand whom I call Stanley is a transsexual man in his thirties who admits that being a man today has a lot to do with not being pregnant; not getting pregnant as a teenager, like his mother did, has allowed him not to repeat a destiny that he claims most girls in his school followed. Today, Stanley is a married man. His wife is a heterosexual woman who never dated anyone queer before meeting him. They have a young daughter conceived by artificial insemination. They are a normal couple whose current problem is that Stanley's wife wants a second child.

My analysand fears he will have a son, and thus, opposes the idea. He thinks it would be more difficult to be the "father of a boy". A revealing slip of the tongue follows: "I cannot be a trans father". But Stanley is already a trans father; he has a daughter. He thinks that caring for a son will expose an insufficiency – his lack of knowledge about masculinity. Stanley regards himself as a "feminist man" – a label that has the other sex – difference – written in its identity. He's not, he says, like a biological man. He feels at ease among men but also feels different (this is important, because he is not psychotic).

Recently Stanley mentioned a dream: "I was making love with a man. He does not know I am trans. I am anxious. I touch his penis but find a weird translucent plastic thing with a red rod in it." He added, as if to explain: "A transparent plastic thing." I stopped the session, repeating back "trans parent plastic thing."

Ultimately, the most radical discovery of psychoanalysis is that sex is tied to the death drive. Stanley's "castration" has to do with his acceptance of his own mortality, a fact not unrelated to his conflicted desire to become a parent. Reproduction proves the mortality of the individual. One does not "duplicate" in sexual reproduction, as we often think. We do not buy a share of immortality by having children; quite on the contrary. As Lacan puts it, sexual reproduction means that "the living being, by being subject to sex, has fallen under the blow of individual death." Reproduction does not guarantee immortality through replication but rather shows the uniqueness (and death) of each individual. In Stanley's case, this is made absolutely clear – his wife will get pregnant using sperm from an anonymous donor. And Stanley is aware of this fact. He is quite relieved that, thanks to the artificial insemination, his offspring will not carry the "defective, addiction-prone" genes in his family. For Stanley, the cut of castration or mortality with which he is struggling to come to terms with is also an expression of his singularity as a subject, as a feminist man, as a "trans parent."

For Freud and Lacan, sexual reproduction and death are two sides of the same coin. Sexual reproduction requires more than one individual; one person or partner alone simply cannot produce a new being. In principle, the sexed living being implies the death of the immortal individual. Sexual difference and sexual reproduction account for the constitutive lack in the subject – a lack which Lacan ascribes to "reproduction, through the sexual cycle." As we have seen, there is no pre-programmed "biological" dictate in the psyche that determines why somebody will situate herself or himself, independent of her or his body, as a man or woman; further, there is no "biological" dictate that seeks a "fitting" complement.

Here we see that to occupy a sexual orientation is to accept a primal loss. The major signifiers – "trans," "parent," "plastic" – at work in Stanley's unconscious may perhaps re-knot themselves in a "sinthome". We shall see. This is a case in progress.

This feminist man is at ease in the world because he can pass in his masculine persona. His being a man is never questioned. He is lean, muscular, and good-looking and has all the markers of what, in our society, is seen as virile masculinity. Stanley often says in session that it is "weird" to be a trans-man, that his transition is hard to explain, even to himself, but that he needs to invent something to survive. In the years preceding his transition, he was drinking heavily, and ruminating about suicide. Now he can imagine a future.

Stanley's concerns about the flesh have moved onto the boundaries of the body, pushed onto the body as envelope. "When will I be fine in my own skin?" he asked recently. He added, "When will I feel confident and happy?" Perhaps now the body/ego, the psychic envelope appears removed from the real of the flesh, and could perhaps become more of a metaphor, more prone to a retroactive reorganization. We shall see, as this is still a case in progress.

Beautiful Bodies

Often, gender transformation aims to achieve the beautiful, stable form. The wonderfully tender and intimate documentary, *Beautiful Darling: The Life and Times of Candy Darling, Andy Warhol Superstar*, explores this ultimate aim. This 2010 feature-length focuses on the life of Candy Darling, the moving transgender muse, who appeared in several of Andy Warhol's films and inspired numerous Lou Reed songs. The documentary includes a clip from another documentary, *Bailey on . . . Andy Warhol* (1972) in which Warhol explains the difference between "drag queens" and his stars. Drag queens, Warhol says, "just dress up for eight hours a day. The people we use really think they are girls and stuff, and that's really different." Warhol may have even suggested to Candy that she have a sex-change operation. Candy demurred, "I'm not a genuine woman . . . but I'm not interested in genuineness. I'm interested in being the product of a woman." Thus she dosed herself with the same female hormones that very likely caused her death from lymphoma in 1974. She was twenty-nine years old. Candy is not preoccupied with her genitalia; she's got a beautiful face – it's "I, Candy" or, rather, "Eye Candy." Her face is extraordinary; it's spellbinding, pale and luminous, always impeccably made-up. Candy has the face Roland Barthes sees when he looked at Greta Garbo – a face "descended from a heaven where all things are formed and perfected in the clearest light". To Barthes, Garbo "represented a kind of absolute state of the flesh, which could be neither reached nor renounced."

Candy was supremely beautiful. Her majestic face, though, did not allow her to reconcile the limits imposed on her by her corporeal, sexual being. "I feel like I'm living in a prison," Candy wrote. She noted how she couldn't do certain things – swimming, visiting relatives, getting a job, or having a boyfriend. Her sex life remains a matter of speculation. As she lay dying on her hospital bed, Candy posed for Peter Hujar, who snapped a black and white portrait, later entitled, "Candy Darling on her Deathbed." Death was not far from the lens – Candy died soon after the picture was taken.

She left a note:

> To whom it may concern,
> By the time you read this I will be gone. Unfortunately before my death I had no desire left for life. Even with all my friends and my career on the upswing I felt too empty to go on in this unreal existence. I am just so bored by everything. You might say bored to death. It may sound ridiculous but is true. I have arranged my own funeral arrangements with a guest list and it is paid for . . . Goodbye for Now
> Love Always
> Candy Darling

"Peter Hujar knows that portraits in life are always, also, portraits in death," wrote Susan Sontag of that last image. Photography "converts the whole world into a cemetery," Sontag wrote in her introduction to *Portraits in Life and Death*, the single book Hujar published during his life.

It is the tension between beauty and death that I want to underline here. One should explore the role of beauty as a denial of death. Death functions as a limit to the promise offered by plasticity of an endless metamorphosis. As any reader of Hegel knows, the philosophy of sexual difference cannot but take death seriously and look it in the face, which however should not exclude a sense of humor.

Is sex nature's joke?

Perhaps nature has a sense of humor. Nature, Hegel tells us, "combines the organ of its highest fulfillment, the organ of generation, with the organ of urination".

Žižek uses Hegel's comment as a jumping off point for his Phenomenology, a critique of phrenology. Žižek (1989) refers to what he calls Augustine's theory of the phallus. For Augustine, sexuality is not the sin for which humans are punished but rather a punishment for "man's pride and his want of power" (p. 222). The phallus embodies the punishment, "the point at which man's own body takes revenge on him for his false pride" (p. 408). Man may be able to master movement of all parts of his body except one – the phallus acts on its own, has its own volition and will.

Žižek reverses this paradox and entertains us with a vulgar joke: "What is the lightest object on Earth? – The phallus because it is the only one that can be elevated by mere thought." In this divine levitation, any punishment can be dialectically overcome. The phallus is less the way in which the flesh is humbled than the signifier of the operation by which the power of thought over matter is made manifest. Thought, words, images can be mobilized and avoid the sad fate defined by anatomy.

Let us recall that Freud avoided the trap of having to choose between anatomy and social convention. For psychoanalysis, sex is never a natural event, nor can it be reduced to a discursive construction. Sex or gender is a false alternative. Sexual difference is neither sex nor gender because gender needs to be embodied while sex needs to be symbolized. There is a radical antagonism between sex and sense, as Joan Copjec persuasively contends. Sex is a failure of meaning, a barrier to sense.

I want to emphasize the strong drive to beauty within the transsexual transformation as a legitimization in the search of authenticity. We encounter many trans folk who hope to be seen or read in the gender with which they identify. These folk talk about passing or not passing. I cannot help but wonder: is this a purely imaginary beauty, or one like that of Antigone, in whom Lacan sees sheer radiance or "unbearable splendor" (Lacan, 1992, p. 247), that is a beauty purified of the imaginary? In his description of Antigone, Lacan regards Antigone's beauty as a protective "barrier" that "forbids access to a fundamental horror"; for Lacan, her beauty is a screen that protects us from the destructive power of the Impossible, which Lacan calls the Real. Beauty can be a limit to reckless jouissance and an intermediary site between two deaths. This may lead us to conclude that transgender individuals want to be recognized in their being. When they say "I am beautiful" the stress is more on "I am" than on "beautiful". Theirs is ethical as well as an aesthetic concern.

To conclude, the sex and gender division was taken up by the feminists of the 70s as a political tool but let us not forget that this distinction emerged from the early sex change operations performed at clinics during the 60s like that lead by John Money at Johns Hopkins. Their work was initially aimed at correcting bodies they saw as "botched" by nature – intersex babies whose physical gender markers were not clearly male or female. Money's clinic was shut down partly due to the highly publicized failed case of a twin baby boy who suffered a botched circumcision and his family agreed to a sex change as treatment. The sex change treatment of David Reimer failed. David never accepted his sex change and never identified with his new gender. When finally informed of his medical history, he made the decision to live as a male and for that needed to undergo once again a sex-change protocol similar to that of many trans folk. His life, however, ended tragically in a suicide.

Why such a need to correct "what ain't broken"? When a baby is born with ambiguous genitalia, it is considered a medical emergency (Fausto-Sterling, 1999, p. 45). According to the current standards of treatment, within the first 24 hours after birth the child will have to have a declared sex. Today's practitioners, "unlike the doctors of the nineteenth century . . . do not search deeply into an intersexual's body in hopes of finding a material marker of ontological 'true' sex" (Domurat Dreger, 1998, p. 181). The answer is not skin deep but foreskin deep. According to the medical protocol, a girl cannot have a too noticeable "phallus" (as the scientific literature calls it) (Muram & Dewhurst, 1984; Newman, Randolph, & Anderson, 1992). Indeed, the medical decision concerning the assignment of sex is made on the basis of "phallic" size: "Infants with male-like structures are assigned to the male sex, while those with smaller phallic structures (micropenises or 'normal' clitorises . . .) will be assigned the female sex" (Kessler, 1990, p. 13). A phallus less than 1.5 cm long and 0.7 cm wide results in an assignment as female (Donahoe et al., 1991, cited in Fausto-Sterling, 1999, p. 57). Anne Fausto-Sterling (1999) dubs this standard "phallo-metrics" (p. 59).

First, let us emphasize that the semantic use of "phallus" in current medical terminology for cases of ambiguous sex is revealing; it exhibits all the properties of the Lacanian phallus while proving that grown up medical doctors are not far removed from Little Hans who believed that his sister's *Wiwimacher* was going to grow into a penis. All share infantile sexual theories about sexual difference.

I started with the missed encounter of Freud and Hirschfeld. Today, a new enlightenment is ushered in: we are becoming less intolerant about gender non-normative expressions and identities. However, this democratization of transgender, as I called it, has been captured as a marketing strategy, in which gender transition is approached as another consumeristic choice. The whole process is predicated on the American belief in technology and self-reinvention; this belief converts gender transition into a commodity, a personal choice available to those who can afford it.

What would be more democratic, more American than changing your gender on demand? Is this "democratic" ideal presented as another form of a more perfect union, a union that denies the lack of rapport, the fact that there is not such a thing as a sexual/social relation?

Of course, you will notice that I quoted the preamble to the American constitution: what is a more perfect union? What utopia does this promise entail? This would have us probe more deeply the ideologies surrounding what I have called the democratization of transgenderism, its mixture of progressive liberalism aiming at less repressive attitudes facing sexuality, and a confused and often mystifying scientific utopia offering new infantile theories for the future.

Lacan's path toward a deeper understanding of sexuality proves that one can be Freudian and keep progressing while remaining close to the clinic, keeping an openness to ethics and aesthetics. So-called masculine and feminine positions are predicated on contradictory systems; they follow dissymmetrical logics that are two ways of exemplifying how language fails to signify sex. Let me reiterate my point: sexual difference is neither just the body (as biological substrata) nor the psychic introjections of the social performance of gender (a socially constructed role). Neither the perspective of biological essentialism nor that of social constructivism can solve the problem of unconscious sexual difference. Because sexual difference is neither sex nor gender, sex needs to be symbolized, and gender needs to be embodied. What matters is not having a body or being in a body but becoming the body that will embody being.

Note

Several passages from this text have been published in Gherovici, P. (2017). *Transgender Psychoanalysis: A Lacanian Perspective on Sexual Difference*. New York: Routledge.

References

Adams, P. ed. (2003). *Art: Sublimation or Symptom*. New York: Other Press.
Bailey, D. (1972). "Bailey on . . . Andy Warhol," Transcript of David Bailey's ATV Documentary. Bailey Litchfield/ Mathews Miller Dunbar Ltd., London.
Bullough, V. (1994). *Science in the Bedroom: A History of Sex Research*. New York: Basic Books.
Domurat Dreger, A. (1998). *Hermaphrodites and the Medical Invention of Sex*. Cambridge, MA: Harvard University Press.
Donahue, P.K., Powell, D.M., and Lee, M.M. (1991). Clinical Management of Intersex Abnormalities. *Current Problems in Surgery*, 28(8):513–570.
Edmonds, A (2010) *Pretty Modern: Beauty, Sex, and Plastic Surgery in Brazil*. Durham, NC: Duke University Press.
Fausto-Sterling, A. (1999) *Sexing the Body: Gender Politics and the Construction of Sexuality*. New York: Basic Books.
Feinberg, D.L. (1980). *Journal of a Transsexual*. New York: World View.
Gay, P. (1998). *Freud: A Life of Our Times*. New York: W.W. Norton & Co.
Griggs, C. (1998). *S/HE: Changing Sex and Changing Clothes (Dress, Body, Culture)*. Oxford, UK: Berg.
Hausman, B. (1995). *Changing Sex: Transsexualism, Technology, and the Idea of Gender*. Durham, NC: Duke University Press.
Hines, H. (2007) *TransForming Gender: Transgender Practices of Identity, Intimacy and Care*. Bristol: Policy Press.
Joyce, J. (1992) *A Portrait of the Artist as a Young Man*. New York: Penguin.
Kessler, S. (1990). The Medical Construction of Gender: Case Management of Intersexed Infants. *Signs: Journal of Women in Culture and Society*, 16(1):3–26.
Lacan, J. (1992). *The Seminar of Jacques Lacan: Book VII: The Ethics of Psychoanalysis, 1959–1960*. Edited by Jacques-Alain Miller. Translated by Dennis Porter. New York: W.W. Norton & Co.

Lacan, J. (2005). *Le séminaire: Livre XXIII: Le sinthome 1975–1976*. Edited by J.A. Miller. Paris: Seuil.

Lewins, F. (1995). *Transsexualism in Society: A Sociology of Male to Female Transsexuals*. Melbourne: Macmillan.

Mock, J. (2014). *Redefining Realness: My Path to Womanhood, Identity, Love, and So Much More*. New York: Atria Books.

Morel, G. (2003) A Young Man Without an Ego: A Study on James Joyce and the Mirror Stage. In *Adams*. pp. 123–146.

Morris, J. (1986). *Conundrum*. New York: Holt.

Muram, D., & Dewhurst, J. (1984). Inheritance of Intersex Disorders. *Canadian Medical Association Journal*, 130(2):121–125.

Newman, K., Randolph, J., & Anderson, K. (1992). The Surgical Management of Infants and Children with Ambiguous Genitalia: Lessons Learned from 25 years. *Annals of Surgery*, 215(6):644–653.

Salamon, G. (2010). *Assuming a Body: Transgender and Rhetorics of Materiality*. New York: Columbia University Press.

Sterling, A.F. (1999). *Sexing the Body: Gender Politics and the Construction of Sexuality*. New York: Basic Books.

Stryker, S. and Whittle, S. (2006) *The Transgender Studies Reader*. New York: Routledge.

Thompson, R. (1995). *What Took You So Long? A Girl's Journey to Manhood*. New York: Penguin.

Žižek, S. (1989) *The Sublime Object of Ideology*. New York: Verso.

Chapter 17

Repudiation of femininity and the aftermath on the female sexual body

Vaia Tsolas

According to the *New York Times*, Debbie Reynolds died of *a broken heart* one day after the death of her daughter Carrie Fisher. Dying from a broken heart is a well-established occurrence known as Takotsubo syndrome, the Japanese term for octopus trap where the heart, caught in an overflow of stress hormones, 'is stunned' and can't take it. This causes a temporary weakening of the heart muscle and a massive heart attack in some cases. This *New York Times* article highlights the relationship between the body and mind, which has been a topic of fascination since antiquity.

For Freud, drives were the solution to the dichotomy of mind/body. It is neither the biological body, nor the mind alone, that we psychoanalysts are mostly concerned with, but rather the body of the Freudian drives and its productions, namely, unconscious fantasies. The body of the Freudian drives is a metapsychological construct defined by Freud "as a measure of the demand made upon the mind for work in consequence of its connection with the body" (Freud, 1915, p. 122). This demand is a constant pressure for satisfaction originating in the erogenous zones of the body; in his masterpiece Three Essays on the Theory of Sexuality (Freud, 1905) Freud explains this beautifully by elaborating his theory of infantile sexuality. Infantile sexuality threatens to break through the ego, demanding the mind to work by binding libido into representations via the stages of psychosexual development.

Shocking his contemporaries with the notion, Freud defined infantile sexuality as a much larger concept of sexuality; love for life and libidinal satisfaction. "A child sucking at his mother's breast has become the prototype of every relation of love" (Freud, 1905, p. 222). Infantile sexuality, however, continues to be the unwanted step-child of mainstream contemporary psychoanalytic theorizing precisely because it is conflictual by nature and disruptive to the ego's pre-genital defenses.

> Constant pressure is first manifested in the ego by the presence of anxiety. The fact that the drives exert pressure constantly, while the ego is periodic in nature, implies that the latter 'has work to do'. The link between them is therefore antagonistic. The issue then becomes: what kind of effort can the ego deploy in order to equip itself with respect to this constant pressure

through every one of the interconnected events that constitute the test of reality for psychosexuality?

(Schaeffer, 2011, p. 5)

For Schaeffer, the constant pressure of the libido is disruptive, but it is also nourishing to the ego, expanding its capacities from the anal to the genital ego in falling ill less and living a fuller life. The capacity of the ego to allow itself to be penetrated and enriched by drive energy is named by Schaeffer as the *feminine dimension* for both sexes. Feminine dimension stands for sexual difference and otherness. "What I call the feminine sphere is internal and invisible; rejecting it may coincide with the deeper refusal of any difference between the sexes and of female genitals as carrying all the fantasies related to opening up and driven-based desire" (p. 45). The female sex as invisible is the receptacle of projections of castration when one tries to conceive of it in an anal or phallic way. Schaeffer further elaborates on otherness as it is represented by sexual difference and the erotic and genital aspects of psychosexual development in the creation of ecstatic sexual pleasure.

Both men and women, for Schaffer, face the challenge of allowing their ego to be penetrated by something that feels foreign; in this case, the constant pressure of the drive and on a bodily level, their genitals. The penis operates periodically and has to allow the constant pressure to awake it and carry this energy to the female body by penetration, creating pleasure and ecstasy. The female genitalia, on the other hand, needs to allow the penetration, the opening up, the breaking through, which her ego's anal sphincter defenses hate. She views Freud's concept of repudiation of femininity (penis envy in women and fear of a passive homosexual attitude in men) as the failure of the ego to overcome its anality, but unlike Freud she does not see this obstacle as insurmountable.

Repudiation of femininity, for Schaeffer, takes its energy from castration anxiety and exists only to deny, dominate, destroy or run away from the feminine dimension. For the female, the discovery of the feminine dimension, on the other hand, is constructed through a shared creation with a partner, which can come about only thanks to the fact that the partner conquers the woman's anal and phallic defenses and tears them away from her, helping the woman to leave behind the pregenital mother. In order for the partner/lover to be able to let go of his own anal and phallic defenses and to be dominated by the constant thrust of his libido that he will carry into the woman's body, he must first overcome his own fear of women and his own omnipotent phallic mother.

Moreover, for Schaeffer, the working towards the feminine dimension for both sexes requires a path towards opening up libidinally on a physical and psychological level and using this drive energy for sublimation and ecstatic pleasure. The following dream of an eight year old girl exemplifies the struggle for the girl to separate from the pregenital phallic mother and to transcend the ego's anality in sublimation. "I was swimming with my best friend, K, and as we were swimming together, this octopus came around and it wrapped its tentacles around us. The octopus thought the two of us, with our eight combined limbs, were one of its babies. I did the breast stroke and K did the crawl and swam to shore. During the swim one of the legs of the octopus fell off because of the pressure of holding us. We used the ink for the typewriter at school that we are trying to fix." The fallen leg, as it stands for female castration, transforms itself here through the psychic work of representations into ink, the libidinal sublimatory jouissance and creation.

This chapter presents a less favorable outcome of negotiating the feminine dimension; two clinical cases of female patients whose anal ego-superego restricts the penetration of libidinal energy, with the result that the unbound energy returns to the body to imprint an unsymbolized defectiveness. Both patients share a domineering mother and a weak father who becomes in turn idealized. The idealization of the father attempts to facilitate the getting away from the omnipotent mother, which in succession intensifies the devaluation of female genitalia, penis envy and the glorification of the phallic mind. Moreover, the hypercathexis of these patients' intellectual capacities serves as a perverse response to the repudiation of the feminine dimension where the 'smart mind' stands for the erect phallus pushing away incestuous wishes and oedipal guilt associated with matricide and uniting with the father in thinking, overvaluing thought and signification. Both patients suffer from the beatings of an early, harsh, and hypervigilant maternal superego, the narcissistic wound and humiliations of having a defective feminine body that does not work and the overflow of jouissance that breaks through as unbearable realistic anxiety.

The first patient, Anna, is a successful writer who presented initially to treatment suffering from vaginismus and a masochistic relationship with a long term boyfriend. Her recent immigration from the east to the west, from a culture that prioritized the needs of the family over the individual's, to a culture that valued the opposite highlighted Anna's conflict over sacrificing her adult female sexuality for the father. It is important to note that the father in this paper is not the Oedipal triangular father who is potent enough to take away the girl from the claws of the pregenital mother, but rather he is the archaic father who stands as a mere replacement for the phallic mother; the mother who possesses the destructive anal phallus.

The second patient, Matilda, is diagnosed with terminal cancer around the same time her father was diagnosed with cancer. Matilda, in the intergenerational chain of female subjectification and reactive rage to male domination, assumed the role of the one who is supposed to set the record right; be like a man and prove how it is possible for a woman to do it all. A successful business woman who managed to get married and to be a mother later in life came too close to prove to all generations before her that she was, in fact, the woman who had it all, until the moment that a very aggressive tumor came to return her to the mark of her birth. Was she being punished because she stole the phallus from her father? Was she dying instead of the father, dying for the father? Was her tumor a symbol of her defective femininity or the stolen phallus that was supposed to be returned to the father? Matilda brings to her analyst an overwhelming urgency at the intersection of life and death to mentalize what feels too real to be contained.

Anna – female sexuality at the altar of the father

The only true love is the love of sacrifice, Anna often told me, describing the love she had felt she was taught by and had received from her father, as well as her love for him and the way his, in return, was conditional upon her sacrifice. Her life, long prior to her immigration, had revolved around this everlasting tension between loving another in the most profound sense of love (the love of sacrifice) and saving something for herself, her own very sense of being.

Anna, the youngest of two sisters, was the only one in her family that chose immigration to create a life for herself. Her family, deeply Caucasian and Orthodox, of Georgian descent, remained true to their roots. Anna intuited that in the simple act of crossing borders, one questions the pre-established order of motherland as unsatisfied, incomplete, and lacking. "I always wanted to run away from my family and I always felt so guilty." She loved her family to death she told me but couldn't take them for long. Hanging out with her friends had been her escape, but this time she wanted to study abroad but nonetheless to return upon graduation. The matricide that was implied in the act of leaving was tolerated by the tantalizing fantasy of a return, as if murder was not to be executed yet, but rather suspended into the future. Anna's fantasy of matricide elaborated in a form of parricide by making life choices in the new land of which her father not only would disapprove, but even could be killed if he were to find out. She imagined that her life could fully begin only when her parents had peacefully passed away without being aware of her transgression, which was choosing a boyfriend from a different culture and religion; a Jewish man, a profane travesty in Anna's Christian orthodox family.

Carrying the weight of hostile attacks towards her intrusive domineering mother, Anna felt from very early on that the only redemption was to side with her father and to repair her father with her mind and to excel academically. Driven to succeed, Anna's immigration continued the legacy of academic success and upon graduation she decided not to return to her country of origin since she was offered a wonderful opportunity to remain as a textbook writer. "If I caused all this pain in my family by leaving, I had better do something with myself," Anna told me, making clear that her success was not a surprise and that failing was not an option. Her mind was working fine, but her body was not, Anna told me in tears; her vaginismus was the bodily mark of sacrifice and punishment for choosing a boyfriend against her father's approval.

Anna came to treatment because she wanted to fix her vaginismus, which followed her as a bad stain, a stain she could not wash off. This symptom that revealed Anna's sexual life, told of her incestuous relationship and unconscious loyalty to her father, her debasement of her mother and anything that stands for the feminine, and her wish to sacrifice her body and receive her punishment.

In its Latin roots, sacrifice is an act that makes sacred. Freud speaks about sacrifice on several occasions. In *The Psychopathology of Everyday Life*, Freud (1901) interprets the accidental breaking of a precious little marble Venus.

> That morning I had learned that there had been a great improvement, and I know I had said to myself: 'So, she's going to live after all!' My attack of destructive fury served therefore to express a feeling of gratitude to fate and allowed me to perform a *'sacrificial act'* – rather as if I had made a vow to sacrifice something or other as thank-offering if she recovered her health!
> (p. 169)

In *Civilization and Its Discontents*, Freud (1930) speaks of sacrifice as linked to renouncing our instinctual satisfactions again for some other gain, this time to maintain group cohesion. In *Totem and Taboo*, Freud (1913) presented the prehistoric murder of the father of the primal horde by his sons to take possession of his powers but this parricide mobilized guilt and the need to restore the father by the totemic sacrifice. In the sacrifice an animal was killed, offered to the higher good, and then devoured. In observing taboos, one needs to give up certain wishes and, if and when one breaks a taboo, one has to repair the damage by renouncing some instinctual gratification. The sacrifice here is intended to diminish guilt and restore good relations with God.

As a little child, Anna used to hide under her bed when she would provoke her father to give her a beating. She remembers her sibling being beaten, but yet her father would never touch her. Anna felt she held a hidden special place in her father's heart, but still the mother had proven to be more powerful, manipulating the father with her tears. "She would cry about almost anything and run to her room. He would become like a little boy. I hated her tears. It made us feel all responsible. Now, I hate when I cry." Anna liked her body looking more boyish; small breasts, thin, very tall with short blond hair, and facial characteristics similar to her father's, all of which contributed to the overt paternal idealization and identification.

Anna invested analysis with enthusiasm and curiosity and I received her with affection and care. An idealized and beating father and an intrusive and devalued mother appeared early in the analysis. My silence made her anxious and paranoid of my judgments. She liked my comments, but my talking made her anxious that I might reveal how much I didn't know. Her attempts to correct me, and to make herself understood, left me with frustration at times. The raising of her voice, the subtle jerking of her upper body in defiance, her complaints that I did not get her, all entered in this early sadomasochistic dynamic with a unique focus on anally controlling the unknown. Soon enough, her vaginismus entered the analytic space and my interpretations felt like unwanted penetrations. Her reaction of dissolving into tears like her mother added an additional layer onto her no-entry anal defenses. She reacted to my interpretations as if I were giving her "beatings," releasing her masochistic jouissance in response.

Not surprisingly, Anna felt her boyfriend, an unsuccessful painter, was more 'feminine,' soft, gentle and overly emotional. She portrayed him as castrated himself with an overly dominant powerful mother in his mind. He attached to her like a little boy; not ambitious, and too dependent on her. Her busy life left him frustrated that he was not her priority. His weakness, his insecurities, his failings and his complaints made Anna feel guilty, especially because she couldn't give herself fully due to her vaginismus. Anxious about the new edition of her old crime, Anna responded to the complaints with a sacrificial submission and intense resentment.

It was with a lot of shame and after working together for a year, that Anna told me about her masturbatory fantasies of being raped. "Being taken against my will, violently," she admitted. She wondered if her difficulties to be penetrated served this fantasy. She explained that similarly to provoking her father for a beating, she was aroused by the idea that she provoked a rape. "I seduce the man and without him knowing that it is I provoking the assault, he rapes me." She was disappointed but relieved that her boyfriend never succumbed to sexual violence that in her mind was translated as sexual potency. She was successful though in provoking him to fight with her and to feel beaten by his verbal assaults.

Anna described their sexual life, however, as "passionate, and hot." She often initiated sex aggressively. Sex consisted of foreplay; mutual manual or oral masturbation. She felt furious when he would 'drop her' as he reached orgasm without caring about her pleasure. She felt he was justified not to take care of her as she was not taking care of him by withholding intercourse. She 'took care of business alone the way she knew how' after such droppings. She took pride in her elevated libido as the stolen paternal phallus that was supposed to compensate for her vagina not working.

Janine Chasseguet-Smirgel (1964) discusses times when sexual penetration is experienced as an intolerable desire for the ego because it goes against self-preservation. This occurs when the penis stands in phantasy for the invading, annihilating, destructive and primitive maternal phallus that Chasseguet-Smirgel equates to the maternal phallus of the anal phase. In these cases we cannot speak of a change of object and we see paranoia in women as persecution and passive homosexual desires. The transfer to the father has failed and the two objects are inadequately separated in phantasy; the paternal penis is the maternal phallus.

When Anna tried to wear tampons, her masochistic phantasy was of her female mentor looking at her and laughing about how pathetic she looked. In sessions, when she talked of her genitals and her sexual life, she appeared extremely anxious, licking her hair and smelling her fingers. Her body posture, fidgety and edgy, stood in contrast to her overt presentation, as neat, well-kept and stylish. She lay on the couch in a fetal position and kept her head tilted towards me, so she could watch me watching her. She associated to my watching her with a paranoid overtone. Being observed, she recalled the humiliating memories of her mother intruding into her private matters, listening to her phone calls and reading her journals.

Anna described the primal scene as her early memory of witnessing her parents locking their bedroom door in the middle of the day. She was frightened by the ensuing noise, worrying that the mother was being beaten up by her father. She associated this fear to her fear of being alone in her apartment worrying that a scary man would break through the window and rape her.

Kristeva (2008) in her article "A father is beaten to death," provids a more optimistic outcome for the girl in her differentiation from the pregenital mother in reaching towards the father of signification. In her reading of Freud's "The child is being beaten," she suggests that "the guilt that underlies the murder of the father is the other side of the desire for him." For Kristeva, the fantasy of the child being beaten marks the beginnings of individuation, of sexual difference, of a speaking subject. The little girl differs from the boy in the way she protects herself from incestuous love for the father (he loves me) and her defensive masochism (no, he doesn't love me; he beats me) by projection into another who shares the same sex as the father 'he is beating a boy.'

Parallel to the fantasy that another is being beaten, Kristeva emphasizes that the little girl transfers the intensity of her incestuous love for the father, her own desire, to speaking, thought, representation and mental activity. This transfer is not simply a perverse defense against guilty genital desires, but also the creation of a new source of sublimatory jouissance (as the dream illustrates above).

The complication for Anna rested not only on the hypercathexis of her intellectual world, the repudiation of femininity and with that the rejection of her feminine body, but also on her choice of a weak man who was the beaten boy and at the same time the beaten father, who stood as an equal in the suffering. In this choice, Anna was able to pacify her incestuous guilt and to find her masculine weak twin, her double, to fuse love, guilt and punishment together. Therefore the new man in her life, her boyfriend, came to embody the second part of her fantasy of the father being beaten to death. He was not only the demanding, beating and prohibiting father, but also her equal who suffers the same prohibition and punishment as she. She then could enjoy the first phase of her Oedipal fantasy of "I love him and he loves me." As Kristeva says, "we are both in love and guilty; we both deserve to be beaten to death. Only death will bring us together again" (p. 237). In Anna's words, "we love each other to death, if I leave him, I am afraid I am not going to find this kind of love ever again." He had sacrificed sexual genital pleasure for her and she sacrificed her father's approval for him. This mutual sacrificial love seemed to suspend the incest taboo in Anna's mind through the suffering of the two lovers and to disentangle incestuous desire from guilt, which in turn enabled it to reach the ideality of this love being divine.

Similarly, the rape fantasies kept separate incestuous desire and guilt, since it remains ambiguous who is the rapist/beating one and the raped/beaten other; Anna both provokes and receives the assault. In other words, it is her double who tries to break through her window, her hymen, and force her into a feminine position. And this is the paradise of masochism for Anna, the paradise where behind the masquerade of the rapist, she rapes/beats herself and enjoys herself in the position of the father being beaten to death without the complications of the primal scene, parricide and incest. In sum, repudiation of femininity and sacrifice of female genital sexuality in this case comprises not only a way to appease guilty feelings for parricide, but also a divine union with the father that is free from instinctual gratification. And it is because of this that Anna declares that there is no love as pure as the love of sacrifice.

Matilda – repudiation of femininity with a brisk tone of dealing with life and death

Matilda came to see me initially because of performance anxiety at work and frustration with her self-perceived inadequacies. She held a high position in the corporate world, managing a large number of employees. She was a boss that treated her subordinates with 'tough love,' which made her appear controlling, intense and intimidating. Her superiors had great respect for her, but still Matilda worried that it was only a matter of time before her flaws would be discovered and she would be humiliated. Shame and guilt were Matilda's long life companions. She compensated for her guilt and shame with hard work that left her feeling bitter and resentful. Matilda, even though tears rolled down her eyes every time she spoke of how hard she worked for others, was aware that the hard work was not an attempt to appease others, but rather that harsh, critical and demanding part of herself; her own cruel superego.

In his chapter "Introduction to the study of the early superego" Bela Grunberger (1989) makes a useful distinction between the later Oedipal superego and the early maternal superego by bringing the latter back to the body and especially to the anal-sadistic phase and sphincter training. "A child with an ego . . . which cannot be perceived or recognized in its totality, cannot channel the emotional mass that is reactivated by the introduction of conflict . . . and its only solution is to eject anything that is a source of unpleasure and to attribute it, together with the unorganized and elementary aggressivity . . . to its mother" (p. 107). This projection contains the roots of the early superego that gives its harsh maternal coloring. In other words, the early maternal superego a) preserves the child's narcissism and omnipotence and protects the child from its primitive aggression by projecting into the mother and b) this maternal imago associated with the anal active phase and sphincter control is what the child, in turn, assimilates and identifies with.

If all goes well, due to good enough mothering, conflicts associated with the anal phase are resolved, and the child then can, with the help of the paternal functioning, begin the constitution of the later superego (the heir of the Oedipus complex and its dissolution). Discussion of the development and nature of the early superego is beyond the scope of this paper. It is mentioned here only as a vehicle to examine repudiation of femininity and its consequences for the female body in its relation to an early anal maternal superego that still exercises its power on the basis of the sphincter control of the drives.

Matilda climbed the ladder of the corporate world very quickly. Coming from working class, blue collar, uneducated parents, Matilda saw education as her passport to a better life. She had graduated with an MBA from an Ivy League school and did not have any difficulty falling into a prestigious career. Working long hours left her very little time for anything else. She occasionally dated men, but even these sexual encounters did not lead to any meaningful relationships.

Matilda was an only child who grew up in an impoverished part of New York City. Her parents were immigrants from Romania; her father worked as a cab driver and her mother was a stay at home mom. Her mother, however, had educational and professional aspirations, but early on found herself in a prearranged marriage with a husband whom she tolerated. She rebelled against the derailing of her imagined life "like a defiant adolescent boy; wearing jeans, smoking cigarettes and hanging out with her American friends."

Matilda's birth signified the maternal ambivalence over marriage and motherhood. Matilda was told that she would have killed her mother and one of them would have survived if a complicated Cesarean had not succeeded in saving both mother's and baby's life. Matilda was born with a scar on her forehead as a result of her fight to leave the maternal uterus. That was the birth mark that came to signify the maternal projections of aggression against an intergenerational tradition of male supremacy and children coming to stand for malevolent phalluses accentuating the underlying sense of female castration. The physical scar, however, disappeared in infancy.

Matilda was a resilient child after this bad beginning. She took charge of her family as a replacement mother by 'picking up the slack' and taking care of the household. She recalls coming from school and having to make her own dinner while the mother was on the phone chatting with friends. Matilda remembers always hating her mother for not being like her friends' mothers. In stark contrast to the devalued mother, the father stood as calm, normal and stable, in her words the pillar of the household. However, Matilda recalls, her mother was jealous of the father's independence. The maternal penis envy was expressed by the mother's pathological jealously over the father's imagined sexual affairs. "There was no evidence of him cheating on her; he adored her, but nonetheless she insisted that he was cheating." Therefore, in terms of power, the mother was a phallic mother; in Matilda's words, "she wore the pants in the family," while the father appeared castrated. "He could never leave her despite her making his life and mine a complete nightmare."

Resentment was mixed with loyalty towards the mother during the parents' quarrels. Matilda, as if she was joining the mother in power and madness, spied on her father when mother asked her. Compensating for guilt for betraying the father and reality, Matilda remembers projecting into the future some reparation to the father when she would be away from her mother's clutches.

Matilda was a tomboy growing up, following in the mother's footsteps. She could not imagine herself marrying anyone or having children of her own. However, fantasies of repudiating femininity did not protect Matilda from the dangers of sexuality. Matilda was molested in latency by an older cousin over the period of a year, which she kept as her intimate secret. Shame and guilt accentuated

Matilda's sense of defect during latency and complicated even further her entrance in her puberty and adult sexuality.

When I met Matilda in her late thirties, she wore conservative business clothes, very little makeup and short hair. Her body language was rigidified, but with a masochistic inclination, ending every other sentence she uttered with tears about her sense of victimization and sorrow towards herself. She narrated her life in a captivating way, revealing her level of education, insight and the potency of her mind. At this stage of her life, Matilda wanted a husband and a family, but still she struggled articulating this to herself as if she would betray all the victimized females that came before her in her family. However, one year into the treatment Matilda fell in love with an accomplished man who valued her for her professional endeavors and at the same time found her attractiveness enticing. This relationship progressed as quickly as Matilda was progressing in her treatment and ended in marriage and pregnancy two and a half years later. Matilda ended her treatment at this point. Shortly after, she communicated to the therapist that she had given birth to a beautiful girl and that she was feeling content with the therapeutic work accomplished. It is worth noting that during this time of courtship, marriage and motherhood, her physical presentation transformed by a removal of the masculine camouflage of her femininity.

It was a decade later that Matilda contacted me again complaining of anxiety. This time Matilda was in a war with the pregenital phallic mother, but now it was represented by her aging mother-in-law who had moved into the same building as Matilda in order for her son to attend to her physical ailments. Matilda complained of feeling hostile toward her husband who reminded her now of her castrated father in his repeated submissions to her mother. Matilda was living with her parents once again even though they were now played by different actors. Her husband's preoccupation with his mother's care combined with his demanding work schedule brought Matilda back to her indifferent mother. Her hostility towards her husband mixed in with pre-menopausal hormonal changes made Matilda's sexual life feel barren and this, in turn, brought back her self-perception of being masculine, aggressive, unwanted and defective.

Matilda, however, wondered how much she had brought back this unhappiness as a punishment for finally having more than her mother and for evoking primitive maternal envy. She said that she had everything she had ever wanted, a wonderful daughter, a loving husband and a skyrocketing career. We focused this time in treatment on her unconscious sense of survival guilt and fear/wish for punishment. We examined this sense of guilt in relation to her aggression towards her husband and becoming like her castrating mother, stealing sadistically and anally incorporating the paternal phallus.

Matilda's anxiety and guilt were quickly diminished, but not for long this time. Her family drama unfolded quickly again, this time as her father was diagnosed with terminal cancer. Matilda met the news with denial as she spoke of this loss being unimaginable. What would her mother do? Her father's loss implied the shattering not only of her family's cohesion, but also of her own internal sense of stability and strength. While going through this unimaginable loss, Matilda was diagnosed with terminal cancer marked by an aggressive tumor that situated itself like a buried relic under the very place her birth mark had been so many years before. The timing and the coincidence of father's-daughter's diagnoses felt too surreal to be true. The father's cancer went into remission as Matilda's cancer brought her to the footsteps of her death very rapidly.

"It is like I had said, I owed him this one," Matilda told me in tears, revealing the sense of her archaic crime; she had betrayed her father in her loyalty to her mother and finally had to pay with her own life in order to restore him. The few months that followed after her diagnosis were too painful at times to be mentalized as I felt the urgency of her inexorable death and the wish to save her. As I was vacillating in the countertransference between dying with her/for her and living and thinking with her/for her, Matilda began writing a journal that she shared in sessions in a rush-to-say-it-all fashion, to extend her life and to find a way to turn this fatal misfortune around. She opened a dialog with her tumor.

She had a hard time naming her tumor in her writings as one has a hesitation naming the male organ, she said. She associated her tumor to the masculine part of herself, her own phallus. She had stolen this from her father and had to send it back to him. "But as a cancer? No!" she muttered. She was happy with her father's remission. However, she did not want to die for him. Her upcoming surgery signified removing the phallus-tumor in order to get a real chance for life, perhaps for the first time. Her mind was her strength, her phallus, which she had prided herself on for her entire life, to the extent of repudiating her own femininity in compliance with the maternal demand. Guilt and reparation now appeared focused on the stolen phallus that had turned bad and cancerous. This removal/castration she imagined would bring her face to face with real limitations, and depending on her psychological adjustment to these limitations, could determine the length of her life.

> One explanation of female masochism is to be found in its link with the guilt of incorporating the penis in a sadistic-anal way, as though women, in order to achieve this incorporation, had to pretend to offer themselves entirely, in place of the stolen penis, proposing that the partner do to her body, to her ego, to herself, what she had, in fantasy, done to his penis.
> (Chasseguet-Smirgel, 1964, p. 598)

Due to the length and purpose of this paper, I will not go into the enormous gravity and complexities of the transference-countertransference unfolding in this treatment, but rather I would like to isolate one aspect that I find relevant for the examination of repudiation of femininity on the altar of the pregenital phallic mother. Up to this point, in the transference, the protective ideal ego had appeared as the one who shielded Matilda from her harsh maternal anal superego and allowed her the chance of becoming a mother and a wife. However, with her fatal diagnosis, this transference regressed to that of the castrated impotent father who was unable to protect her from the return of the archaic-witch mother who this time had come back for blood. This return made Matilda's aggression, combined with destructive envy, reveal itself in the transference; she assumed the place of the witch with hostility towards me and envy toward my cancerous-free life.

As mentioned earlier, Matilda had aimed to actualize the mother's dreams by aspiring to combine professional success with motherhood and female sexuality. The closer she came to this aspiration, however, the more she felt she was the mother's phallus and the more she feared evoking maternal envy and punishment by the archaic mother (witch) for having stolen the phallus for herself. The projected maternal penis envy and ambivalence that had marked Matilda at birth and was cast as punishment returned with its sphincter controlling character; however, this time it was wiping out her own life, emerging under the vanished traces of her scar.

In the subsequent months of Matilda's battling with her tumor and going through surgeries and radiations, it was if she was in a battle with the omnipotent destructive phallus that literally was squeezing out of her skull the healthy part of her brain as it progressively took command; and once again Matilda had to fight for her life as in the uterus. She imagined that the removal of this cancerous phallus would give her a chance for a second life, a life where she could live for herself and not for her mother. She envisioned a 'real' mourning of her own sense of limitations and a separation-individuation that would render the ghastly battle one worth having fought, however Pyrrhic the victory might feel. This separation from her pregenital anal mother had to be a life and death matter for her, just as her birth mark had foretold the story in a similar fashion.

In a similar manner to that which I called the mother-witch earlier, Schaeffer (2011) uses the metaphor of the Sphinx, as the mythical female phallic pregenital mother. She utilized the etymology of the greek word "Sphinx" as deriving from *sphingein* which means to squeeze, to bind tightly and to strangle. "How can we transform a menacing Sphinx, the anal strangler, into a libidinal woman whose sex organ is a "lost soul" that demands to be conquered and possessed but whose ego and anal narcissism abhor defeat?" (p. 10).

Matilda's husband was failing in killing his own maternal Sphinx and in the face of Matilda's impending death, he was verging on withdrawing completely. Matilda's mother was the one who came to nurse Matilda during her difficult treatment days. "I had to come this far, to have to die in order to make my mother be a mother to me," Matilda articulated with her usual hateful tone. Her defeat at the hands of the maternal Sphinx brought her to the brink of her own death. Repudiating of the feminine sphere, in this case, came to be repudiation of love for life in general, as the ego in the face of the fear of death, closed down with his sphincter control any libidinal movement and the anal superego demanded 'you must do your duty to love me.'

It is a challenge for every subject, independent of sex and gender, to transcend anality and with that to modify the early phallic maternal superego in negotiating need for punishment for the dangers of incest and parricide. However, it is an extraordinary journey for the girl to change objects and to struggle and to defeat the maternal Sphinx of her early anal superego. Repudiation of femininity, therefore, is her resistance to this challenge. This resistance can manifest itself in various ways depending on the prophesy of signification (unconscious phantasy) and can impede the psychological work of opening up, varying from fear to hatred of anything foreign that can enter the body and the ego.

In the cases of Anna and Matilda, the thrusting libidinal drive energy, which will carry her to the arena of adult sexuality and ecstatic pleasure, felt as a threat to the self-preservation of the body and ego. The transcendence of the maternal sphinx demanded a partner who was not afraid of women and an ego that was not hateful of the drives. The dream of the eight year old girl above beautifully illustrates this journey of partnership to meet the feminine as Other, sexual difference and libidinal creation.

References

Chasseguet-Smirgel, J. (1964). Feminine Guilt and the Oedipus Complex. In Birksted-Breen, D., Flanders, S., and Gibeault, A. (eds.), *Reading French Psychoanalysis*. London and New York: Routledge, pp. 563–600.

Freud, S. (1901). The Psychopathology of Everyday Life: Forgetting, Slips of the Tongue, Bungled Actions, Superstitions and Errors. *The Standard Edition of the Complete Psychological Works of Sigmund Freud, Volume VI (1901): The Psychopathology of Everyday Life*, London: The Hogarth Press, pp. VII-296.

Freud, S. (1905). Three Essays on the Theory of Sexuality. *The Standard Edition of the Complete Psychological Works of Sigmund Freud, Volume VII (1901–1905): A Case of Hysteria, Three Essays on Sexuality and Other Works*, London: The Hogarth Press, pp. 123–246.

Freud, S. (1913). Totem and Taboo: Some Points of Agreement Between the Mental Lives of Savages and Neurotics. *The Standard Edition of the Complete Psychological Works of Sigmund Freud, Volume XIII (1913–1914): Totem and Taboo and Other Works*, London: The Hogarth Press, pp. VII-162.

Freud, S. (1915). Instincts and Their Vicissitudes. *The Standard Edition of the Complete Psychological Works of Sigmund Freud, Volume XIV (1914–1916): On the History of the Psycho-Analytic Movement, Papers on Metapsychology and Other Works*, London: The Hogarth Press, pp. 109–140.

Freud, S. (1930). Civilization and Its Discontents. *The Standard Edition of the Complete Psychological Works of Sigmund Freud, Volume XXI (1927–1931): The Future of an Illusion, Civilization and its Discontents, and Other Works*, London: The Hogarth Press, pp. 57–146.

Grunberger, B. (1989). Introduction to the Study of the Early Superego. In Macey, D. (ed.), *New Essays on Narcissism*. London: Free Association Books, pp. 105–121.

Kristeva, J. (2008). A Father Is Beaten to Death. In Kalinich, L., and Taylor, S. (eds.), *The Dead Father*. London and New York: Routledge, pp. 175–187.

Schaeffer, J. (2011). *The Universal Refusal: A Psychoanalytic Exploration of the Feminine Sphere and Its Repudiation*. London: Karnac Books.

Chapter 18

Concluding remarks

Christine Anzieu-Premmereur

On the Body was been written by and for the international multi-disciplinary community of psychoanalysts who understand the profound significance of research in psychoanalysis that can enhance our ability to join in and treat the pain of today's patients whose disconnection from their Bodies and Body Egos leave them feeling confused, disoriented and often hopeless.

With the aim of encouraging us to reflect deeply about the theoretical and clinical efforts needed to keep psychoanalysis alive, *On the Body* covered a broad range of intersecting topics: the body in the changing family, subjectivity in a world of communication without bodily presence, the sexual body lost in disorganization of and disconnection from a sense of identity, the sick body and the speaking body so muted by narcissism that its voice is no longer heard, as well as the immeasurable toll levied on psychoanalysis by the widespread disavowal of infantile sexuality as the core of the mental organization.

The body remembers both early and traumatic experiences. Suffering, illness and loss of body unity interfere with the building of the Ego. Like pain, intense sensations leave a scar on the Ego. The powerful associations among body sensation, body image and mental life demand a central role in the mind of the therapist. In an era of tattoos, piercings, plastic surgery, gender transformation, advanced technology for restoring damaged bodies, the treatment of both children and adults mandates an unwavering focus on the narcissistic and libidinal qualities of the body as the essential sources of mental life.

In recent years psychoanalytic thinking has witnessed a renewal of interest in the unconscious forces behind the contemporary burgeoning of identity pathology; work with disturbances in identity, autistic features, eating disorders, addiction, and gender issues has reinforced the unassailable association between a loss of the connection with the body and archaic anxieties. When the capacity for adequate mental and emotional development finds itself at risk, sensation and action intervene to decrease anxieties linked with primitive non-mentalized experiences. The psychoanalytic connection between emotional growth and bodily experiences resounds when emotional disturbances manifest themselves in a distorted relationship to the body and its functions.

In the post Freudian era, the narcissistic and borderline patient supplanted the neurotic patient at the center of analytic thinking and practice. Currently, we focus more on crises in identity, returning psychoanalysts to fundamentals of the Ego and the sense of self: the body. We talk less about narcissism as a secondary process than about primary narcissism. In the early psychic functioning of primary narcissism in the absence of a securely attuned environment, the body proffers itself as a last resort when mothers themselves are dealing with depression and narcissistic failures, more preoccupied by their own identity crises than by emotional connection to their newborns. Group dynamics also play an important role in the consolidation of subjective being, resulting in the proliferation of social media as a force that serves to mirror and maintain the fragile subject that was "neglected" in early development.

The body presents as the first vital object of reference at the time of the process of unification of the different autoerotic, partial drives into a singular unit that will become the Ego. The encounter between primary narcissism and the pleasure principle is driven by homeostatic leveling of excitement and feelings, to which Andre Green added negative narcissism, rendering the identity complex already a conflicted one. As for Lacan, when the narcissistic subject can never be found because of the dependency towards the maternal ideals, the identity conflict is associated with narcissism and eroticism, and is reworked by language and analytic process.

As repressed sexuality has waned in the contemporary world, the urgency of working through repression has been supplanted by the endeavor to reveal the unconscious to the conscious through thinkable processes. The analyst confronts the task of facilitating representation not only of the patient's unconscious landscape, but also the quality of the patient's body-mind in an era of mechanical ways of being and confusions in identity that often remain estranged from symbolic development. From Freud to modern psychoanalytic theories, the symbolic function remains inextricably associated with the theory of infantile sexuality. Play in children is a beautiful demonstration: the body in sensation, in action, in relation to others and the world, is played through and represented by metaphors. Metaphors that are also the tool for the psychoanalyst. Analytic work in its quality of listening and sharing, mirroring and transforming, while dealing with defenses and destructiveness, insists that patient and psychoanalyst find ways to live more fully in their own skin. This book is about a perspective that places the body and sensorial working through in the foreground, with the many implications of the specific modalities of clinical approaches.

Index

2001: A Space Odyssey 31

Abraham, Karl 159–160
actuality testing 150
actual neurosis 130–131
Adler, Alfred 88
affect 130–138
aggression 8, 34, 39, 94, 96, 120–121, 126, 181–185
AIDS 167
Aisenstein, Marilia 132
alexithymia 131
Alone Together: Why We Expect More from Technology and Less from Each Other 5
Aloupis, Panos 8, 103–104
American Psychoanalytic Association 43
anality 175, 185
Anzieu, Didier 1, 3, 54
Anzieu-Premmeneur, Christine 7, 64, 65
aphasia 152–153
aprè-coup 97, 104, 134, 155
Arensberg, C. M. 35
Aristophanes 117
Aron, Lewis 4
autistic defenses 89
autoeroticism 91, 95, 97, 126, 166, 188
autopoesis 32

babies 56–57, 76–87, 92–96, 170–171, 182
Balsam, Rosemary 5, 6, 16, 46
Banfield, Edward 34
Barahona, R. 53
Barthes, Roland 66, 169
Bataille, Georges 71, 72
Baudelaire, Charles 69
Beautiful Darling: The Life and Times of Candy Darling, Andy Warhol Superstar 168–169

beauty 56, 168–170, 183, 186
Benedek, T. 47
Benjamin, Jessica 4
Bergmann, Martin 42
Better Angels of Our Nature, The 75
Beyond the Pleasure Principle 154–155
Bibring, G. L. 47
Bick, Esther 92, 95
biological essentialism 45
Bion, Wilfred 81, 90
birth control pill 30
bisexuality 80–82
Blade Runner 31
Blakeslee, S. 151, 153
Bleichmar, Sylvia 52–53
body, the: as an organism 106–108; changing pronouns and 47–49; desire and jouissance and 108–109; ego, sibling (*see* sibling body-ego); flexible genders and 43–44; interactions with technology 15, 17–18; material body 6, 16, 43, 45–47, 51; mourning of the natal body 54; multiple genders, the imagination and 53–57; phantom limbs and phantom pain in 147–151; postmoderns and 45–46; psychoanalytic theory of 1–5, 187–188; sensori-experience of 90; soul and 105–118; as a surface 105–106
body-ego: latency of 84–85; lateral 85–86; mother-infant interaction and 89–98
body-psyche 146–147; aphasia and 152–153; general view of 156–158; phantom limbs, phantom pain in 147–151; post-traumatic states 154–155; psychic reality and 151–152

Bollas, Christopher 52, 87
boredom, feared 19
Boyd, Robert 32, 33
Breuer, J. 109–110
Brousse, Marie-Hélène 64
Buhler, Charlotte 87
Butler, Judith 45, 165, 167
Butterfield, Ardis 48

cancer 11, 43, 144–145, 166, 176, 183–185
Capek, Karel 30
cardiac disorders 123–125
Carson, Rachel 18
cell phones 18; empathy apps 20; what we are allowed to avoid using 19–20
Chasseguet-Smirgel, Janine 11, 179, 184
Chodorow, N. 51
Christian, Brian 52
Civilization and Its Discontents 27, 33–34, 178
clinical use of "they," "zie," 49–51
Cloak 25
Clouds Over Sidra 25–26
consciousness 110–111, 114–115
Copjec, Joan 170
cosmetic surgery 42, 53–54, 166–167
countertransference 136
culture of forgetting 17

Damasio, A. 91
Danish Girl, The 161
Darling, Candy 168–169
David, Christian 132
death drive 104, 127–128, 167; clinical vignette 123–125; the heart and 125–127; trauma and 120–123
de-cathexis 122, 125
defusion 120
depressive hedonia 109
Descartes, Rene 30, 52, 111, 114, 117
desire and jouissance 108–109
destructiveness 8, 89, 120, 122, 126, 144, 188
Deutsch, Helene 47
digital culture 15, 63–64; analysts falling for empathy machines and 23–24; assault on empathy 18–19; avoiding presence in 22–23; as a culture of forgetting 17; empathy machines 18, 20–22; fantasies of the fiction-free larger culture and 24–25; and phones allowing us to avoid 19–20; as robotic moment 18; virtual reality (VR) in 25–27
divided subject 109–110
division as the human condition 114–115
Dolezal, Rachel 38–39
Domurat Dreger, A. 171
drive(s): autoerotic, partial 188; to beauty, within transsexual transformation 170; death 104, 120–128, 167; defense mechanisms and 76; demand of the 138; derivatives 46; as desire 115; destructive 77; feminine dimension and 175; Freudian 4, 106–107, 130–131, 143, 148, 174; fusion of 115–117; homoeroticism 69; infantile 72, 92, 135; instinct and 1–3, 43; life 42; the Other and 110; phallic 117; primacy of the 8; procreative creative power 57; repression and 151–152; sexual 157; as solution to dichotomy of mind/body 174; in theory of the drives 80–82, 103, 105, 108, 130
dual inheritance theory 5–6, 15–16, 31–34; in action in ethnography 34–36; changes in attitudes about sex and 29–31; introduction to 28–29; new sexual ethos and 37–39; psychoanalysis and 39–40
dualism 114–115, 117–118

early maternal superego 10, 144, 176, 181
eating disorders 2
eczema 96–97
Edmonds, Alexander 166–167
Ego 187, 188; Ideal 138; psychology 16; *see also* body-ego
Ego and the Id, The 91, 105
Elbe, Lilli 161
Embodied Subject: Minding the Body in Psychoanalysis 5
embodiment 9–10, 15, 20, 46, 143–148, 154, 157, 160–164
empathy, technology's assault on 18–19
empathy apps 20, 26
empathy machines 18, 20–22; analysts falling for 23–24
Eros, Thanatos, and "Triebmischung" 115–117
erotic, the 34, 39, 42–43, 98, 108–109, 126, 175
essential depression 122, 125, 131

ethnography, dual inheritance in action in 34–36
excitation 3, 8, 104, 120, 122–123, 127–128, 130, 134, 143

Facebook 52, 63, 162
FaceTime 17, 24
Fain, Michel 126
Fausto-Sterling, Anne 165
feared boredom 19
fear of disintegration 89
Feinberg, Leslie 165
female phallus 143, 154, 179
feminine dimension 11, 175
fertility 29–31; *see also* dual inheritance theory
fetish 10, 153–154
"Fetishism" 154
fighting by text 22–23
Fisher, Carrie 174
Fisher, Mark 109
fixed sexuality 166
flexibility, gender 6, 42–57
Fliess, Wilhelm 80, 82, 151
Fogel, G. I. 47
Freud, Sigmund 105, 120; on anxiety neurosis 123; on aphasia 152–153; on bisexuality 80; on body boundaries 97; changes in attitudes about sex from time of 29; on contrast between individual psychology and social or group psychology 86; on the divided subject 109–110; on double function of the individual 39; on drive 2; on the Ego and the Id 91, 105; on Eros and Thanatos 116; on fetishism 154; on fulfillment of needs 2; on health versus illness 111–112; Hirschfeld and 159–160; on intertwining of body and psyche 1; introduction of infantile sexuality 75, 174–175; on libidinal energy 33–34, 98; on the "mischief maker" 42; on pain 148–149; parentality connected to 69–74; on place of sex in civilization in 1930 28–29, 31; on psychic reality 151–152; psychoanalytic theory 1–4; on psychosomatic illness 130–131; Q-hypothesis 107; on repression 112–114; on repudiation of femininity 156; on sacrifice 178; on sexual reproduction and death as related 168; on sociocultural versus biological notions of sex 45; Strachey's erroneous translation of 2; on trauma 120–122, 154–155; on the unconscious 111, 114
friction-free, fantasies of the 24–25
Friston, Karl 155
fusion 70, 92, 103; of drives 115–117

gender: affirming surgery 161; the body and 43–44; body trouble 160–162; botched encounters in psychoanalysis and 159–160; case example 55–57; clinical situation 49–51; constructing sex and inventing 159–172; contemporary questions on 47; contemporary social climate for changes in 51–53; familial confusions with 51; fluidity 162–167; identity and flexibility 6, 42–57; the imagination, the body, and multiple genders in 53–57; introduction to 42–43; mutability 162; plurality 42; postmoderns and the body and 45–46; pronouns 47–49, 164; sexual difference and 82–84; *see also* transgender persons
George, Robert 37–38
Gherovici, Patricia 10, 143–144
Giddens, Anthony 166, 167
Goldstein, Kurt 153
Google glass 26
Green, Andre 9, 122, 130–131, 188
Greer, Germaine 84
Groddeck, Georg 111
Grotstein, J. S. 92
Grunberger, Bela 181
guilt 10–11, 103, 109, 113, 131, 176–184

hair pulling 96
hallucination 143, 150
health versus illness 111–112; affect and representation in psychosomatics of 130–138; AIDS and 167; aphasia and 152–153; choice of a fetish and 153–154; death drive and 120–128; phantom limbs and phantom pain in 147–151; post-traumatic states 154–155; psychosomatic illness case example 132–138
heart, the 123–125; death drive and 125–127; Takotsubo syndrome and 174
Hegel, G. W. F. 167, 169
Hello Barbie 21
Helmholtzian machine 155
helplessness 122, 125, 156

Henry II, King 49
Hines, Sally 162
Hirschfeld, Magnus 159–160, 161
Hoffer, Willy 93
homeostasis 112
Homer 138
homoerotism 70
Hujar, Peter 169
Hurst, Rachel 53
hypospadias 55–56

Ideal Ego 124, 126, 138
illness versus health *see* health versus illness
imagination, the 53–57
impingement 8–9, 121
implantation (of the sexual) 157
imtromission (of the sexual) 157
infantile sexuality 75, 92–94, 143–144, 174, 188
Inhibitions, Symptom and Anxiety 81
Internet, the 24, 51–52, 97, 162–163
Interpretation of Dreams, The 109
intersexuality 170–171
inter-subjectivity, lateral 86–88
in-vitro fertilization (IVF) 5, 15–16
Ireland 34–36

Jackson, Hughlings 152–153
Jenner, Caitlyn 161, 162
Jolie, Angelina 166
Jones, Ernest 85
jouissance 8, 103, 105–108, 115–116, 176, 180; beauty as limit to reckless 170; excessive 164–165; experienced today 109; heroic aspect of 107; masochistic 178; overflow of 11
Joyce, James 164
Jung, Carl 160

Kaes, Rene 86
Katan, Maurits 153–154
Kernberg, O. F. 95–96
kibbutzim 34
Kimball, S. T. 35
Kinsey, Alfred 163
Klein, Melanie 77, 82
Kohut, H. 92
Kristeva, Julia 6–7, 11, 47, 63, 65–67, 180

Lacan, Jacques 1, 66, 75, 103, 115, 130, 188; on beauty 170; on body image 164; on gap between body and soul 8; on mirroring 86, 105; on origin of the *Je* 106, 117–118; on sexuality and sexual identity 10, 159, 163, 172; on sexual reproduction and death as related 168; on sexual versus non-sexual reproduction 116–117; version of Freud's Eros and Thanatos 107–108
Langer, Marie 47
Laplanche, Jean 143, 145, 156–158
latency, body-ego of 84–85
lateral body-ego 85–86
lateral inter-subjectivity and mirroring 86–88
Laurent, E. 63
Law of the Mother/Law of the Father 7, 64, 66–67; prohibition of 79–80; sibling body-ego and 75, 77; *see also* parentality
Leclaire, Marie 150
Lemma, Alexandra 4
Levinas, Emmanuel 156
Lévi-Strauss, Claude 69
Lewins, F. 165
libidinal energy 34, 95, 144, 176
limbs, phantom 147–151
Litowitz, B. E. 52
Loewald, H. 55
Lombardi, Riccardo 90
love of sacrifice 177–181

Mahler, Margaret 94
malleability 43–44, 166
marriage: dual inheritance theory and 28–40; parentality and 69–74; same-sex 37–38, 70
Marty, Pierre 122–123, 125, 128, 131–132
masochism 10, 121, 122, 178, 180, 184
material body 6, 16, 43, 45–47, 46, 51
maternal phallus 144, 179
maternal Sphinx 185–186
Maturana, H. R. 32
McDougall, Joyce 90
mediation of feelings 91
Meng, H. 120
mentalization 54, 103, 123
Merleau-Ponty, M. 147–148, 150, 151, 152, 153
metaphors 90–91
Mieli, P. 2
Milk, Chris 25–26
Milner, Marion 98

mind-body integration 89
Minding the Body: The Body in Psychoanalysis and Beyond 4
mirroring 86–88, 94, 103
Mirror Stage 8, 103, 105–106, 108, 117, 144, 164
Mitchell, Juliet 7, 64; *see also* sibling body-ego
Mitchell, Stephen 4, 37
Mixed Messages 32
Mock, Janet 161
Money, John 43, 45, 165, 170
Morozov, Evgeny 25
Morris, Jan 165
Morris, Rob 24
mortality 21; acceptance of 167–168; Brazilian women and 167; denial of 144
mother-infant interaction 89–98; difficult to treat patients and 89–90; during feeding 92–94; mother as "auxiliary" ego in 92; mother as protective shield in 91
motor traces 150, 153
Muller, John P. 5

NAACP 38
narcisissm 92, 95, 122, 134, 181, 187–188
natural selection 34
Nebenmensch 156
neurosis, actual 130–131
neurotic state 123

Oedipus complex 11, 46, 73, 88, 103, 105, 181; latency and 84–85; sibling body-ego and 77, 80, 82–84
omnipotent fantasies 44
On Aphasia 152
operational closure 146, 157
operatory somatic patients 122–123
ORLAN 43
Other, the 106, 108, 110

pain, phantom: phantom limbs and 147–151; psychic reality and 151–152
Papageorgiou, Marina 9, 104
parentality 6–7, 66–67; defined 68; neither modern nor traditionalist new version of 73–74; theoretical fable 68–71; What is a father? What is a mother? and 72
Pasteur, Louis 111
paternal function 144–145, 181
patriarchal order, decline of 63–65

Paul, Robert 5–6, 15–16
penis-envy 83
performance anxiety 181–182
personal pronouns 42, 47–49, 164
Pfister, Oscar 120
phallus: Augustine's theory of the 170; body and self in antagonistic tension and 161; guilt and paternal 183; hallucination of female 143, 154; malevolent 182; penis representing maternal 144; plastic sexuality and 166; primitive maternal 179; sex assignment based on size of 171; stolen paternal 176, 179; -tumor 184–185
phantom limbs 147–151
Picard, Rosalind 24
Pinker, Stephen 75
plasticity 167, 169
plastic sexuality 166
plastic surgery 17, 43, 53–54, 98, 187
Plato 111, 117
Please Select Your Gender: From the Invention of Hysteria to the Democratizing of Transgenderism 10, 159
pleasure principle 107
plurality, gender 42
political wars in psychoanalysis 43
Pollock, Jackson 73
Pontalis, J.-B. 146
Portrait of the Artist as a Young Man, A 164
postmoderns and the body 45–46
post-traumatic states 154–155
presence: avoiding 22–23; power of 5
primal loss 8, 117, 144, 168
primary maternal preoccupation 121, 127
primary narcissism 188
primitive aggression 181
progressive disorganization 131
pronouns 42, 47–49, 164
Prosser, Jay 164
pseudo-drive 151
psychic pain 143
psychic reality 151–152
psychisation 70–71
psychoanalytic theory 1–5, 187–188; addressing the changing world 63–65; bisexuality and 80–82; botched encounters with non-normative expressions of gender 159–160; difficult to treat patients and 89–90;

dual inheritance theory and 39–40; ego psychology and 5, 16; empathy machines and 23–24; language of 146–147; parentality and 69–74; political wars in psychoanalysis and 43; sexology and 143–144, 159, 161; synthesis between neuroscience and 146; work with children 91–96
Psychopathology of Everyday Life, The 178
psychosomatic illness 130–131; case example 132–138
psychosomatics 4, 8–9, 68, 76
Pythagoras 111

Q-hypothesis 107
Quinodoz, Danielle 50, 57

racial identity 38–39
Ramachandran, V. S. 147, 149, 150–151, 153
rape fantasies 180–181
Raphael-Leff, Joan 47
reality, psychic 151–152
reality testing 150
Realness 161
Reclaiming Conversation: The Power of Talk in a Digital Age 5, 15
reel game 97
Reimer, David 171
Reisner, Steven 42–43
Relational Perspectives on the Body 4
representations 89–91, 95–98
representative presentation 86
representative repression 104
representatives, psychic 121–122, 130–131, 152
repression 112–114, 188; phantom limbs and 150
reproduction 2, 5–6, 15–16, 31–39, 63, 116–117, 144, 166–168
repudiation of femininity 156, 174–177; in dealing with life and death 181–186; love of sacrifice and 177–181
Reynolds, Debbie 174
Richerson, Peter 32
rites of passage 79
robotic moment 18
robots, sociable 21–22, 24
rocking 94–95
Roe v. Wade 30
Rowling, J. K. 84

sacrifice, love of 177–181
Saketopoulou, Avgi 54
same-sex marriage 37–38, 70
Sandler, J. 92
Scarfone, Dominique 9, 143, 145
Schaeffer, J. 11, 175, 185
Schiele, Egon 106
Schilder, P. 93
seduction 69, 156–157
Segal, Hanna 2
self-injury 96
self-preservation 179
self stimulation 94–95
sensations, physical 7, 56, 89–92, 95, 98, 135, 143, 187–188
separation trauma 78
sex: bisexuality 80–82; changes in attitudes about 29–31; Freud on place of 28–29, 31; Freud on sociocultural *vs.* biological notions of 45; inventing gender and constructing 159–172; as nature's joke 169–171; new ethos of 37–39; social context for changes in attitudes about 29–31; theory of the phallus and 169–170; Victorian views of 108–109, 113; *see also* dual inheritance theory; gender; infantile sexuality; parentality
sexology 143–144, 159, 161
sexual, the 10, 143, 145
sexuality as mischief maker 42
sibling body-ego 75–76; bisexuality and 80–82; gender and sexual difference in 82–84; inner framework 80–82; of latency 84–85; lateral body-ego and 85–86; lateral inter-subjectivity and mirroring and 86–88; outer framework 76–78; prohibition of Law of the Mother and 79–80; sibling trauma and 76, 78–79
Siri (Apple) 20
skin 53–56, 78, 89–90, 92–96, 104, 123–124, 128; tattoos 43, 98, 187
Skype 17, 23–24; analysis by 23
Smadja, Claude 9, 126, 132
sociable robots 21–22, 24
social media 19, 26, 51–52, 87, 188
somatics 111; disorders 104, 110, 122, 124–126; equilibrium 112; sexual function 123
somatization 9, 65, 73, 126, 132

soul, the 105; body as an organism and 106–108; body as a surface and 105–106; and body versus consciousness and the unconscious 110–111; desire and jouissance and 108–109; divided subject and 109–110; division as the human condition and 114–115; from dualism to circular but non-reciprocal dialectic of 117–118; Eros, Thanatos, and "Triebmischung" and 115–117; illness versus health and 111–112; repression and 112–114
speech residues 152, 154
sphincter 97, 175, 181, 185
Spinoza, B. 114
Spiro, M. E. 34
Spitz, R. A. 92, 95
Steinach, Eugen 161
Stern, Mark Joseph 38
Stoller, Robert 43, 45
Stryker, Susan 162
Studies on Hysteria 112, 115
sublimation 55, 71, 134
Superego 138, 181
Symposium 117

Takotsubo syndrome 174
tattoos 43, 98, 187
technology *see* digital culture
texting, fighting through 22–23
Thanatos 115–117
Thatcher, Margaret 49
theory of the phallus 169–170
Thompson, Raymond 164
"Three Essays" 45
Tillman, Jane G. 5
Totem and Taboo 178
transference 135
transgender persons 49–51; aiming to achieve beautiful, stable bodies 168–169; body trouble 160–162; botched encounters with psychoanalysis 159–160; case example 167–168; gender fluidity and 162–167; theory of the phallus and 169–170; transitioning by 165–166; *see also* gender
translation 152–153, 156, 157
trauma 9, 103, 156–157; death drive and 120–123; post-traumatic states and 154–155; separation 78; sibling 76, 78–79
traumatic neurosis 121
Tremblay, R. 75
Triebmischung 115–117
Tsolas, Vaia 10, 144–145
Turkle, Sherry 3, 5, 15, 30; *see also* digital culture
Tustin, Frances 91, 93
Twain, Mark 33

unconscious, the 110–111, 114
unpreparedness 154–156

vaginismus 176–179
Vanity Fair 161
Varela, F. J. 32, 146, 148
Verhaeghe, Paul 7–8, 103
Victorian sexuality 108–109, 113
virtual reality (VR) 25–27

Warhol, Andy 168–169
Wegener, Einar 161
Weininger, Otto 80
Winnicott, D. W. 55, 127; on impingement 8–9, 121; on mirroring 94; on penis-envy 83; on primitive anxieties 92; on separation trauma 78
Women's Bodies in Psychoanalysis 5, 16, 46